(Noo)

THE REALITIES OF WORK

0333636406

The Realities of Work

MIKE NOON

and

PAUL BLYTON

First published 1997 by
MACMILLAN PRESS LTD
Houndmills, Basingstoke, Hampshire RG21 6XS
and London
Companies and representatives
throughout the world

ISBN 0–333–63640–6 hardcover
ISBN 0–333–63641–4 paperback

A catalogue record for this book is available
from the British Library.

This book is printed on paper suitable for recycling and
made from fully managed and sustained forest sources.

10   9   8   7   6   5
06 05   04 03 02 01 00

Printed and bound in Great Britain by
Antony Rowe Ltd
Chippenham, Wiltshire

Contents

Acknowledgements

The authors and publishers wish to thank the following for permission to use copyright material: The Controller of HMSO and the Office for National Statistics for Tables 2.2, 2.4 and 2.5 from *Labour Market Trends*, January 1996, Table 2.3 from *Employment Gazette*, October 1995 and Table 4.1 from *New Earnings Survey*, 1995, Table A 28.2; Rivers Oram Press for Table 4.2 from Patricia Hewitt, *About Time: The Revolution in Work and Family Life*, Rivers Oram Press, London 1993. Every effort has been made to trace all the copyright-holders, but if any have been inadvertently overlooked the publishers will be pleased to make the necessary arrangement at the first opportunity.

List of Figures

List of Tables

1 Exploring the Realities of Work: An Introduction

WORK – A MODERN MYTH

Here is a modern myth about work. Contemporary workplaces are peopled by high performing, highly committed individuals, bound together into a common cause by a corporate mission enshrined within a strong organisational culture. Workplaces themselves have been 'transformed' by new technologies, new forms of organisation and a new generation of management thinking that stresses flexibility, quality, teamwork and empowerment. The workers in these establishments are motivated by ambition and a sense of purpose, and by the individually-designed financial rewards they receive – part of those rewards taking the form of a financial stake in their organisation, either as shares or as profit-related bonuses. Employees are guided by self-interested individualism, and no longer see a role for collective organisation and representation, hence the demise of trade unions.

This representation of work is one implicit in much of the current management literature and is enthusiastically propagated by management gurus. In the UK, this depiction of work has been reinforced by the rhetoric and practice of the Governments from the late 1970s onwards: specifically the promotion of self-interested individualism in an 'enterprise culture' – a culture based partly on the creation of a (so-called) 'share-owning, property-owning, democracy'. Moreover, this has been accompanied by fundamental shifts in the character and location of much of the work that is now undertaken: in particular, a sharp decline in the late 1970s and 1980s in the proportion of the total labour force engaged in traditional, large-scale, heavy industries (such as shipbuilding, dock working, coal-mining and iron and steel production) and a continuing rise in a wide range of service sector activities, many of these undertaken by small-scale businesses. As a result of these developments, the nature and experience of work itself is said to have been fundamentally and irreversibly transformed, leaving an 'individualised, self-actualising' workforce to face the challenge of a new millennium.

A starting point for writing a book about the realities of work was to challenge this myth: a myth by which, in one form or another, implicitly or explicitly, we are increasingly confronted in books and other literature on aspects of management and organisational behaviour. Further, it is a representation of work which is profoundly misleading. Our combined research experience of over thirty years has involved talking to workers, union representatives and managers, reading workers' own accounts of their lives, and exploring the findings of researchers studying work in different parts of the world. All this convinces us that while ambition, satisfaction, fulfilment and cooperation are commonly present in the office and on the shopfloor, they continue to co-exist alongside (and in many cases remain secondary to) feelings of frustration, boredom, resistance and the pursuit of strategies designed to make it easier to get through the working day. Likewise, just as a formal management rationality may be identified to a greater or lesser extent in all workplaces, so too can a more informal workers' counter-rationality: less immediately visible perhaps, but a counter-rationality that has just as much, if not more to do with understanding how workers experience work than anything deriving from management. As we shall see, this counter-rationality takes several different forms, ranging from gaining additional (unofficial) rest periods to organising work in ways to achieve an easing of work pressures, increased income and/or a sense of control. The pervasiveness of such counter-rationalities, and their significance for those involved, indicates the importance of analysing these aspects of work behaviour not as temporary deviations from a management orthodoxy, but as persistent and rational responses of groups of workers whose interests only partially coincide with those of management, and who have a vested interest in, for example, preserving their energy, maximising income, having fun and gaining a sense of control over their work situation.

What this book is anxious to avoid, however, is the trap of replacing one myth about the realities of work with another. Just as work is not, for the majority, as it is portrayed or implied in most contemporary management texts, so too no single contrasting representation would be any more accurate. What is needed to a much greater extent than has usually been recognised, is to capture the *diverseness* of work experience – the fact that workers experience, in varying degrees, both satisfaction *and* alienation, demonstrate both cooperation *and* resistance, display both common interests *and* opposing ones, and perceive their distinct interests in both individual *and* collective terms. The challenge that faces us is to explore the *varied* experiences of work – in short, the realities of work. But this needs some explanation, so first we must set out our analytical frame of reference.

The Analysis of Work

Any analysis of work and working lives involves addressing a range of concepts that often seem to be competing with each other. In other words, there are inevitable tensions associated with the different ways the subject can be approached, so it is important to make clear at the outset the position we are adopting. Our aim is to explore the variety and diversity of work experiences, and in so doing we have tried also to reveal the diversity of ways that work can be investigated. Just as there are many realities of work, so too there are many ways of exploring those realities. The plurality of the experience of work is matched by a plurality in ways that work can be studied. We will clarify (and qualify) this pluralist perspective below, but first it is important to identify the key tensions (see Figure 1.1) and explain how we are approaching them.

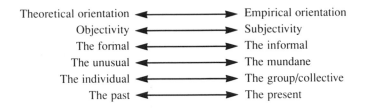

Theoretical orientation	Empirical orientation
Objectivity	Subjectivity
The formal	The informal
The unusual	The mundane
The individual	The group/collective
The past	The present

Figure 1.1 *Key tensions in the study of work*

Theoretical Orientation — Empirical Orientation

Given the central role of paid work to industrial capitalism, and to the individuals therein, it is not surprising that the subject has given rise to extensive theoretical consideration which, at best, offers a stimulating variety of ideas. However, no single theory successfully captures the cross-cutting nature of work experience: the ways in which work encapsulates both conflict and cooperation, satisfaction and alienation, tension and accommodation. What we have found useful is to draw upon the most relevant theories at different points in the argument, focusing attention on the value of different theories for locating and interpreting work experiences and worker behaviour within a broader conceptual framework. In this way, then, the book does not advocate or adopt a single theoretical perspective but is informed by a range of theories, and seeks to tread the difficult – but what is felt to be ultimately the more rewarding – route of incorporating different theoretical insights without on the one hand becoming shackled to a single orthodoxy, or on the other hand being guilty of inappropriately cobbling together convenient bits of different theories to form an illogical pastiche.

We have also attempted to achieve a balance between theory and empiricism. There is a rich empirical tradition in Anglo-Saxon academic research that has informed our understanding of the experience of work. Moreover, empirical studies display a true plurality of research methods, all of which are legitimate and worthy attempts to explore the realities of work – although, of course, they vary in quality and rigour. Throughout the chapters, we have tried to show how different research methods have been used to address a variety of questions: methods which range from the ethnographic approach of qualitative researchers to the statistical analyses of their quantitative counterparts. Similarly, there is diversity in the levels of analysis: from detailed studies of particular workplaces to international comparative surveys. In some instances too, these different methods have been used to address the same research question, producing a plurality of interpretations that compete with one another for theoretical supremacy; nowhere is this better illustrated than over the issue of skill discussed in Chapter 5. As committed, active researchers ourselves, we have a strong conviction that theory and empiricism have a symbiotic relationship: an empirical account devoid of theory is as inadequate as a theory without data.

Objectivity—Subjectivity

The plurality of empirical study also reveals a deeper tension between, on the one hand, researchers whose concern is to explore the objective conditions, processes and causal effects surrounding work, and those who seek to interpret subjective experiences and the meanings that people derive from their work. We have drawn from both perspectives, and have sought to show the increasing importance of recognising a balance between considering the extreme objectivist position of one concrete, measurable truth, and the extreme subjectivist view of a multitude of intangible, impressionistic, equally valid truths. As noted above, we reject the notion that the essence or 'true' experience of work can be distilled into a single thesis or argument. It is one thing to identify common properties, general influences and widespread constraints, but it is another to postulate grand theories supposedly encapsulating the 'reality' of work. For a central problem is that the world of work, and work people's objective and subjective locations within that world, are more complex than that. Not only do the activities which constitute work take highly diverse forms, are conducted in a wide variety of settings, with those taking part displaying the full range of character and biographical variation, but in addition it is clear that people subjectively experience work in a host of different ways. Hence, as the book's title indicates, what needs to be sought is an understanding of the reali*ties*, rather than any all-embracing reality, of work. This is not to dismiss the possibility of unearthing various widespread influences or common characteristics of work in contemporary industrial society. But while identifying and assessing these, it is equally important in a book of this nature to give recognition to the diversity of work realities.

Inextricably interwoven with theory—empiricism and objectivity—subjectivity are the next three, largely self-explanatory tensions listed in Figure 1.1 above:

> the formal   —   the informal
> the unusual   —   the mundane
> the individual   —   the group/collective

Again, our intention has been to strike a balance. So, we contrast the formal policies and procedures of employment with the informal practices enacted on the shop and office floor, exemplified by the strategies to get through the working day discussed in Chapter 8 and the counter-control of time in Chapter 4. We encounter the unusual, such as the deviant work in Chapter 10, and the mundane, like the routine tasks of the assembly-line in Chapter 6. We examine both the individual and the group, attempting to pull these two perspectives in and out of focus to provide a more detailed, dynamic overall image. Indeed, in all the chapters, our concern lies with the relationship between the individual experience and the collective understanding of work. In particular, we will explore how collectively negotiated understandings permeate the work setting, disadvantaging some individuals and groups, and benefiting others.

The Past—The Present

Throughout the discussion we have attempted to give a sense of history. All too often management texts fail to acknowledge the historical traditions of work and working, which means that the reasons why particular practices, policies or ideas came into being are obscured. At worst, such an ahistorical approach has meant that each issue is dealt with as a contemporary problem that can be solved by a quick-fix solution: typically in the form of the latest buzz-word or policy to emanate from self-styled management gurus. It is little wonder that the result is at best a mixed success. Moreover, such an approach shows a contempt for the past that is both ill-advised and anti-academic. In contrast, we have tried to imbue our analysis with a respect for the past in terms of ideas, practices, theories and research. Our concern is to show that the realities of work are embedded with resonant themes, abiding struggles and unresolved problems; 'new' issues and ideas are often in practice a new expression of the dilemmas and concepts of a previous period.

However, this does not mean that important changes have not occurred in the world of work. If there are good reasons for writing a book which seeks to underline the realities of work experience and the variance of those realities from that suggested in parts of the extant literature, there are good reasons too for undertaking such a project at the present time. Prominent among these is the need to reflect important changes in work which have been occurring in recent years and the prospects for further significant changes in the future. At their most general these involve very broad issues relating to eras or 'regimes' of industrial capitalism and whether or not the current period is one where emphasis is shifting from key sectors of work being organised on the basis of large-scale, standardised, mass production operations (with all that entails in terms of the size of organisations, the nature of jobs and patterns of control) to smaller-scale, more flexible forms of organisation, taking full advantage of more flexible technologies to service less standardised, more fragmented and more volatile product markets (see for example, Aglietta, 1979; Piore and Sabel, 1984). Whether or not the entire thesis regarding a shift towards 'flexible specialisation' can be sustained – the evidence is far from conclusive – what is clear is that a combination of factors, including changes in levels of competition, the nature of markets and available technologies, are resulting in significant changes in the character of many work organisations.

In other, more immediate ways too, the character of work has been changing markedly in recent years. Nowhere is this change more apparent than in the growing feminisation of the workforce to a point where, in the UK for example, almost half (and in the foreseeable future, over half) of the labour force is comprised of women. Indeed, as we examine in more detail in Chapter 2, in various regions and industry sectors in the UK, women already constitute the majority of workers. With the sociology of work criticised for being unreflective of women (see, for example, Tancred, 1995) and with many individual studies criticised (rightly) as being written largely by men about men working in factories, this point in industrial history, when the balance is shifting to a majority of the workforce being female, makes it an appropriate time to consider more closely the contemporary realities of work for both women and men.

If many industrial societies are reaching a point in their history where women outnumber men in the workforce, they are far beyond such a turning point in terms of the respective sizes of their manufacturing and service workforces. The dominance of the latter as the larger source of employment is well established, and in a country such as the UK there are now four times as many people working in service activities as in manufacturing (see Chapter 2). Yet, despite their respective sizes, the research attention focused on work in service organisations remains less than might be expected. Further, besides a general need to reflect more accurately the realities of work in the whole range of work contexts, there is need to represent new aspects of work which the expansion of services has brought about. For example, the increase in activities involving direct contact with the public, coupled with a greater emphasis by management on the importance of those dealings (and the delivery of 'customer care' as a key source of competitive advantage) has given rise to work activities entailing not just mental or manual work, but also 'emotional' work – work where an explicit part of the job is to display a particular set of emotions (Hochschild, 1983). Such labour has long been part of many – particularly female-dominated – occupations such as nursing, but it is only comparatively recently that questions have been raised about the implications of such labour for the nature and experience of work (emotional labour is the focus of Chapter 7).

EMPLOYMENT RELATIONS: MANAGEMENT–WORKERS

Central to the analysis throughout the book is a further fundamental tension that warrants introduction here: that of the employment relationship between management and workers. In this regard, we are intentionally seeking less of a 'balance' because we are concerned centrally with the way that work is experienced, rather than how labour is managed. Moreover, we are concerned with the diversity of the employment experience between employees.

Nevertheless, it is important to recognise that management and workers can be characterised as two groups engaged in a structural conflict. Workers' interests only partially coincide with those of management and apart from a common 'zone of interest coincidence' incorporating aspects such as organisational survival, each of the parties maintains their own distinct interests and agendas. Thus, while management's key concern, for example, lies with labour's *performance*, labour's concern may be seen to lie in protecting other interests in the face of any drive for improved performance – for example, avoiding over-work, gaining satisfaction, maximising income and achieving a sense of control or enjoyment. Yet at the same time, since management can only hope to achieve their performance objectives by securing active workers' consent – for it is not possible for them to obtain continued higher performance solely through the exercise of control over labour – the effect is in practice to remove the option of seeking to suppress all workforce activities not directly related to the accomplishment of managerial goals. Such suppression, while unlikely in any event ever to be more than partially successful, would be likely seriously to endanger the consent that management requires from its workforce. As a result of these two factors – the partial coincidence of interests and the need for management to secure active workers' cooperation in the production of goods and services – the relationship between management and workforce is 'not simply one of (management) control versus (worker) resistance, but a more problematic mix of dissent and accommodation, conflict and cooperation' (Blyton and Turnbull, 1994: 31).

This is not to argue that the two parties share a symmetry of power in their relationship to each other. On the contrary, the employment relationship is characterised by a distinct asymmetry of power, encapsulated in the employer's key ability to hire and fire labour. What does result from the distinctiveness of the two sets of interests, however, is a co-existence of management rationalities and workers' counter-rationalities. Further, the common element of management and worker interests, and the interdependencies which exist between the two groups, indicate the bases of co-existence of the two sets of rationalities, with little attempt by one to usurp or suppress the other. It is the combination of these factors – the partial coincidence/partial difference of interests, management's need for active workforce consent as well as control, and the resulting tension and accommodation between management and workforce rationalities – that help to shape many of the aspects of how work is experienced.

METHODOLOGICAL PLURALISM

It will be apparent from the discussion so far that our concern with seeking to explore diversity and variation in the work experience, our acceptance of the many interests and struggles of the employment relationship, and our appreciation of the varied theoretical perspectives and methods of research and analysis, places us as methodological pluralists. Having been out of fashion, the rise of individualism, the challenge of postmodernism and the political hegemony of the right in advanced capitalist economies, has given fresh impetus to pluralist approaches, not least as a platform from which to critique prevailing orthodoxies. It is our conviction that a pluralist framework of analysis also offers an alternative to the drift towards postmodernism, perhaps helping to alleviate the fears of those who bemoan postmodernism as a rigorless, distracting, obscure exercise in navel gazing (see for example, Best and Kellner, 1991; P. Thompson, 1993). In a recent analysis of pluralism, McLennan (1995: 99) suggests that an important feature of what he describes as 'new pluralism' is the way it can address and even resolve the dilemma, ambivalence and paradox in society – a sentiment we share and hope to demonstrate in this book.

Our approach of *methodological pluralism* warrants a little more explanation. McLennan (1995: 57–76) argues that the methodological pluralist has to take a position with regard to ontology (the nature of reality) and epistemology (the way of knowing). This involves deciding whether there can be a pluralist ontology (many realities), a pluralist epistemology (many ways of knowing) or both (many ways of knowing many realities). Consequently, the methodological pluralist can take one of three positions, which McLennan (1995: 73–4) sums up by using three slogans:

1. 'Many versions, many (constructed) worlds'
2. 'Many (fragmented, temporary) versions, one enduring world'
3. 'One (true, valid) version for every single world, but many worlds'.

The first slogan reflects the acceptance of both epistemological and ontological pluralism, whilst the second accepts epistemological pluralism, but rejects ontological pluralism. However, it is the third slogan that reflects the position we adopt here: the rejection of epistemological pluralism, but the acceptance of ontological pluralism. To quote McLennan (1995: 74) again:

[This perspective] maintains that each of the many worlds is perfectly *real*, not just imagined, and for each of these worlds there will (eventually or in principle) be only *one* comprehensive valid theory. Of course, at any given point there are likely to be several plausible versions for each of the various worlds, but it is never legitimate to regard all of these versions as equally valid in principle. [Emphasis in original.]

Having defined our approach to the subject, it is now necessary to specify our field of enquiry. So, a brief word on the definition of work before we map out the overall plan of the book.

WHAT IS WORK?

A definition of work is the 'application of effort or exertion to a purpose' (Concise Oxford Dictionary). If we are not sleeping, eating or engaging in leisure activities, what we are likely to be doing is work, in one form or another. In practice, the boundaries are rather less clear cut than this because many leisure pursuits – such as gardening or woodworking – can also be categorised as work; indeed, for some (landscape gardeners and carpenters) these activities represent not a leisure activity but their main source of paid employment. Hence, the same activity may represent a leisure activity in one context and paid work in another. Thus, it is not the activity itself which defines whether or not it is work, but the circumstances under which the activity is undertaken.

Most books on work confine their attention to paid employment. Clearly, given the number of people involved, the time devoted to it and its importance as a source of income, this is an important component of work. Further, it is paid employment in the sphere of visible work that society views as the principal form of work – 'real' work in these terms is seen to be that which is remunerated. But at the same time, such a focus obscures as much as it reveals: the concentration solely on paid work ignores huge areas of work which, if paid for, would equal or exceed the total value of paid work which is undertaken. The main areas of unpaid 'hidden' work are household-based work (cooking, cleaning, child-rearing, home improvement, and so on) and a range of activities falling under the heading of voluntary work. Work may also be 'hidden' if it involves illegal activities, or is undertaken for payment which is not declared to the tax authorities. What is needed is to strike a balance which gives a greater recognition to the different activities which constitute people's work. Further, such a balance is necessary not only because of the scale of the different spheres of work but also because of the key links between the different spheres of paid and unpaid, visible and hidden work. The fact that unpaid work is undertaken disproportionately by one group (women) and the implications of work in the unpaid sphere for access to paid work, makes the study of the different areas of work more important still. Thus, while several of the issues in the book require primary consideration to be given to work in the form of paid employment, at the same time and at several specific points, recognition is given to a broader definition of work, both to underline the significance of the different spheres in their own right, as well as the significance of hidden work for a fuller understanding of the nature and character of paid employment.

OUTLINE OF THE TEXT

Space prevents equal consideration being given to all conceivable aspects relating to the analysis of work experiences, and it has been necessary to select what are judged to be the main issues and themes in the light of our overall focus. In so doing, it was felt that certain issues needed to be woven through the fabric of the text, rather than being separated out into individual chapters. Perhaps most important in this regard is the issue of gender. The studies of the significance of gender at work convincingly demonstrate that it must be seen as 'a major organising principle' (Cockburn, 1985: 251) and consequently should be included at every stage of analysis of work. So, there is no chapter on 'gender' because it represents an important issue within each chapter; indeed, in Chapters 5, 7 and 10, for example, gender emerges as the most significant analytical concept. A similar approach has been taken with regard to the impact of technology on work, and changes which have taken place under the title of flexibility – changes which range from the way tasks are grouped together to new employment contracts and work patterns. The pervasiveness of a number of recent developments indicated that, rather than being located in one part of the book, they needed to run through the book as a whole, surfacing at various points in the analysis.

Two themes which do not figure in the book are managerial work and industrial relations processes. The former was omitted not only because of space limitations but also because of the qualitatively different position held by managerial workers compared to most of the other groups on which the book focuses. Recent accounts of managerial work (for example Hales, 1986; Jackall, 1988; Reed, 1989; Scase and Goffee, 1989; T.J. Watson, 1994) may usefully be read in conjunction with the present text. In terms of industrial relations, the significance of collectivism and trade union organisation is identified at many points throughout the book, both at a general level (for example, the implications for the broader context of work of the weakening of trade unions in the 1980s and 1990s) and in more specific terms (such as the role of trade unions in influencing particular patterns of skill definition). What has been left to others, however, is an assessment of recent developments in industrial relations structures, processes and outcomes which, while having a bearing on actual work experiences, require separate and detailed treatment rather than what here would necessarily be rather too passing a reference (see Blyton and Turnbull, 1994).

These boundaries having been clarified, the themes outlined earlier inform the analysis contained in the remaining chapters. Overall, the aim is to examine the contemporary realities of work, identifying the factors affecting those realities. To this end, the separate chapters relate to specific aspects of work experience, such as what meanings people attach to their jobs; how people experience time at work; what factors affect whether jobs are defined as skilled or not (and whether jobs increasingly require more or less skills); how new forms of work performance are being expected of employees; how different groups and individuals use various coping mechanisms to deal with the more unpalatable aspects of their work; how work becomes a site of hostility and unfairness for some people; and how work is experienced outside the boundaries of conventional employment.

Our discussion begins by locating the different aspects of work within a broader perspective. Chapter 2 presents an overview of the changing political, economic and industrial contexts of work, together with key aspects of labour market development. Using the example of the UK, the aim of this chapter is not simply to locate more micro-level developments within a broader setting, but to draw links between the nature of work performed and broader industrial, economic and political developments. It is argued, for example, that the types of work available and overall levels of skill development in a society can be related in part to choices over broader competitive strategies, reflecting either a search for competitive advantage based on improved performance (resulting, for example, from skills enhancement) or alternatively on minimising cost (via, for instance, maintaining low wages and/or minimising expenditure on training).

In Chapter 3, the meanings attached to work are explored, raising important questions about why people work, and considering the possible existence not of a single but of multiple work ethics, and the possible relationships between these work ethics and the nature of contemporary work. The significance of aspects of working time for the overall experience of work is considered in Chapter 4. This chapter examines the development of a time-discipline among workers, and the importance of recent trends in the duration, arrangement and utilisation of working time. In this chapter too, consideration is given to whether or not work is becoming more intensive, as employers seek a higher utilisation of time through, for example, reductions in the amount of non-productive time.

Chapter 5 examines the concept of skill, identifying its problematic basis and the need to view the ways in which jobs are defined as skilled or non-skilled through a process of social construction – a process which, in the past, has worked more in favour of some groups (notably men and trade union members) than others. The question of skill is continued in Chapter 6, which considers the issue of the routinisation of office and shopfloor work. The chapter explores whether, as a result of management strategies and technological changes, work is becoming deskilled or whether recent qualitative and quantitative data allow a different interpretation to be applied: upskilling and reskilling.

Chapter 7 considers a growing aspect of work – emotional labour – which refers to job demands that require the performance of a particular emotional display: a display which, in many occupations, has become increasingly central to the delivery of 'customer care'. As this aspect of work has so far been given little consideration in texts on the subject, we examine not only the nature and development of emotional labour, but its possible effects on those required to perform it as part of their jobs. Studies of emotional labour have identified a range of coping mechanisms which workers employ to handle the demands of prolonged performance of emotional labour. Other aspects of 'survival strategies' are the subject of Chapter 8, which reviews different ways in which workers 'manage' the pressures and monotony which characterise many occupations. These coping mechanisms can take various forms, ranging from informal rules, games and jokes, to fiddling and sabotage. In these activities, issues of group identity, sub-cultures and social closure are prominent, underlining the importance of informal groups for understanding the dynamics of workplace behaviour.

Chapter 9 focuses on the issue of discrimination at work. While several other chapters highlight ways in which women have been disadvantaged in the past (for example, in relation to the way skill has been defined) in this chapter the focus on gender is broadened to explore the experience of discrimination by drawing from research on race and ethnicity. The process of discrimination at work is theorised, and competing theoretical perspectives on equal opportunities are examined, together with a consideration of provisions adopted in the workplace.

In Chapter 10 the focus shifts to work lying beyond paid and visible employment. By considering both 'unrecognised' work (in the domestic and voluntary spheres) and work which is paid but remains 'concealed' (either work which is performed 'off the cards' to avoid tax payments, or work which is clandestine primarily because it is wholly or partially illegal) the chapter allows a fuller consideration of the broad range of work activities, and also the important ways in which work in the formal sector is closely interrelated with the hidden work sector. Finally, in Chapter 11 the discussion is broadened out to reflect on key themes that have emerged from this exploration of the realities of work.

2 The Changing Context of Work

INTRODUCTION

The comment is often made that the world of work has undergone dramatic changes over the past 20 to 30 years. Some commentators have gone so far as to characterise these changes as representing a fundamental shift in the nature of capitalism itself: a shift from 'Fordist' to 'post-Fordist' forms of production, from mass production systems to flexible specialisation, from industrial to post-industrial society, or from modern to post-modern forms of organisation. Such broad characterisations usefully signal both the depth of changes taking place and also the ways myriad individual changes can be interpreted as part of much broader trajectories. At the same time, it is important to examine the specific changes themselves because such generalising shorthands constantly run the danger of obscuring as much as (or more than) they reveal. Not only do they encourage (over)generalisations about the direction in which society is heading, they also (and often more implicitly) embody sweeping assumptions about where it has been.

In this chapter it is necessary to cover a lot of ground fairly quickly, for its purpose is to present an overview of how the context of work has been and is changing, and in so doing offer a broad landscape within which to locate the more specific experiences of work that are discussed in later chapters. Even an overview must be selective, however, since contexts can be defined at several levels – an individual worker is located in a particular work setting, but in turn that workplace is situated within a local economy, which itself is embedded in national and international economic contexts. Further, these economic contexts are interrelated with, and influenced by, political contexts also operating at each level. Thus, in this chapter it is necessary to review some of the main changes that have been taking place in the political context of work over the past two decades, as well as both broad changes occurring within the economic context, and changing patterns of employment. Many of the issues raised in this chapter feed directly into more specific arguments covered in more detail later. For the moment though, the need is to capture a sense of the breadth of change occurring at the different levels.

The chapter is divided into three sections. First, the broad changes occurring in the political context of work over approximately the last two decades are reviewed, followed in the next section by a similar examination of the central (and often closely related) changes occurring within the economic context, together with some of the main responses to those changes. The major

developments occurring in the structure and patterns of employment are explored
in the third section. To illustrate this discussion we draw primarily on the case of
the UK, though for the most part the trends and patterns identified are also
similarly evident within other industrial societies.

CHANGES IN THE POLITICAL CONTEXT

It is impossible to analyse work without giving some consideration to the
political context within which work is located. More accurately, it is necessary to
consider a series of political contexts embedded within one another: the
international political environment, the national political context and local
politics. Each of these are considered briefly below in an attempt to apply some
broad brush strokes to the political backcloth against which the realities of work
may be examined. The discussion is confined to the aspects of the political
context that have impacted upon the workplace.

The International Political Environment

In Europe, one of the most important cross-national political developments has
been the establishment of the European Union (EU). Member states are subject
to a growing body of European law which is increasingly impacting upon work
organisations by obliging employers (and countries as a whole) to comply with
European legislation, even if individual national governments are reluctant. For
example, the European Court of Justice has in the past forced the British
Government to enact additional equal pay provisions to take into account the
European Community legislation covering work of equal value (Rubinstein,
1984). More recently (1995) the UK Government has been required to change the
law on employment protection to give part-time workers the same qualifying
period as their full-time counterparts in respect of statutory employment rights
concerning, for example, redundancy pay and unfair dismissal compensation
(Dickens, 1995: 209).

The political logic behind introducing EU-wide legislation is to enhance the
free movement of labour by harmonising the conditions and rights of employees
across national boundaries. This is particularly important for the more prosperous
states such as Germany which might otherwise fall victim to 'social dumping' – a
process whereby companies transfer elements of production to countries within
the EU which have lower wages, less employment protection and fewer employment rights, thus decreasing the costs and overheads of labour. Such differentials
exert considerable pressure on those member states with favourable employment
terms and conditions to lower them in order to provide a competitive environment
for the companies located there. The logical consequence of this is a spiralling-
down of employment protection, with Europe becoming a domain of decreasing

employment rights and increasing insecurity and exploitation – a politically and morally undesirable outcome within most member states.

In the process of enshrining European-wide employment rights and better conditions, a key development has been the establishment of the European Community Charter of the Fundamental Social Rights of Workers (known as the Social Charter). In 1989 it was accepted by 11 of the then 12 member states (the UK refusing to sign) as a political proclamation, with no formal legal status. However, it established the direction in which social policy was to develop, and by 1992 the 11 member states acted to begin the process of implementing the Social Charter through the EU institutions by signing a Protocol on Social Policy (the social chapter). Again Britain refused to be a signatory, and this 'opting out' has led to the notion of a 'two-speed' Europe in regard to social policy and employment rights, with the UK in the slow lane (for a fuller discussion, see Towers, 1992).

A related international political issue concerns the extent to which the concept of the 'nation state' is being challenged as the most significant body of governance. As stated above, the transnationalism of the EU is having an impact in the workplace, but there is an additional supranational influence that is also becoming increasingly pervasive: the multinational corporation. The growth of multinational organisations has meant that increasingly it is possible to identify a global division of labour, with the amount, type and quality of employment differentiated across the world under the guidance of corporate management. The stability and credibility of politicians has come to be guided as much by corporate interest as accountability to an electorate – particularly so when investment in a particular region means jobs and local economic prosperity. Moreover, the dependency of many developing nations on the continued investment by multinationals is well illustrated by Shell in Nigeria, or the desperate search for western capital by countries of Eastern Europe and the former Soviet bloc.

The National Political Context

In spite of the growing significance of the supranational context, however, the national political context still represents an important influence in the advanced capitalist economies of the west. Nowhere is this more so than in the UK which stands out as having experienced a series of governments in the 1980s and 1990s dedicated to pursuing employment policies distinct from (and frequently in direct opposition to) the trends in the rest of the European Union. Successive Conservative Governments since 1979 sought to deregulate the labour market in an attempt to allow employers to operate more freely. This policy of deregulation has been underpinned by theories of neo-classical economics which hold that economic revival is dependent on allowing market forces to operate free from any 'artificial' constraint or government intervention. It is argued that competitiveness has been hampered in the past by high labour costs caused by the restrictions and rigidities imposed on employers by employment protection legislation, and the power and influence of trade unions. Both these factors are seen to raise labour costs artificially and stand in the way of allowing market rates and forces to prevail. Seduced by this reasoning, successive Conservative Governments from 1979 onwards embarked on a series of incremental changes that sought to deregulate employment and restrict the influence of trade unions.

Deregulating employment has had the effect of shifting the balance away from employment protection towards employment flexibility – a flexibility which carries a number of consequences for those both in and out of work. However, in identifying the full extent and implications of deregulation, care needs to be taken, for it is something of a misnomer to talk of the government in the UK 'deregulating' the relations between capital and labour. Indeed, relative to many other economies, the labour market and employment relationships in the UK have *never been* highly regulated. In the UK, legislation on such basic employment issues as the maximum hours a worker is permitted to work, or the minimum number of days' holiday a person is entitled to, is notable by its absence. The same holds for the type of employment contracts that an employer can offer – for example, unlike various other countries there is no requirement for employers in the UK to justify the offering of temporary rather than permanent contracts. A similar picture has also been true in regard to the representation of employee interests, with no statutory regulation requiring employers to conduct negotiations with trade unions, and if negotiations are conducted and agreements struck, nothing in law to say that these agreements are legally binding contracts.

In these circumstances, the deregulation of labour markets which has taken place in the UK since the early 1980s is all the more significant: it removes and reduces regulations in a context already characterised by a low degree of regulation. Further, in a country where labour market regulation is in any event only modest, the further diminution of that basis of regulation has considerable *symbolic* significance regarding the perceived relations between capital and labour and the lack of any need to protect the latter against the powers of the former.

Governments have acted to deregulate the labour market in various ways. Prominent among these has been the extension of employees' qualifying period from six months to two years to achieve various (modest) employment protection rights, such as the right to question whether or not a dismissal has been practised fairly. The result of this is to leave workers with less than two years service more vulnerable to dismissal. There are many instances, for example, of employees being dismissed a few weeks before their two-year qualifying period has been worked, and new workers set on, in order that the employer avoids employment protection responsibilities, such as the requirement to make maternity provisions. Indeed, this was blatant at EMI where packers were offered temporary contracts of one year and 364 days – completely legal, although somewhat morally questionable (BBC *Panorama*, 17 May 1993).

Other direct deregulation has had the effect of, first, restricting the coverage of, and subsequently abolishing Wages Councils (for a fuller discussion of the reasoning, see Dickens *et al.*, 1993). The principal role of the Wages Councils was as minimum wage-setting mechanisms in industries poorly served by trade unions or collective bargaining. The Wages Act (1986) excluded workers under the age of 21 from coverage by Wages Council decisions, and reduced the degree to which Councils could specify different wage and overtime rates. Subsequently, the Trade Union Reform and Employment Rights Act (1993) abolished the Wages Councils still remaining (with the exception of agriculture) which means that the UK is the only European Union country with no form of legal protection for low-paid employees (see Table 2.1).

Successive Conservative Governments since 1980 also acted to deregulate labour markets by imposing restrictions on the operations of trade unions. The argument by the state is that 'over strong' trade unions have created 'rigidities' in labour markets by using their power to push up wages artificially, beyond competitive rates, and generally to influence recruitment policies, staffing levels, and work organisation in ways deleterious to competition. Two areas specifically targeted as requiring restriction were the abilities of unions to operate closed shops (where trade union membership is a condition of employment) and the abilities of unions to take strike action. During the 1980s, legislation had the effect of virtually removing the closed shop in Britain altogether. In 1984, it was estimated that around three and a half million manual workers were covered by closed shop agreements; by 1990 (and following restrictive legislation in the form of the 1980, 1982, 1988 and 1990 Employment Acts) this coverage had fallen to between one third and half a million (Millward *et al.*, 1992: 99). Similarly, a series of six pieces of legislation between 1980 and 1993 related to strike action which cumulatively had the effect of heavily circumscribing the conditions under which strike action can take place – an important (though not the sole) reason for the dramatic fall in numbers and size of strikes. The number of strikes in the 1975–79 period, for example, averaged 2310 annually with an average annual number of days lost around 11.7 million. However, by the early 1990s, the number of strikes and amount of days lost had fallen to less than one-tenth of these former levels (Blyton and Turnbull, 1994: 274; Sweeney and Davies, 1996).

Deregulation has not just applied to the private sector; indeed, one of the objectives of the Conservative Governments has been to inject a stronger free market ideology into the public sector. A guiding belief in this was that public sector organisations were inherently inefficient because they were not exposed to the rigours of the market. The Conservative solution was to embark on a programme of extensive privatisation, including: British Airways, British Steel, British Telecom, the public utilities (gas, electricity and water), and British Rail. Those parts of the public sector which could not be privatised (because it was politically too sensitive or too dangerous to do so, such as local authorities,

Table 2.1   *Minimum wage arrangements in Europe*

Austria	legally binding industry agreements	98% of workers covered
Belgium	legally binding central agreement	less than 10%; most covered by sector/company agreement
Cyprus	sectoral agreements, some statutory minima	85% by collective agreement; 5% on statutory minima
Denmark	legally binding sectoral agreements	80–85% of workers covered
Finland	legally binding sectoral agreements	85–90% of workers covered
France	statutory minimum	9% on minimum rate; most covered by sector agreements
Germany	legally binding sectoral agreements	90% covered
Greece	statutory central agreement	most lower level agreements improve on national minimum
Ireland	statutory minima covering 15 sectors	covers low paid sectors such as hotels and catering
Italy	legally binding industry agreements	pay negotiations cover vast majority
Luxembourg	statutory minimum	around 10% on minimum
Malta	statutory minimum	no reliable statistics
Netherlands	statutory minimum	5% on wage around minimum
Portugal	statutory minimum	about 8% directly affected by minimum
Spain	statutory minimum	around 10% of workers affected
Sweden	legally binding industry agreements	collective agreements cover most workplaces
Switzerland	industry collective agreements	50% of private sector; 350,000 public employees on minima
UK	Agricultural Wages Boards only	around 200,000 farmworkers – 1% of total workforce

Source: *Labour Research*, July 1995, taken from *New Review* of the Low Pay Unit, September/October 1994 and *OECD Employment Outlook*, July 1994.

schools, hospitals and the police) have been exposed to quasi-markets, encouraged to act like private companies by purchasing goods and services from different operating units, and obliged to contract out their operations wherever financially advantageous, through the process of compulsory competitive tendering (CCT).

In the past, one important way the state regulated employment within and around the public sector was via adherence to Fair Wages Resolutions which were based on the principle that when a private sector firm was awarded a government contract, its employees should be paid at a level commensurate with equivalent work being undertaken by public sector workers. This was part of a broader state approach to acting as a 'good employer' and promulgating its practices more widely. The good employer approach also extended to its encouragement of trade union representation, leading to very high levels of union organisation throughout most of the public sector. The introduction of commercialism into those activities remaining in the public sector, however, has occurred alongside the abandonment of Fair Wages Resolutions. Moreover, the growth in CCT has resulted in most tenders being won on the basis of least cost, with low wage levels being an important means of keeping costs down when tendering. Thus the increase in CCT and the ending of the concept of 'fair wages' has removed further 'rigidities' from the labour market concerning wage rates for employees working on government contracts.

As well as deregulation, privatisation and the commercialisation of the public sector, the political context of employment in the UK has been altered in a further significant way over the past two decades. The political willingness, underpinned by neo-classical economics, to abandon full employment and tolerate high levels of unemployment has made the experience of being out of work far more common. Further, for many school-leavers their first experience of the world of work is a government training scheme with no job at the end of it. Redundancy and unemployment are examined separately below, but it is useful here to note the political as well as the economic dimension of unemployment. If one of the ways the context of work has changed is in the overall reduction in job security and notions of the permanency of employment (and we believe this to be the case; see below) this can be traced back in part to political decisions relating to 'acceptable' unemployment levels. Indeed, it is the local impact of unemployment in the deregulated environment that highlights the need to consider the local political context.

Local Politics

One of the most vivid examples of how local politics can have an impact on work is the extent to which it encourages (or inhibits) capital investment in an area. In terms of encouraging capital investment, an example from the 1980s of local politics playing a key role relates to the location of the Nissan car company in the north-east of England. In this instance, various parts of the local state (the local authority, the county council and the local Development Corporation) acted to purchase land in sufficient quantity (over 900 acres) as to attract the car-maker with the prospect of being able to expand their operations on the site much above their originally stated plans (Crowther and Garrahan, 1988).

In the UK the local political context has also proved to be a site where an alternative political agenda can by orchestrated from that prevailing at national level. For example, the Greater London Council and local authorities such as Liverpool and Sheffield implemented policies that sought to boost local employment yet ran counter to the political intentions of the Conservative Governments in the early 1980s. Until the 1987 Transport Act, for example, Sheffield ran a subsidised bus service which was out of line with the free market policies of the Government (see also Goodwin and Duncan, 1986). Similarly, Liverpool City Council continued its massive building programme for council housing in spite of the Conservative Government's avowed goal of creating a 'home owning democracy' through a freeze on council-house building and the implementation of a 'right to buy' policy for existing tenants. Such examples must be treated with caution, however, for whilst they illustrate the potential importance of local politics in the UK, the overall tendency over the past two decades has been a reduction of local political influence through increasing centralisation at Whitehall (Hoggert, 1996).

CHANGES IN THE ECONOMIC CONTEXT

Just as significant changes can be identified in relation to the political context, so too important developments have characterised the economic context of work in recent times. One of the most marked economic changes over the recent past has been the increased internationalisation of trade in goods and services. Just as earlier periods of industrial development witnessed a gradual shift in the extent to which enterprises were oriented towards national rather than local markets, the last quarter-century has seen a marked increase in the cross-national nature of goods and service production. Indeed, it has become increasingly common to refer not just to an internationalisation of production but to its 'globalisation', conveying a sense that the entire world is coming to be viewed as a single production centre and market-place. In part, this increase in scale and breadth reflects the growing number of countries figuring in an increasingly industrialised world, with countries such as Korea, Taiwan, Singapore, Brazil, Mexico and recently Malaysia, Thailand, India and China becoming prominent industrial producers and major international traders. Globalisation also particularly reflects an expansion in multinational operations, with companies from a growing number of countries establishing production and operating facilities within an increasing number of 'host' countries. Driven by such factors as the differential cost and availability of labour, favourable exchange rates and the importance of being situated within, rather than outside, multi-country free trade areas (such as the European Single Market) the scale of multinational activity has continued to grow (Stopford and Turner, 1985). Throughout much of the twentieth century, the United States was unchallenged as the source of most multinational companies, but while the US remains prominent, the last quarter of the twentieth century has seen a growing proportion of multinational activity originating from elsewhere – most notably from Japan (Campbell and Burton, 1994). In Britain by the early 1990s, for example, 200 Japanese companies had been established, including major employers such as Toyota, Sony, Nissan and Honda. Increasingly too, multinational companies originating from other South-East Asian countries such as Hong Kong, Korea, and Taiwan, together with European countries such as Germany, have become increasingly evident.

The spread of industrialism, the increased presence of multinationals and the growth of large free trade zones have contributed to an intensification of competition in many markets over the past generation. A growing number of local and domestic markets have become exposed to wider competition, either as a result of international trade or through activities of multinationals producing for the 'host' country market. So much so that a worker in the UK Midlands, for example, could work at the Rover Longbridge car plant (now German owned), or the (French owned) Peugeot Ryton plant, travel to and from work in their British manufactured Ford or Vauxhall car (both US multinationals in the UK), do their shopping at lunchtime in their local (German owned) Aldi supermarket, and travel into Birmingham at the weekend to purchase household goods at the local (Swedish owned) Ikea superstore, before returning home to watch their UK manufactured (Japanese owned) Hitachi television, picking up a hamburger from the local (American owned) McDonald's on the way.

Besides the pervasiveness of multinationals, other factors too can be seen to have fuelled the intensification of competition, not least an accelerated diffusion of new technologies, generally resulting in more restricted technological advantage being enjoyed by individual companies for a more limited time. Related to this, technological advances in telecommunications have accelerated the speed with which companies can effectively operate in geographically dispersed markets, thereby undermining any advantage of proximity and exclusivity which local producers might previously have benefited from.

The effects of intensified competition on work and workers can manifest themselves in a variety of ways depending on how employers respond to the competitive pressure. Decisions such as positioning in markets through acquisition, divestment, or change in location, which markets to operate in, which products to develop or abandon and which technologies to employ, are all likely to be influenced by the nature and intensity of competition. At the same time, however, in the search for competitive advantage and efficiencies, labour and labour costs frequently play a central role. This is often not only true where labour costs represent a high proportion of total costs, but also where labour costs form a much smaller proportion, but are more open to manipulation (at least in the shorter term) than other, more fixed costs. In the international air passenger transport industry, for example, labour costs represent only between 25 and 35 per cent of total operating costs (Doganis, 1994: 18); however, many other costs (for example, the cost of aircraft and fuel prices) are less open to manipulation, thus making labour one of the few 'variable' elements of cost, at least in the short term. As a result, in the face of deregulation and growing competition in the industry, there is strong pressure on airline managements to improve competitiveness via cuts in their overall labour costs (Blyton and Turnbull, 1996).

There are essentially two contrasting strategies that employers may adopt towards labour in their search for competitive adavantage: on the one hand, by increasing the output that labour achieves; or on the other, by reducing its cost. In practice, of course, these two strategies do not represent the sole choice available. Rather, they are located at each end of a continuum of responses, with employers likely to seek improvements in their competitive position by a mixture of responses designed to increase performance *and* reduce costs. Variation, therefore, is likely to be not between one extreme and the other but rather between the relative priorities given to performance improvement and cost reduction. Yet, it is helpful to delineate the two ends of the continuum in a little more detail, for they indicate how broad economic (and political) strategies have important ramifications for labour. At one extreme, seeking competitiveness through improved performance presupposes the creation of a highly trained and competent workforce, capable of utilising a high level of skill to yield increased levels of output. The other extreme, of a labour strategy based on lowest cost, is likely to entail minimising expenditure on training, resulting in a low-skill, low-productivity, low-cost workforce. The choice between these strategies (or the relative weight given to each within more complex strategies) is not only an economic choice but also reflects political policies and constraints. An important reason, for example, why employers in Germany have generally pursued a 'high skill, high performance' strategy is partly because state policies on training and vocational education have resulted in an extensive training infrastructure, and a comparatively high level of skill development among the labour force. Added to this, alternative strategies such as minimising labour costs by hiring in workers when demand is strong, then firing them when demand drops, are less readily available to German employers, because of statutory restrictions governing redundancy and dismissal. This contrasts with the UK where there is little regulatory constraint on employers' ability to hire and fire. Given this, and the comparatively low development of national training and vocational education provision in the UK, it is evident how political policies in the two countries have influenced markedly different labour strategies (Boyer, 1988; Brunhes, 1989).

It has been widely argued that the UK in the 1980s and 1990s has been in the vanguard of those countries pursuing a low-cost competitive strategy, with consequences for levels of investment in skills, wage levels (including non-wage labour costs such as sick pay and pension contributions) and the (low value-added) nature of much of the productive activity taking place (for a discussion, see Blyton and Turnbull, 1994). The low wage levels and widespread availability of labour (due partly to high levels of unemployment: see below) have been important factors encouraging a high level of foreign direct investment into the UK compared, for example, to other EU countries. Much of this investment has required only low or modest levels of skill development, with many activities (for example, in the motor components and consumer durables) involving assembly operations of one form or another. The paucity of the education and training structure in the UK compared, for example, to many of its western European counterparts, has been well documented (see, for example, Keep, 1989 and 1994) as has the UK's level of productivity and performance (see Blyton and Turnbull, 1994: 37–44). The broader point for our present discussion, however, is that many of the salient aspects of work – types of jobs available, levels of income, extent of training and skill development, and degree of job security – can only be fully understood within the broader context of overall competitive strategies and the political and economic milieux within which those strategies are formulated and pursued.

Aside from the question of overall strategies aimed at higher performance or lower cost, in other ways too, greater competition and the search for more efficient operations have led to significant changes in how organisations approach the tasks of goods and service production. For example, the twin factors of advances in technological capability and the search for greater efficiency have stimulated the development of more advanced forms of production control, with production processes being 're-engineered' or 're-configured' to improve the sequencing and integration of different stages of productive activity within organisations and the efficiency with which production 'flows' through an organisation with the minimum of bottlenecks. Partly, this involves the supply of materials and the timing of manufacturing processes being matched more closely to customer orders, so that goods are produced 'just-in-time' to meet delivery requirements, thereby reducing the amount of capital tied up in stocks of raw materials, work-in-progress and finished goods. In terms of the possible impact on people's experience of work (and as discussed further in Chapter 4) one effect of just-in-time operations could be an increase in work intensity, or at least a reduced ability to create greater control over work pace by building up 'banks' of part-finished items that can be drawn upon to ease work pressures at a later point.

Closely associated with these changes in production processes has been an increased emphasis on output quality, with Japanese manufacturers such as Toyota leading the way in making the management of quality a key component in overall production and competitive strategy. The increased emphasis on quality has manifested itself in a variety of management initiatives such as quality assurance, quality circles and total quality management (TQM) (Deming, 1982; S. Hill, 1991; Juran, 1979; Oakland, 1989), and has given rise to additional phrases in the management lexicon such as 'continuous improvement', 'zero defects', 'internal customers' and the more commonplace 'right first time'. Much emphasis has come to be given to assuring quality at the point of production rather than at final inspection, in an attempt not only to ensure a better quality product, but in particular to avoid the cost of re-working defective output. As discussed in more detail in a later chapter, among the effects of these changes for the experience of work has been an increased emphasis on quality assurance and a requirement for workers to take greater responsibility for inspecting their own work and that of their work colleagues.

CHANGES IN INDUSTRIAL STRUCTURE AND EMPLOYMENT

The structure of employment is never static but reflects and delineates patterns of change in particular industries and broader sectors of activity. The pace and some of the contours of change vary from one industrial society to another; nevertheless a number of broad developments are evident, reflected in the changing structure of employment. Measurement of the structure and location of economic activity, the characteristics of the workforce, the nature of employment contracts and patterns of unemployment and redundancy indicate the aggregate nature of employment and the ways this is changing over time. A number of measures are interconnected: the simultaneous growth in service sector, female and part-time employment, for example. Also, some of the trends which can be identified are influenced not only by structural shifts in the economy but by cyclical factors which act to accelerate or inhibit certain longer-term changes at particular periods. At the same time, what is revealing is the robust nature of many of the structural changes: cyclical effects such as economic recession have, in many cases, had only a modest influence on several of the aspects of employment change (for example, the growth in part-time working) slowing some of the trends but rarely causing even a temporary reversal in longer-term developments. This is true even of those aspects of the employment experience, such as redundancy and unemployment, which in the past were closely associated with recessionary conditions, but in more recent times have become rather more loosely tied to overall economic conditions.

Employment in Service and Manufacturing Industries

The period since the mid-1970s has seen the continuation – and at times such as the early 1980s, the marked acceleration – of a long-running trend towards a reduction of employment in productive industries (manufacturing, utilities, mining and agriculture) and a rise in the proportion of employees working in service sector activities. In the quarter-century between 1971 and 1995, the number employed in manufacturing in Britain fell by over 4 million or more than half (Table 2.2); in the same period, the number employed in services rose by more than four and a half million. As a consequence, by 1995, more than four times as many people were employed in the service sector in Britain as worked in manufacturing. When all industries are taken into account (agriculture, forestry and fishing; mining; electricity, gas and water supply; construction; as well as manufacturing and services) the proportion of the overall workforce engaged in the service sector in Britain stood at over three-quarters (75.7 per cent) by

Table 2.2   Changes in employment in manufacturing and services in Britain
1971-95 (selected years) (thousands)

	Manufacturing	Services
1971	7 890	11 388
1975	7 351	12 545
1981	5 677	13 525
1985	4 895	14 089
1991	4 215	15 802
1995	3 845	16 138
% change 1981–95	–33.3%	+19.3%
% change 1971–95	–51.3%	+41.7%

June totals, seasonally adjusted.
Source: *Labour Market Trends*, January 1996.

September 1995, up from just over half (52.6 per cent) of the total employees in employment who worked in services in 1971. In contrast, manufacturing employment by 1995 had fallen to just over one in six (18 per cent) of the total in employment.

Within the service sector, employment in some industries has grown far more rapidly than in others. While employment in the banking, insurance and finance sector, for example, more than doubled between 1971 and 1991, and the numbers employed in hotels and catering rose by almost four-fifths, employment in other sectors showed more modest increases over that period, including retail distribution (where employment increased by 9.7 per cent), public administration (11.2 per cent increase) and transport (16.7 per cent increase) (Blyton and Turnbull, 1994: 48). Likewise, the decline in employment in production industries in the 1970s and 1980s was also very unevenly distributed with the rate of decline in some sectors (for example, coal mining, metal manufacturing and textiles) more than double that found in others (for example, paper, printing and publishing) (Blyton and Turnbull, 1994: 47).

This increasing predominance of service sector employment is also reflected in other characteristics of the employed workforce, particularly the proportions of male and female, and full and part-time workers in the workforce. Just as the past generation has been characterised by a growth in the service sector, it has also been characterised by a growth in the proportion of the workforce that is female. Several factors are important in accounting for this change, reflecting changes in both the demand for, and the supply of labour. Demand-side factors, however, are dominated by the shift to service sector employment and the increased opportunities for employment among women in service industries. This has been a key factor behind the increase in women's overall share in the workforce over the past generation. In the late 1950s, women comprised just over one-third of the total employed in Britain. By 1995, this proportion had risen to almost one-half: of the 21.3 million employees in employment in Britain in June 1995, 10.56 million (49.5 per cent) were women. As the rate of participation of males in the labour force continues to stagnate or slowly decline, and as the participation rate of women continues to rise, the realisation of a feminised workforce, where a majority of the employees in employment are women, is imminent. Indeed, the 1993 Census of Employment in Britain identified twenty-five counties and Scottish regions (out of a total of 66) where the number of female employees outnumbered their male counterparts (Thomas and Smith, 1995: 369). A workforce where the majority are female is a reality too in various industries in the UK; and in the service sector as a whole, well over half of all employees are female (see Table 2.3).

Table 2.3   *Employees in employment: results of the 1993 Census of Employment (proportions of males and females in service and non-service industries) (percentages)*

	Production industries, construction, agriculture, forestry and fishing (%)	Service industries (%)
Males	35.9	64.1
Females	13.7	86.3
Total – all employees in employment	25.0	75.0

Source: *Employment Gazette*, October 1995.

A major aspect of this growth in the service sector and in female employment has been the growth in the number of part-time jobs. By 1995 two in every seven jobs in Britain were part-time (Table 2.4). Of these, four-fifths (80.3 per cent) were held by women, and while just over one in ten male employees worked part-time, among females the proportion was over four in every nine. According to the Census of Employment figures, in 1993 more than nine out of ten (93 per cent) of these female part-time jobs were located in the service sector (see Naylor, 1994, for a detailed historical examination of the growth of part-time working in Britain).

Self-employment

As well as changes in the employed workforce there have also been significant developments in the extent of self-employment over the past two decades. Between 1971 and 1981, the number of self-employed rose only slightly, and in

Table 2.4   *Part-time working in Britain, 1995* (thousands)*

	Female	*Male*	*Total*
Part-time	4 923	1 209	6 132
Full-time	5 640	9 569	15 209
All employees in employment	10 563	10 778	21 341
% of employees working part-time	46.6	11.2	28.7

* September figures.
Source: *Labour Market Trends*, January 1996.

terms of their proportion within the total labour force remained constant (Table 2.5). However, in the following decade the numbers of self-employed increased by almost half, and by 1995 over one in nine of the labour force was self-employed.

Some of the factors bringing about such a rapid increase in self-employment in the 1980s are not difficult to identify. First, the high level of unemployment and rate of redundancies in the early 1980s, coupled with a lack of job prospects, led many to seek a living by self-employment. Among the unemployed this was supported by a minimum subsidy (£40 per week for twelve months) by the state under its Enterprise Allowance Scheme, designed to move people from being unemployed to self-employed. In addition, as part of their efforts to cut direct labour costs, many companies in the 1980s abandoned employment contracts in favour of commercial contracts by requiring some of their workers to alter their status from being employees to being self-employed. This occurred, for example, among workers operating outside the main workplace, such as service engineers and milk roundsmen, and particularly in the construction sector (see Evans, 1990). Where self-employed individuals are simply selling their skills to an organisation they are sometimes referred to as 'labour only subcontractors'

Table 2.5   *Self-employment in Britain, 1971–95 (thousands)*

	1971	*1981*	*1991*	*1995**
Self-employed	1 953	2 058	3 066	3 244
Total labour force	24 637	26 028	27 614	27 211
Proportion of labour force which is self-employed (%)	7.9	7.9	11.1	11.9

* September
Source: *Labour Market Trends*, January 1996.

and these comprise a high proportion of the 2.6 million enterprises with no employees at the end of 1993 (Dale and Kerr, 1995: 462).

The growth in self-employment was heralded by governments in the 1980s as a mark of success and testimony to its 'enterprise culture'. In practice, however, much of this newly created self-employment involves low remuneration and long hours. In 1993, for example, full-time self-employed people worked, on average, around 7 hours per week more than employees (Butcher and Hart, 1995: 218). Small businesses are also prone to high rates of business failure and probably attest more to a lack of employment prospects and firms accepting only self-employed labour, rather than any significant desire for autonomy within an enterprise culture.

The Location of Employment

Size of employing organisation
Whilst it is commonplace to think of a 'typical' employing organisation as one that is fairly or very large, in fact of the 992 000 enterprises with employees operating in Britain at the end of 1993, four out of five employed less than ten people while only 17 000 (1.7 per cent of the total) employed more than 100 employees. Of these, 14 000 were medium-sized (100–499 employees) and just 3000 were large (500 or more employees) (Dale and Kerr, 1995: 462). However, these 3000 largest businesses accounted for over one-third (37 per cent) of total non-government employment. Large-scale enterprises predominate in the energy and water sector, mining and quarrying, chemicals and parts of the financial sector. Small firms on the other hand, are particularly numerous in parts of the manufacturing sector (including printing and publishing, furniture and fabricated metal products) as well as in agriculture, construction and most service industries (including business services, entertainment, catering and vehicle maintenance and repair) (Dale and Kerr, 1995: 463).

In terms of trends in firm size, there is some indication that average firm size is declining and that the proportion of total employees working for smaller firms is gradually increasing. In part, this reflects the shift from manufacturing to service activities (smaller firms being more prevalent in service industries) and the closure of many formerly very large establishments (such as steel plants and shipyards) over the past two decades. Restricted longitudinal data (covering the period 1988 to 1991) collected by the Organisation for Economic Cooperation and Development (OECD) suggest a modest trend throughout the main industrialised countries towards a larger share of employment being concentrated in smaller firms. In the UK between these dates, for example, the share of total employment located in firms with less than 100 workers rose from 47 to 49 per cent (OECD, 1995: 124). Smaller firms also figure prominently in statistics on employment creation. As the OECD (1995: 128) notes, however, 'volatility in employment levels... appears to be an intrinsic characteristic of small businesses'. In other words, smaller firms figure prominently in statistics of gross job gains *and* gross job losses (see also Shutt and Whittington, 1987).

Location of employment
As employment in production industries, particularly traditional industries such as coal, steel and shipbuilding, has declined, so too has the proportion of total employment located in the main industrial conurbations. There has been a growing tendency to establish and expand service activities and new manufacturing projects on 'greenfield' sites, often in semi-rural areas (Massey, 1988: 61; see also Sayer and Walker, 1992). Further, for a significant minority of workers, their work is located in their own home. The 1994 Labour Force Survey (LFS), for example, gives an estimate of over 640 000 people working at home in Britain. The earlier 1991 Census put this figure much higher (almost double the LFS figure), though the definition of homeworking used in the Census also included those resident in a workplace (such as hotel workers, agricultural workers, farmers and those 'living over the shop') which increases the total significantly (Felstead and Jewson, 1995).

Unemployment

Trying to draw an accurate comparison of present-day rates of unemployment with those of earlier periods is complicated by the many changes made to the basis on which unemployment statistics are calculated; since the late 1970s, for example, there have been over twenty such changes (see Denman and McDonald, 1996: 18; and Department for Education and Employment, 1995a: 398–400). Despite these difficulties, however, important long-term trends in the rate of unemployment remain evident. Average rates of unemployment increased slowly from the late 1950s onwards, with a much greater increase in the early 1980s (Table 2.6). While rates dropped to slightly lower levels during the late 1980s and early 1990s, they remained far above those experienced before 1979. The higher rates of unemployment after 1979 cannot be accounted for simply by reference to the effects of economic downturn: even in periods of growth such as in the late 1980s, the unemployment rate failed to decline to levels previously witnessed in other growth periods. Thus, overall, whilst during the period 1945–74 the average annual unemployment rate in Britain never reached 4 per cent in any single year, after 1979 there were only three years (1980, 1989 and 1990) when unemployment fell below double that figure, and for eight of the fifteen years between 1980 and 1994, annual unemployment averages remained above 10 per cent.

Despite falls in unemployment over the previous two years, by the end of 1995 there remained over two and a quarter million people registered unemployed in the UK (8 per cent of the workforce). This continuing high rate of unemployment in the 1990s is despite a marked reduction in the number of young

Table 2.6   *Unemployment rates in the UK 1945-94 (five year averages)*

Year	Yearly average (%)
1945–49	2.1
1950–54	1.7
1955–59	1.7
1960–64	1.9
1965–69	2.1
1970–74	3.1
1975–79	5.6
1980–84	11.1
1985–89	9.7
1990–94	8.7

Source: Calculated from J. Denman and P. McDonald, 'Unemployment statistics from 1881 to the present day', *Labour Market Trends*, January 1996, pp. 5–18.

people entering the labour market, as a result of both demographic trends and an increased tendency for 16- and 17-year-olds to remain in full-time education.

Unemployment impacts more upon some groups than others: the young, unskilled and those from ethnic minorities, for example, are disproportionately represented in the official unemployment figures. However, the 1990s has also seen a broadening of the impact of unemployment. During the previous decade, unemployment had primarily affected those regions (the north and west) more reliant on employment in traditional manufacturing industries, but the early 1990s recession brought unemployment to the service sector in general, and those service activities located in south-eastern England in particular. The result has been a more even spread of unemployment across the various regions of the UK than has typically been the case in the past (Department for Education and Employment, 1995b: 351).

The unemployment level at any one time, however, fails in various ways to adequately reflect the level and impact of job shortages that has come to characterise the UK since the 1970s. In the first place, the proportion of the total workforce which has experienced a period of unemployment in recent years is considerable. The prevailing level of unemployment at any particular time comprises the difference between those coming onto the unemployed register and those leaving it. Over a year, these unemployment 'flows' are far greater than changes in the unemployment rate might suggest. During 1994, for example, the overall level of unemployment fell by just under 400 000 (from 2.89 million in January 1994 to 2.50 million in January 1995). This figure, however, is the product of an inflow of new unemployment registrations of *ten times* that amount (just over 3.85 million) during the year and an outflow of 4.25 million (Department for Education and Employment, 1995b: 354). In a proportion of the cases, the same individuals become unemployed (and re-employed) more than once in any given year, thus figuring several times in the inflow and outflow statistics: studies have shown that between one-third and two-fifths of new registrations are likely to have previously been unemployed during the same year (Department for Education and Employment, 1995b: 355). What the magnitude of the flows also underlines, however, is the breadth of experience of unemployment within the workforce as a whole. It also reflects the lack of employment security partly associated with a deregulated labour market (see also below).

The level of unemployment does not reflect the total picture of job shortage, however. In addition to those officially counted as unable to find work, there are millions more who have become prematurely (and involuntarily) retired or otherwise dropped out of the labour market because of a perceived lack of prospects of finding work. Changes in the participation rates of men in the labour market indicate the scale of this discouragement effect. The proportions of males of working age who are active in the labour market (in work or registered unemployed) has fallen steadily over the past two decades, to a point where more than one in four males of working age in the UK, and not in full-time education, are not active in the labour market – a level of inactivity which Hutton (1995:1) identifies as having 'incalculable consequences' for the overall level of well-being and social cohesion in the country.

Two further points are worth making in regard to unemployment. First, the level of unemployment and the extent to which people have been made unemployed, impacts both materially and psychologically upon not only those directly affected. The impact is extended by a general heightening of awareness of job insecurity and the perceived difficulties that can be experienced in gaining employment once unemployed – difficulties clearly expressed in the scale of long-term unemployment (at the beginning of 1996, for example, over 35 per cent of those unemployed had been out of work for at least a year, and over 14 per cent had been out of work for at least three years: data from *Labour Market Trends*, March 1996), together with the disproportionate presence of some groups (such as older workers) among the long-term unemployed. The effects of high levels of unemployment on people's attitudes to work and feelings of job insecurity were vividly summed up in the 1980s by Ron Todd (then Chief Negotiator at the Ford Motor Company and later General Secretary of the Transport and General Workers Union) who commented that 'we've got 3 million on the dole and another 23 million scared to death' (quoted by Bratton, 1992: 70). The second point is that the rate of flow onto unemployed registers, and the continuing high rate of unemployment, have been influenced by the amount and circumstances under which redundancies have been declared over the recent period. It is to a more detailed consideration of redundancies that we now turn.

Redundancies and Job Insecurity

Labour Force Surveys in the UK indicate that between 1990 and 1995 over four million redundancies took place in in Britain. Redundancies are nothing new, of course. What *is* new in the 1990s, however, is the causes of redundancy. In the past, redundancies have been a consequence of economic difficulty, as Capelli (1995: 577) comments: 'Firms clearly laid off workers because of cyclical downturns or other situations where their business declined, but reductions in other situations were extremely uncommon'. However, increasingly common is the tendency for employers to announce redundancies as a cost-cutting measure even at times when the business and the economic outlook are buoyant. Quoting Capelli (1995: 577) again, 'workforce reductions are increasingly "strategic or structural in nature" as opposed to a response to short-term economic conditions'. The experience in the UK in recent years reflects this: firms announce redundancies when they are doing badly *and* when whey are doing well, with the constant shaving of workforce totals being used as a method of cost control. A key reason for this, Capelli argues, is that outside the organisation – and particularly among shareholders and investment markets – cutting workforce levels has come to be taken as a sign of restructuring, efficiency-saving and likely improvement in profitability. The upshot is that redundancy announcements can improve share prices. Capelli (1995: 571) quotes one US study, for example, (by Worrell *et al.*, 1991) which found that stock prices rose on average by about 4 per cent in the days following lay-off announcements that were part of general restructurings.

In conjunction with the higher average levels of unemployment over the past two decades, this high level of redundancies signals an increased likelihood both of employees personally experiencing redundancy and unemployment and an increased likelihood of working in an organisation where redundancies have been, and are, occurring. The effect is likely to have been to make job insecurity a more prominent concern to workers in contemporary workplaces than it was to a majority of their counterparts a generation ago. The level of insecurity has also been fuelled by a tendency for more jobs to be offered on the basis of fixed-term contracts, rather than as indefinite employment contracts. As Allen and Henry (1996: 66) point out, the growth of subcontracting in the private sector and the move towards contracting out of public services has led to a growth in 'precarious employment', where jobs are secure only for the length of the contract. The effect, as these authors note, is the creation of 'an atmosphere of pervasive insecurity' (Allen and Henry, 1996: 67).

At the same time, it should be noted that many employees continue to spend a significant part of their career with a single employer. In 1995, for example, 50 per cent of employees in Britain had at least five years' service with their employer, and a fifth of these had worked for the same employer for 20 years or more – a figure slightly higher than the proportion (19 per cent) registering at least 20 years' service with their present employer in 1992 (*Labour Market Trends*, February 1996: 39). Thus, a significant proportion of those in employment build up long service with a single employer. For others, however, work is a much more precarious affair with insecurity, redundancy, temporary contracts and unemployment contributing to an overall experience of a fragmented, rather than a unified, working life.

CONCLUSION

This chapter has illustrated some of the ways in which broader influences and developments affect the everyday realities of work. Political policies, from local planning decisions to national strategies on deregulation to the harmonisation of employment conditions across countries, have significantly influenced the context within which work is performed. With the growing integration of many national economies into multi-nation associations such as the EU, it may be anticipated that the political influences on work will be increasingly evident at the transnational level in years to come – possibly at the expense of both national and local political mechanisms.

This increasing economic and political association between different blocs of countries has also been one of the influences on levels and patterns of competition within individual sectors and markets. The growth in competition in general may be seen to have affected the experience of work in various ways: in particular, through a more intensive managerial search for both performance improvement and labour cost reduction – objectives which manifest themselves in a variety of managerial strategies in relation to the workforce, and which also reflect broader political conditions, such as the degree of statutory regulation of employment and the national provision of education and training. Competitive pressures from rising industrial nations has also been a major factor bringing about fundamental restructuring of most mature industrial societies, with the latter experiencing a decline of many of the sectors on which their industrialism was initially built (such as coal, steel, textiles and shipbuilding) and the growth of other, primarily service sector, industries. This shift has been reflected not only in a decrease in manual and rise in non-manual jobs, but also in major changes in workforce composition: the prominence of male manual workers has given way to an increasingly feminised workforce, and one in which a significant proportion of employees work part-time.

In addition, an important change in the overall context of work over the past generation has been the degree to which work has, for many, become a more precarious activity. Indefinite employment and long service with a single employer have, for many, given way to a more fragmented job history. Much higher levels of unemployment, coupled with high redundancy rates and job insecurity, have resulted in a growing proportion of the workforce experiencing paid employment as an intermittent, rather than a regular, activity. One of the issues this raises is whether, as work becomes more fragmented and as the experience of non-work becomes more common, the values associated with work show signs of being in decline. It is to an examination of work values that we now proceed.

3   The Meaning of Work

When we are children, we frequently get asked the question, 'What do you want to be when you grow up?' And full of the idealism of youth, we eagerly reply that we are going be an astronaut, a fashion model, a footballer, or maybe a computer games designer. Years later, when we are adults, the question is rephrased to, 'What do you *do*?' We mutter that we are in insurance, or work on the check-out at the local supermarket, or maybe we're employed in the local benefits office. Moreover, a large number of people are having to say they are unemployed, or have taken early retirement.

These two common questions are significant because both underline the fact that paid employment is generally considered to be a central defining feature of ourselves as individuals. As children we are being judged in terms of our employment aspirations, and as adults we are being assessed in terms of our employment status. In short, paid work is one of the principal means by which we evalute other people. In this chapter we explore the concept of work and assess why so much emphasis is placed upon what a person does for a living. Our main concern is to analyse the reasons behind why people work. We begin by exploring the *economic necessity* of work, and review evidence to suggest that people would carry on some form of work even if they had no financial need to do so. Next, we assess the *moral necessity* of work through a discussion of the 'work ethic'. This leads us to question whether or not the work ethic is in decline and if it has any relevance for contemporary society.

THE ECONOMIC NECESSITY TO WORK

Intuitively, we know people work in order to earn money to live; it is through paid work that basic needs are satisfied because it provides money for subsistence (food, housing, clothes, and so on). However, there is a major problem with accepting this argument as it stands: can we really talk about the need to work for the purpose of subsistence when society provides a welfare state that (in theory at least) prevents people from falling below the basic level of subsistence? Social welfare provision in the form of unemployment benefit, housing allowances and free medical care were specifically designed to act as a safety net, preventing people from plunging into destitution. It is the prime example of the state intervening to prevent its citizens from being left totally at the mercy of market forces. Indeed, politicians of both the right and left have argued that the benefit system can act as a *deterrent* to work because it provides a supposedly satisfactory standard of living. The problem arises because someone can undertake a week's work in a low-paid job and receive the same or lower income than someone claiming benefits. Moreover, when people take a low-paid job after being on unemployment benefit, they often lose their entitlement to other allowances, such as housing benefit, and as a consequence find themselves financially worse off at the end of the week: this is the classic poverty trap. In other words, the benefit system can act as a financial disincentive to work, even though the person may be keen to be employed.

In the UK, governments have recognised this problem of financial disincentives, and have introduced a range of 'in work' benefits: means-tested allowances that can be claimed whilst in employment. Critics of this policy argue that it exacerbates the problem by effectively susidising employers who pay low wages; indeed, it actively discourages them from increasing wages as the employee would lose benefit, and the employer would have to take up the supplement currently funded by the taxpayer. There are two alternative policy solutions which both focus on increasing the differentials between paid work and benefit, although they differ dramatically in their approach. The first views high benefit levels as the problem, suggesting the need to lower unemployment allowances to increase the incentive to work for low wages, thus making unemployment seem 'less attractive'. Conversely, the second approach is aimed at increasing low wages, typically through setting a national minimum wage, which would similarly increase the differential between those who were in work and out of work, but which would be aimed at making low-paid work more attractive.

As this discussion suggests, in western capitalist economies it is not simply the case that people need to work to subsist; rather, people work to earn money to acquire consumer power. Money is the means to the goal of consumption, whether that be commodity consumption (houses, cars, video recorders, dishwashers, and so forth) or service consumption (for example, drinking, gambling, eating out, and holidaying). The central distinguishing feature between those people in work and those who are unemployed is that the former have much higher (although varied) levels of consumer power, and consequently more choice about their lifestyles. This rise of consumption has been one of the fundamental developments of the twentieth century. Chapter 6 examines the importance of mass production in shaping people's working lives, but worth noting here is the sometimes overlooked fact that mass production develops alongside mass consumption – increasingly the people who produced the goods were those who consumed the goods. It has been suggested that the nature of consumption has changed in recent years, from mass to niche markets (Piore and Sabel, 1984), which has helped to sustain consumption as one of the defining features of our identity. Moreover it perpetuates and elevates the importance of getting money to engage in a shopping experience that is increasingly being seen as a leisure activity in its own right (Featherstone, 1990).

Given the importance of the link between work and spending power, it is

hardly surprising that, when asked, most people will say that earning money is
the prime reason they go to work (or want to work in the case of the
unemployed). This unremarkable observation was recently verified in the UK by
researchers working on a major project entitled the Social Change and Economic
Life Initiative (SCELI), to which we make reference on several occasions
throughout the book. The researchers questioned people about their reasons for
wanting a job, and from analysis of over 5000 responses they found that the
majority (68 per cent) said they worked for the money, either to provide for basic
essentials, or, in the case of 27 per cent, to buy extras things and enjoy some economic independence from the primary earner in the household. Perhaps most surprising is that the figure is not higher than 68 per cent; indeed, to uphold the
(intuitive) assumption that people work simply for extrinsic reward (money for
shopping) we might have predicted the figure to be 95 per cent or more. However,
an astonishing 26 per cent said that they did not work for money
reasons, but for 'expressive' reasons, in other words for the intrinsic rewards
work brings, such as enjoyment, satisfaction and a sense of achievement.
Moreover the percentage of people indicating these expressive reasons remained
very similar irrespective of the gender or employment status of the respondent.
(See Table 3.1 for a summary, and M. Rose, 1994, for a comprehensive analysis
of the SCELI data.)

The analysis so far suggests that the majority of people say they work for
economic reasons, so logically it follows that if, by some stroke of luck, someone acquires a fortune, they would leave work to live a life of leisure. It might be
logical to think like that, but empirically it has been shown not to be the case. Let
us look at the evidence, first by examining another recent study in Britain, and
then assessing a larger international study.

The *Employment in Britain* survey (Gallie and White, 1993) assessed the
attitudes of 3855 people in 1992 regarding a wide range of issues concerned
with work. One of the questions was directly concerned with employment
commitment and asked respondents, 'If you were to get enough money to live as
comfortably as you would like for the rest of your life, would you continue to
work (not necessarily in your present job) or would you stop working?' In
response, 67 per cent of people indicated that they would continue to work, and
there was very little difference in the replies of men and women (68 per cent compared with 67 per cent). Assuming this sample to be representative of the wider
working population, it suggests that the majority of people derive more from
work than their wage packet. However, it might be argued that such
intrinsic satisfaction from work depends on the nature of the job being done, and
that professional workers would be more inclined to stay at work irrespective of
financial security, than semi-skilled manual workers. Gallie and White (1993)
took this into consideration in their analysis and found that the majority of
people in *all* job categories would continue to work even if there was no financial
need, although the proportions increased the higher the job levels of the
respondents. In addition, the survey revealed that employment commitment was
highest among people in their early 20s and declined with age.

Table 3.1 Summary of the SCELI findings on the reasons for working

	Full-time		Part-time		Self-employed		Unemployed		Housewife returners	Totals
	men	women	men	women	men	women	men	women		
Sample size	1786	1026	21	802	248	118	457	272	480	5210
Monetary reasons (%)	75	69	77	66	69	60	69	65	65	68
Expressive reasons (%)	26	27	28	21	29	34	25	25	21	26
Other (%)	1	7	3	14	2	7	4	10	14	6

Source: adapted from M. Rose, 'Skill and Samuel Smiles: changing the British work ethic', in R. Penn, M. Rose and J. Rubery (eds) *Skill and Occupational Change*, Oxford: Oxford University Press, 1994, p.294.

The general impression is that the respondents were committed to employment, but it is important to note two points: first, this does not mean they were necessarily committed to their particular job; and second, they were not committed to working full-time, but rather stated a preference for a working week of between 16 and 30 hours. The respondents indicated a commitment to the principle of being employed, but this does not imply they wanted to maintain their existing conditions of employment. They may also be reflecting the socially desirable norm of being 'in work' rather than demonstrating an individual commitment to employment. This is an issue we return to later in the chapter when we consider the moral necessity of work, but, for now, let us assume that the respondents are committed to employment. This prompts a further question: 'what is causing this individual commitment to work?'

From their analysis of further questions asked in the survey, Gallie and White (1993: 67–69) isolate seven influences on employment commitment. To summarise their argument, we can say that employment commitment will be stronger (1) the more qualifications the person has, (2) the greater their feeling of having been successful in their career, (3) the higher they value 'hard work', (4) the more they feel they have personal control over their destiny, (5) the higher their preference for their current job, (6) the lower their preference for 'an easy life' and (7) the higher their attachment to their current organisation. Of course this does not imply that all these influences have to be present before a person feels committed to employment, but simply indicates the possible range of factors. Overall, the survey suggests that people in Britain demonstrate a commitment to employment, so, how does this compare with other countries? To answer this question, we can examine the findings of the earlier 'Meaning of Working' survey (MOW, 1987) which provides a comparative analysis of eight countries.

Respondents were asked what they would do about work if they won a lottery or inherited a large sum of money and could live comfortably for the rest of their lives without working. The responses are presented in Table 3.2, ranked according to country. It can be observed that although the majority of people in each country would continue to work, it is in Britain and West Germany that the greatest proportion of people indicated that they would stop working – proportions noticeably higher than the next ranked country, Belgium (around 30 per cent for Britain and West Germany, compared with 16 per cent for Belgium). When examining the proportions of people who would continue in the same job or who would want to work under different conditions, the ranking is virtually inverted, with respondents from Japan and Yugoslavia (and to a lesser degree, Israel) demonstrating the highest commitment to their existing employment. In contrast, respondents from Britain are the least inclined to want to remain in their existing job. Similarly, for the USA, Belgium, Germany and the Netherlands a greater proportion of people would want to continue to work under different conditions than remain in the same job, although the differences between the proportions are much smaller than those in Britain. Taken overall, the MOW data shows that people generally have a commitment to employment (although not necessarily to their current job) and that this is affected by national setting as well as age, occupation, individual differences/life experiences.

Table 3.2   *Responses to the financial security question from the MOW survey*

Percentage of respondents who, if they were financially secure, said they would...

Ranking	Stop working		Continue working in the same job		Continue working but under different conditions	
1	Britain	31	Japan	66	Britain	53
2	West Germany	30	Yugoslavia	62	USA	49
3	Belgium	16	Israel	50	Belgium	47
4	Netherlands	14	Netherlands	42	Netherlands	44
5	USA	12	USA	39	West Germany	39
6	Israel	12	Belgium	37	Israel	37
7	Japan	7	West Germany	31	Yugoslavia	34
8	Yugoslavia	4	Britain	16	Japan	27

Source: Adapted from MOW International Research Team, *The Meaning of Working*, London: Academic, 1987.

The evidence therefore suggests that it is not enough simply to argue that people work for extrinsic rewards. Clearly, income beyond the subsistence level is an important reason for working, but surveys reveal that a large minority of people work for reasons other than money (the expressive needs, noted above) and that the majority of people say they would continue to work even if there was no financial need compelling them to do so. It seems that other factors influence attitudes to work: factors which, some have argued, constitute a moral necessity to work.

THE MORAL NECESSITY TO WORK

Implicit in much of the discussion in the previous section is the notion that work is 'good': a virtuous, dignified and worthy activity for people to engage in. In other words, there is a moral dimension to work, commonly accepted by society, which values endeavour and enterprise through employment, above leisure.

Being 'in work' becomes morally desirable irrespective of any financial or social benefit that may accrue to the individual. This moral dimension to work is usually articulated as a 'work ethic', and has traditionally been associated with characteristics such as diligence, punctuality, obedience, honesty and sobriety. So where does this moral dimension to work come from? And what relevance does it have for our understanding of contemporary orientations to employment?

By far the best account of the development of the work ethic is provided by Anthony (1977). Drawing on Weber (1930) he traces the work ethic from the roots of Protestantism in the seventeenth century, which defined work as a religious calling, either through the Lutheran belief that a state of grace could be achieved through endeavour, or the Calvinist doctrine of predestination whereby work became part of a lifestyle demonstrating one's salvation. The Protestant work ethic became the foundation upon which the ideology of work associated with industrialisation and capitalism was built. As Anthony (1977: 44) argues:

> Work had every advantage. It was good in itself. It satisfied the selfish economic interest of the growing number of small employers or self-employed. It was a social duty, it contributed to social order in society and to moral worth in the individual. It contributed to a good reputation among one's fellows and to an assured position in the eyes of God.

Similarly, in his consideration of the work ethic in the United States, Rodgers (1978: 14) argues:

> The central premise of the work ethic was that work was the core of moral life. Work made men useful in a world of economic scarcity. It staved off the doubts and temptations that preyed on idleness, it opened the way to deserved wealth and status, it allowed one to put the impress of mind and skill on the material world.

Whilst the argument that the work ethic provided the basis of capitalist ideology is seductive, it presents us with an analytical problem: how do we disentangle the notion of a moral commitment to work from that of an economic need to work? Can we really argue that there was a general acceptance of a work ethic in industrialising nations prior to the advent of social welfare systems? And even after the emergence of decent wages, is the moral dimension to work any easier to pin down? To put it another way, 'Are workers on the assembly line related to their work by a "bond based on the need for cash from which all moral commitment is absent and which can be easily broken?"' (Anthony, 1977: 286, quoting Beynon, 1973).

To answer these questions, four key themes associated with the work ethic need to be examined: work as a duty; work as a central life activity; work as conscientious endeavour; and work as disciplined compliance. Each of these will be considered in turn, although, as the discussion reveals, there is a considerable overlap and merging of the ideas.

Work as a Duty

This theme reflects the importance of doing one's utmost to seek paid employment rather than remaining 'idle'. In the UK such an obligation to work is enshrined within the social welfare system because a person must prove they are 'actively seeking work' before they are entitled to any welfare benefits. But studies of the attitudes of the unemployed reveal that there is a widespread desire not to be perceived as 'lazy', even if remuneration levels from work are only marginally higher than unemployment benefit (see for example, Turner *et al.*, 1985). To a large extent this may be the result of the desire to be a 'good provider' for one's family. A study of basic life values conducted in the mid-1960s (Yankelovich, 1973) for example, revealed that 80 per cent of American adults linked the importance of being the breadwinner to masculinity. So, being 'in work' not only conferred economic power on the individual, it helped to forge a masculine identity: a man who was unemployed was not only unable to provide for his family, he was also less of a man. More recently this has been illustrated by a study of the gender-specific consequences of unemployment in a town in Britain (McKee and Bell, 1986: 141):

> The loss of the male economic provider struck deep chords among both wives and husbands and a passionate defence of men's right to provide was invariably raised.... Fundamental emotions concerning self-esteem, self-image, pride, views of masculinity, respectability and authority resounded in the expressions of both men and women.

Alternatively, it might be argued that perception of work as the means to becoming a self-reliant provider for one's family is being eroded in western capitalist societies because of the growth of unemployment. It is a forceful argument, particularly when there has been an abandonment of the political commitment to achieving full employment, meaning that some of the blame can be displaced onto the government for failing to provide enough jobs. In other words, as Offe (1985: 142–3) put it:

> [As] the experience (or the anticipation) of unemployment, or involuntary retirement from working life increases, the more the effect of moral stigmatization and self-stigmatization generated by unemployment probably wears off because, beyond a certain threshold (and especially if unemployment is concentrated in certain regions or in certain industries), it can no longer be accounted for plausibly in terms of individual failure or guilt.

Of course, the opposite view can also be argued: as work becomes more scarce the value placed on it (its scarcity value) rises. This can help to explain why most of the unemployed continue to search for work in conditions which offer little hope of secure, long-term, full-time employment. In a further twist to the argument, it may be suggested that when a person is faced with unemployment, they are likely to cope much better (in terms of their mental health) if they do not see work as a duty (Warr, 1987). In other words, a strong work ethic might help motivate a person to hunt for work, but it might have a deterimental effect on their ability to cope with being unemployed. Conversely, a weak work ethic may help a person to accept being unemployed, but in so doing may inhibit their motivation to gain employment.

An attempt to assess the pervasiveness of 'work as a duty' was undertaken in the international survey concerning the Meaning of Working (MOW, 1987). The researchers examined two issues: obligation to work and entitlement to work. The former represents the view that everyone must work to the best of their ability and thereby contribute to society, whilst the latter reflects the argument that everyone should have the right to a meaningful and interesting job with proper training. These are two separate dimensions, and so an individual's orientation to both can be measured. The MOW researchers were able to plot the responses from each country to demonstrate how the orientation to rights and duties can vary in different national settings. The important aspect to consider from these findings is the overall balance exhibited by respondents from each country. Respondents from Japan and Britain showed an evenly balanced orientation between duties and rights; a similar pattern can be seen in Yugoslavia and Israel, but respondents tend to exhibit an overall higher orientation to both. In the United States people tend to perceive work as more of a duty than a right; in fact of all the countries, it was US respondents who were least likely to see work as a right. In contrast, respondents from the Netherlands were most inclined to view work as a right, and least inclined to see it a duty. A similar pattern of right above duty can be seen in the respondents from West Germany and Belgium, although less extreme. Consequently, the national context seems to play an important role in helping to define this aspect of the work ethic.

Work as a Central Life Activity

This theme stresses that paid work is the most important part of life, being superordinate to all non-work activities. Some of the most revealing empirical evidence can again be found in the Meaning of Working (1987: 79–93) survey. The researchers defined work centrality as 'the degree of general importance that working has in the life of an individual at any given point in time' (1987: 81) and they developed a method of measurement which involved asking people to assess working against other important aspects of their lives: family, community, religion and leisure. Overall, the analysis revealed that in terms of importance and significance, respondents judged work to be second only to family. In the combined national samples, 40 per cent placed family as most important while 27 per cent placed working as most important among the five key life roles (MOW, 1987: 252). Of additional interest are three other significant findings. First, a person's work centrality tends to increase with age. This finding is perhaps not surprising, given that people may be promoted or take on more responsibility within an organisation the older they get, coupled with the tendency for a person's social life to 'slow down' with age, although family is likely to assume a more central role. Second, work centrality varies according to national differences. The data revealed that respondents from Japan were considerably more work-centred than other countries, in particular Britain whose respondents displayed the lowest degree of work centrality.

The third finding is that men typically have higher work centrality than women. Caution should be exercised in interpreting this finding, however, because it does not necessarily mean that women are innately less interested in work; rather it might reflect the different roles widely expected of men and women. It is still the case that domestic obligations (particularly cleaning, cooking and childcare) are disproportionately undertaken by women (see Chapter 10) which not only requires them to be less work-centred (more time and thought must be devoted to the family), but can provide an alternative focus to their lives from which they might derive a sense of fulfillment. As Hakim (1991) points out, there has been a failure to recognise that the female labour force is composed of at least two distinct groups that differ dramatically in work orientations: those who choose full-time work, and those who choose the homemaker role.

> [The first] group has work commitment similar to that of men, leading to long-term workplans and almost continuous full-time work, often in jobs with higher status and earnings than are typical for women. The second group has little or no commitment to paid work and a clear preference for the home-maker role; paid employment is a secondary activity, usually undertaken to earn a supplementary wage rather than as primary breadwinner, and is in low-skilled, low-paid, part-time, casual and temporary jobs more often than in skilled, permanent full-time jobs. (Hakim, 1991: 113.)

Of course, it is debatable whether or not women are really as free to choose their roles as Hakim suggests; indeed, as we shall argue in other chapters, the research on the impact of patriarchy in constraining these 'choices' is convincing (for analysis of the key debates see Walby, 1986 and 1990). Nevertheless, for men, the choice of being homemaker is still not widely accepted by society, so, in this sense, the moral obligation to be work-centred is imposed more upon men than women, and the general expectation by employers is that a man will want a full-time job, whereas a woman will settle for part-time work.

In addition to domestic obligations, there may be structural reasons for the lower work-centrality reported by women. As we note throughout the book, women are disproportionately represented in jobs which tend to have lower pay and benefits, lower status, less autonomy, less responsibility and less job security. Moreover, these poor quality terms and conditions are frequently a feature of part-time jobs, the majority of which are undertaken by women (see Chapter 2). This is perpetuated because the widely held assumption that women (in general) have low work-centrality means a woman in a full-time job is frequently faced with male managers and co-workers who assume she is less committed to a career in the organisation because she will leave to start a family (supposedly deferring to her family-centred values): an assumption largely reinforced through the biological fact that only women can have children.

> Managers' perceptions of job requirements and procedures for assessing merit have been shown to be saturated with gendered assumptions... Feminists can argue (as they have for years) that not all women get pregnant, but it seems unlikely that this will stop managers thinking 'yes, but no men will'. (Liff and Wajcman, 1996: 89.)

Finally, it is worth noting how these possible reasons for lower work-centrality can link together. The imbalance of domestic responsibilities means that many women find part-time work more convenient, and consequently find themselves in jobs which are both intrinsically and extrinsically poorly rewarded. In this instance, employment becomes de-centred, yet is endured to provide either an adequate income for the family, or an independent income for the women. So amongst women working part-time or women not in paid employment, it would not be surprising to find low work-centrality. The only proper comparison to be made to assess whether gender does affect work orientation would be to compare like with like: men and women in full-time jobs with similar status and terms and conditions. This is, of course, an extremely difficult comparison to make, given the deeply gendered horizontal and vertical segregation of labour.

Irrespective of gender, Moorhouse (1984) challenges the view that, for the majority of people, work is a central life activity in any sense other than occupying the majority of their waking hours. He argues there is a need to distinguish between what people find important (qualitatively central) from that which occupies large amounts of their waking time (quantitatively central); it is only the former, he argues, that offers any sociological insight into working lives. However, the MOW research revealed a high work centrality on *both* measures (people found work important and it occupied large amounts of their time). But, like all the surveys of this type, it still leaves us with the conundrum of whether people find work important *because* it occupies large amounts of their time – in other words, to use Moorhouse's terms, whether its quantitative centrality determines its qualitative centrality. In addition, such an approach fails to broach an arguably more interesting question: whether people think work *ought* to be so central (both qualitatively and quantitatively). In part we can address this issue by examining the third theme of the work ethic: conscientious endeavour.

Work as Conscientious Endeavour

Irrespective of the work being undertaken, this theme of the work ethic emphasises the importance of doing a job *diligently*. No matter how menial the task, the individual is encouraged to put effort and care into it in order to produce the best outcome. It is summed up in the maxim: 'If a job's worth doing, it's worth doing well'.

A contemporary expression of this can be seen in the management rhetoric of 'customer care'. Typically, these are initiatives requiring all employees not only to show great respect, but to make customers feel as though they are being individually looked after; this increasingly requires employees to manage their own emotions so as to elicit a good feeling in the minds of the customers. This 'emotion work' is being recognised as so important for the competitiveness of contemporary organisations that even those people in low-paid, low-status jobs, such as shopwork, are required to be increasingly diligent in this aspect of their work. It is an issue which will be explored in detail in Chapter 7.

The theme of conscientious endeavour also implies *activity*, whether this is physical or mental. The extent of activity varies of course from job to job and task to task. People may place different values on different forms of activity – in particular the difference between manual and non-manual work. Those who value the former tend to invoke a notion that there is a dignity in physical labour, and that a person has not really done 'a fair day's work' unless they have got their hands dirty. The stress on the virtue of practical rather than cerebral or emotion-based activity has been frequently used to differentiate work supposedly suited to men from that supposedly best undertaken by women. In effect this has perpetuated the gender division of labour by constructing an artificial gendered notion of what constitutes skilled work (see Chapter 4) and increasingly defining customer contact jobs as emotion based, and therefore more suited to women (see Chapter 7). The importance of the physicality of work for men is neatly summed up in the following quotes from male printer workers in Cockburn's study of technological change in the printing industry.

I like to do a man's job. And this means physical labour and getting dirty, you understand... working brings dignity to people I think, they are doing something useful, they are working with these [he demonstrated his hands] that have been provided for that. That's what it is all about. Craftsmanship. (Quoted in Cockburn, 1983: 52.)

People have to work and get their hands dirty, you get more satisfaction out of it than those people that sit there, you know, like a tailor's dummy at an office desk. (Quoted in Cockburn, 1983: 108.)

The roots of this notion of work are deeply embedded, and are particularly evident in working-class culture, especially amongst men (see for example, Collinson, 1992). This is vividly illustrated by Willis's (1977) classic study of a group of working-class 'lads' which reveals how a counter-school culture constructs and reinforces the value of physical labour over mental work.

> Manual labour is outside the domain of school and carries with it... the aura of the real adult world. Mental work demands too much, and encroaches – just as the school does – too far upon those areas which are increasingly adopted as their own, as private and independent.... Thus physical labouring comes to stand for and express, most importantly, a kind of masculinity and also an opposition to authority.... It expresses aggressiveness; a degree of sharpness and wit; an irreverence that cannot be found in words; an obvious kind of solidarity. It provides the wherewithal for adult tastes, and demonstrates a potential mastery over, as well as an immediate attractiveness to women: a kind of machismo. (Willis, 1977: 103–4.)

Coupled with the importance of *diligence* and *activity* is a further element of conscientious endeavour: the notion that work has some purpose; it constitutes an activity that is valued by others; it is *productive*. This is important because considerable effort may go into activities for which people do not get paid. Indeed, Moorhouse (1987) has argued that people are as productively active (if not more so) in their leisure pursuits as they are in their work. Witnessing the effort that goes into activities as varied as gardening, DIY, renovating old cars, sport, embroidery and amateur dramatics confirms this point. Similarly, as argued in Chapter 10, a huge proportion of highly productive activity is unpaid – notably domestic and voluntary work – whilst the informal, underground economy (from car boot sales to drug dealing) is a vibrant arena of productive (and paid) activity which is rarely acknowledged by wider society.

However, whilst diligent productive activity is possible in a variety of spheres, it becomes entwined with work centrality – the previous theme of the work ethic – and as a consequence is identified with employment. As Jahoda (1979: 313) argues,

> Work roles are not the only roles which offer the individual the opportunity of being useful and contributing to the community but, without doubt, for the majority they are the most central roles and consequently people deprived of the opportunity to work often feel useless and report that they lack a sense of purpose.

The unemployed are therefore not only deprived of the economic rewards derived through work, they are also denied the moral approval of their conscientious endeavour if they use their initiative to find paid work unofficially (for example, cash-in-hand jobs) or fill their spare time with non-paid productive (and self-rewarding) activities like voluntary work, gardening, writing poetry and so on.

Work as Disciplined Compliance

This fourth theme of the work ethic is particularly important since it underscores two components essential to capitalist production: the acceptance of the management prerogative and obedience to time structures.

The 'management prerogative' refers to the right of managers to direct the workforce as they deem fit, based on their 'expertise'. It can be associated with a style of management that stresses the unitary nature of the employment relationship, that is, the absence of any major conflict of interest and the position of management as the sole legitimate authority. This concept of unitarism, originally defined by Fox (1966), has received particular attention during the 1980s with the emergence of a new rhetoric of human resource management (HRM) which similarly emphasises the common goals of employees and managers in organisations. HRM ignores any plurality of interests and imbalance of power in organisations and invokes the nostrums of commitment and cooperation to secure efficient and effective performance directed towards strategically designed corporate goals, invariably embodied in a nebulous mission statement. The employees' disciplined compliance with the values and goals of the organisation is perpetuated by management through the development of employment policies and a corporate culture that stress individualism and either marginalise, or completely remove, any collective representation through trade unions (for a full discussion of the multi-faceted nature of HRM, see Blyton and Turnbull, 1992; and Legge, 1995.)

The second element is disciplined compliance with the time structures imposed by management. The working day provides a time structure which clearly differentiates periods of work and leisure. Traditionally, the Monday to Friday '9 to 5' pattern of working hours provided structure not only to the working day, but to the whole of working (and waking) lives. As discussed in Chapter 4, however, these time patterns are undergoing substantial change in contemporary society. Nevertheless, the majority of people still have a structure imposed by the time routines of their working lives. The importance of this structure is often not evident until people are faced with its removal, particularly through the loss of their jobs. One of the foremost researchers on the effects of unemployment sums it up succinctly:

> Not only manual workers but everybody living in an industrialised society is used to firm time structures – and to complaining about them. But when this structure is removed, as it is in unemployment, its absence presents a major psychological burden. Days stretch long when there is nothing that has to be done; boredom and waste of time become the rule. (Jahoda, 1982: 22.)

For people out of work, the problem becomes how to fill the unstructured days, and how to create new structures to take the place of the one they have lost. It is well illustrated by the following quotes from two different studies of unemployment – one in Scotland, the other in England. The first quote is by an unemployed woman in her mid-thirties, and the second by an unemployed male steelworker of the same age.

> I used to think it'd be great not to work... when I was working... I'd 'imagine having a day off' – it was a treat. Now, I've got every day, and every week, and every month... and maybe every year... to do *nothing*. There never used to be enough hours in the day for me when I was working... now, I know what an hour is... it just drags 'round. (Quoted in Turner *et al.*, 1985: 485, emphasis in original.)

> When you're employed you make use of all your time. You come home from work, have a quick bite to eat, a cup of tea, and get stuck into some job you've got to do. You know you've only got a set time. But when you're unemployed you've got all the time in the world and you think, ah, I won't do that today, I'll do that tomorrow. You take a slap-dash attitude, which is wrong. (Quoted in Wallace and Pahl, 1986: 121.)

If all four themes are put together, the work ethic can be summed up as: the belief that it is the duty of everyone to treat productive work as their central life activity and to perform it with diligence and punctuality under the direction and control of managers. Rarely would such a complete submission to the work ethic be expressed by an individual, but elements of the four themes *are* reflected in attitudes to work, as has been illustrated by the research findings quoted above. The general point emerging from the discussion so far is that work is seen by many people as a worthy activity in its own right, over and above the economic rewards it brings. This leads the analysis into the issue of whether the moral dimension to work is changing; more specifically, whether as a result of changes in the structure and nature of paid employment it is in terminal decline and is ceasing to have any contemporary relevance.

THE DEMISE OF THE WORK ETHIC?

As already noted, recent survey evidence about why people work is inconclusive. It reveals that the majority of people on the one hand state that economic need urges them to work, yet on the other hand say they would continue to work even if there was no economic need for them to do so. Despite this ambiguous evidence, some politicians and academics argue that people are increasingly instrumental in their attitudes to work and suggest that there has been a steady deterioration in the work ethic. Within this perspective it is possible to identify two distinct explanations which allegedly account for the demise of the work ethic: structural-economic change and socio-political change.

Structural-Economic Change

This explanation stresses the impact of economic developments and argues that the work ethic is in decline due to structural change in society which has meant that we have moved from an era of industrialism to a 'post-industrial' age. The argument contends that whilst the work ethic was an appropriate basis upon which to build industry, it no longer has a relevance in a post-industrial society. This approach is most closely associated with two commentators whose broader arguments will be encountered in subsequent chapters. The first, Bell (1973 and 1974) argues that advanced industrial economies are undergoing a shift to become post-industrial societies. This is occurring through changes in the social structure including a transformation in the economic base from manufacturing to services, which leads not only to increasing numbers of people being involved in the delivery of services but also increasing demand for, and consumption of, services: from tourism to participative sports; from psychotherapy to massage parlours. Concomitant with this structural change is an increasing importance on information-handling activities which means more white-collar jobs requiring higher levels of education and training, and the emergence of professionals as the dominant group, deriving influence through specialist theoretical knowledge.

If we apply Bell's thesis, it challenges the notion of the work ethic in two principal ways. First, it means that a work ethic developed for an age of industrial production is no longer relevant for a structurally different society: one based on the increasing consumption of services. Second, he suggests that the post-industrial society is a product of the changing social structure, and increasingly this becomes separated from the culture of a society. In other words, changes are shaped by technological advances, increased efficiency and greater theoretical knowledge, so cultural agents of change cease to have relevance. Under this logic, the work ethic will cease to have meaning because (as we have noted) it is a moral phenomenon embedded in the cultural realm, rather than the economic structure.

Critics of Bell (for example, Webster, 1995: 30–51) would argue that his whole notion of a post-industrial society is misfounded because it creates a false dichotomy between manufacturing and services, when in practice the two are interdependent (Gershuny and Miles, 1983). The service sector is helping to sustain the manufacturing sector through 'producer services' (Browning and Singelmann, 1978) such as banking, insurance, marketing and distribution. What is more, there is an increasing expansion not only of service work, but also of service products, so the move may be towards a 'self-service' economy (Gershuny, 1978). For example, people drive cars rather than use public transport, and buy washing machines and vacuum cleaners rather than using laundry and cleaning services. This more complex picture of social and sectoral change suggests there is a continuity of economic development rather than a dramatic structural shift; so it follows that the work ethic might similarly adapt to reflect these changes in patterns of production and consumption. It also brings into question Bell's assumption that the social structure can be separated from the realm of culture – if there is no structural shift, then similarly there is a question mark over the supposed disjuncture with culture (even if one accepts such a separation as feasible in the first place).

The second commentator, Gorz (1982 and 1985), argues that the work ethic has ceased to have relevance because of the emergence of increased leisure time which is 'liberating' people from work. He argues that technological change has led to labour-saving work processes and the creation of a post-industrial age in which leisure and productive activity outside work are increasingly important. Work ceases to be central in people's lives in terms of hours spent working: Gorz (1985: 40–1) projects a future scenario where people will be engaged in work-sharing with the equivalent of no more than ten years of full-time work during their life. Similarly, it is envisaged that income would not be based on having a job or the amount of work performed; instead everyone would be guaranteed a minimum income in exchange for a right to work (and an obligation to perform socially necessary work). Demand for goods and services would be stimulated by the guaranteed minimum income for all, but consumption would only be one side of the equation because the liberating factor for Gorz is the contraction of economic and market activity, and the 'expansion of activities performed for their own sake – for love, pleasure or satisfaction, following personal passions, preferences and vocations' (1985: 53). This 'autonomous activity' could take any form, providing it stemmed from individual choice, and so, for some, this *would* involve competitive, free enterprise for financial gain. In other words, the purpose of life is self-fulfillment which will differ from person to person, so with less work time and more free time people can be allowed to pursue fulfillment in whatever manner they choose.

To summarise two volumes of work into a single paragraph does Gorz an injustice, not least because his vision of the future is so counter-intuitive to the capitalist understanding of the exchange relations of the market and the social relations of work that it may seem a utopian mirage. Certainly there are many aspects of Gorz's thesis that can be criticised, but the discussion here will be confined to two main problems with the notion of leisure replacing work, and hence representing evidence of the demise of the work ethic. First, there is the difficulty of what 'leisure' means. As explored in Chapter 10, there is a range of activities, from housework to amateur dramatics, for which a person does not get paid yet which fills up their time, but it is questionable whether all such activities could be described as leisure, since most involve (unpaid) effort and many are obligations (especially to the family) rather than free choice. Indeed, perhaps these activities equally demonstrate a work ethic, since they display many of its alleged features. So, if a type of work ethic is evident in leisure activities, the move to a leisure society will not enervate the work ethic so much as refocus it. The second problem concerns the location of the work ethic. Even if it is assumed that more leisure time *will* encourage the majority of people to relinquish any commitment to the moral necessity of work, this does not automatically lead to the demise of the work ethic. As Veal (1989) argues, and as expressed in our criticism of Bell's thesis, the work ethic is a cultural phenomenon and, as such, will not be dislocated easily. On the contrary, the resilience of the work ethic might inhibit the moral acceptability of the type of leisure society that Gorz envisages.

> The possibility remains... that the work ethic exists within the culture – not necessarily in the hearts and minds of the workers, but among the media, educationalists, the ruling classes, and so on. Thus it has an official existence, rather like an established religion, without being embraced by the population as a whole. In that case, it could be hindering progress towards a more 'leisured' society. (Veal, 1989: 268.)

To summarise, the conclusion to be drawn from Bell and Gorz is that the traditional work ethic must be abandoned because it is dysfunctional in contemporary society: it is not suited to the changing patterns of employment which emphasise the service sector and force a redefinition of the roles of work and leisure. Whilst there is evidence to support each writer's analysis of the structural change (much of which was assessed in Chapter 2) it does not necessarily signal the demise of the work ethic. Indeed, some commentators argue that of greater impact are the socio-political changes, to which the discussion now turns.

Socio-Political Change

The second explanation offered to account for the supposed demise of the work ethic focuses on the social and political changes that have occurred during the twentieth century. This argument posits the view that easier-going attitudes to work have developed (in complete contrast to the traditional work ethic) due to a general increase in prosperity, the existance of a social welfare net, greater liberal morality, social permissiveness, and a decline in self-discipline. In the UK, the view has been articulated by Conservative Governments through their policies of the 1980s and early 1990s and the call for a return to 'traditional' Victorian values – well illustrated by a Government campaign in 1993–94 for a move 'Back to Basics'.

The distinctive feature of this line of argument is the belief that the demise of the work ethic is a retrograde step, and that it can be managed back to strength by moral education, orchestrated through political intervention. Aside from the rather dubious assumption that a government should be (or could be) the guardian of its citizens' morality, it presupposes that a strong and unitary work ethic is desirable for an increasingly diverse society. Moreover, it is arguable that the rhetoric invokes traditional values (supposedly widely held) that are, in practice, wholly inappropriate for contemporary society. To take two of the central values: anti-indulgence and thrift. In the case of the former, this is based on principles in direct opposition to consumerism, mass consumption and the pursuit of pleasure, that characterise the hedonistic culture on which many businesses thrive. Indeed, the *raison d'être* of a marketing department in an organisation is to *encourage* indulgence and convince people their lives are incomplete without the goods or services the company has on sale. Likewise, thrift and deferred gratification are diametrically opposed to current patterns of consumption which depend on credit and instant gratification. Further, the boom in financial services is not due to people saving more money: rather, it results from people seeking loans and credit that will allow them to spend beyond their means.

So, the values suitable in an era of industrialisation are not therefore necessarily appropriate in an industrialised society, let alone, some would argue, a post-industrial society. Assuming the ethic of work and the ethic of consumption *are* distinct, then advanced capitalist societies require a very different moral orientation among their consumers than among their producers. The puzzle, of course, is how to differentiate such morality when people are simultaneously consumers and producers. In part, this is solved by reconceptualising the problem: the issue becomes whether the notion of 'the work ethic' is simply a red herring.

THE MISCONCEPTION OF THE WORK ETHIC?

It is possible to argue that a supposed 'demise in the work ethic' is without foundation because it is based on the false assumption that a work ethic was generally held by a majority of people in the first place. There can be no overall demise, if there was never any *general* acceptance of a work ethic. As M. Rose (1985: 16) states, 'A possibility is that some sections of the working population did in the past hold work values approximating to a work ethic ... whilst many others were affected in lesser degree by public doctrines about work deriving from it'. Essentially this is an argument for diversity; it suggests that there are, and always have been, numerous orientations to work, and that the notion of a monolithic work ethic misrepresents this diversity. This does not preclude the possibility of changes in work values, but it rejects the view that a general shift has occurred. This emphasis on diversity is argued by Moorhouse (1987) who stresses the importance of gender, class and ethnicity upon work values.

> The meanings of work are not likely to be neat and simple, or form some uncomplicated 'ethic', but are rather likely to be jumbled and variegated, so that any individual has a whole range of types and levels of meanings on which to draw, and with which to understand or appreciate the labour they are doing at any particular moment. (Moorhouse, 1987: 241.)

We have considerable sympathy with this view, especially since one of our starting points in writing this book (as outlined in Chapter 1) is to demonstrate the variety and subjectivity of work experiences. Often, people invoke the work ethic as simply a synonym for a positive attitude to work, even though, as has been shown in the foregoing discussion, it reflects a selection of values, not all of which will be adhered to by those claiming to have a strong work ethic. Our analysis suggests it is probably a gross oversimplification to talk of a single work ethic because the term has a variety of meanings which can easily lead to confusion or ambiguity in interpretation – a type of problem we will also encounter in dealing with other concepts in the study of work, the best example being 'skill' (Chapter 5). However, when any of the themes of the past which constituted the work ethic are in evidence in contemporary society, we may justifiably use the plural term *work ethics* to signify the persistence of a moral dimension to employment beyond the economic need.

CONCLUSION

Throughout, this chapter has been addressing a fundamental question: why work? The evidence indicates that economic need remains an important feature of work, but this does not explain the entire picture. The majority of people say they would continue to work even if there was no economic compulsion to do so, which suggests that work may also be fulfilling other needs. Aside from earning money (extrinsic need) people are likely to cite a variety of intrinsic needs that work helps to satisfy, many of which reflect the moral dimension to work, for example, the search for achievement, creativity and fulfillment, or a sense of worth, purpose or duty. In other words, work is perceived as the right sort of activity to be engaged in; a message that is powerfully reinforced through a shared culture in capitalist societies, and most typically expressed as a work ethic. As has been noted, the work ethic concept has a variety of meanings, but in so far as it characterises a moral dimension to work, it remains an important feature of work orientations, and talk of its demise is somewhat premature.

Clearly work provides an opportunity to socialise with people outside of the family, and virtually all work involves interaction with other people – co-workers, managers, subordinates, customers, clients, and/or the public. We can speculate, therefore that work fulfils an important social need in people. As Jahoda (1982: 24) argues,

> Outside the nuclear family it is employment that provides for most people this social context and demonstrates in daily experience that 'no man is an island, entire of itself', that the purposes of a collectivity transcend the purposes of an individual. Deprived of this daily demonstration, the unemployed suffer from lack of purpose, exclusion from the larger society and relative isolation.

The research evidence reveals that rarely do people express social factors as a reason for working, yet throughout the subsequent chapters numerous examples are evident of the importance of the social dimension of work: how time (Chapter 4) and skills (Chapter 5) can be socially negotiated, how social interaction helps people to get through the working day (Chapter 8), the social phenomenon of discrimination (Chapter 9) and the social isolation which characterises some aspects of hidden work (Chapter 10). For most people, work is a place to socialise, and complex social systems develop within the workplace which often spill over into leisure time. Moreover, whole communities may be socially linked through the workplace where there is a major employer in a locality – for example, a mine, a car plant, a hospital, or a large retail store. Similarly, organisations are often seeking to establish and reinforce their own corporate culture which encourages identity with the organisation through social interaction. In short, work is an important source of social interaction, but for the majority of people the meaning of work lies more in its economic and moral contribution to the human condition.

4 Time and Work

Time is a key component in work, as it is in all aspects of human activity. The way time is experienced is fundamental to an individual's overall experience of work. Having too much time to complete a task can slip easily into feelings of boredom. The sense of having too little time can be a major contributor to work-related stress. Even where tasks can be finished comfortably within a given time, dissatisfaction can still arise if the tempo of work remains unchanging. Indeed, introducing variety into the pace of work is an important means of reducing the monotony inherent in many jobs. Where such variation in the tempo of work does not occur naturally, many employees will seek to create it, at times by speeding up their work pace and at other times by working more slowly. This breaking up of the working period into distinctive segments, each with their own temporal characteristics, is one strategy that many work people employ to 'get through' a monotonous working day (see Chapter 8).

All workplaces function on the basis of an array of overlapping time schedules. These vary enormously, ranging from a few seconds for specific and repetitive tasks (such as on many assembly lines or making up orders in a fast food outlet: see Chapter 6) to many years for the planning, construction and commissioning of major plant, such as a new steelworks, or the siting of a new office headquarters. The clock is critical in every contemporary work organisation, allowing the coordination of multiple, simultaneous, and complex activities in ways which could not be achieved without the close synchronisation made possible by accurate time measurement. This ability to synchronise individual activities within an overall production process has been a key feature of industrial development. The ability to measure time in finely divided units has allowed greatly improved levels of co-ordination, and thereby a growth in the scale and complexity of operations. This has brought with it an unleashing of productive capacity through a much increased division of labour. Indeed, for writers such as Mumford (1934: 14), 'the clock, not the steam engine [was] the key machine of the industrial age', the critical innovation which set the industrial revolution firmly in motion. So too for Hassard, who comments that,

> As the machine became the focal point of work, so time schedules became the central feature of planning. During industrialism the clock was *the* instrument of co-ordination and control. The time period replaced the task as the focal unit of production (1989: 18, emphasis in original).

Just as organisations as a whole function by utilising many different time-scales, individual workers operate on the basis of a diverse set of time schedules. These may range from the short cycle times of a machine-paced task to the length of their working day, working week, working year and ultimately working life. Further, working time is experienced in both an objective and a subjective way. For example, for many workers, particularly those working in factories, the working day is punctuated by bells or buzzers, objectively signalling the start and finish of defined working periods, mealtimes and rest breaks. In addition, however, the clock subjectively dominates many workers' thoughts about work; its hands or digits often advancing all too slowly for those locked in laborious tasks and wishing to be elsewhere.

As we discuss later in the chapter, three aspects of working time particularly affect the overall experience of work. First, the *duration* of the working period importantly shapes individuals' overall experience of time at work. Since the early nineteenth century, the issue of the length of the working period has been a major focus for employment relations, with campaigns by workers and social reform groups to reduce working time regularly confronting employers opposed to any reduction in the length of productive activity. Second, of equal importance to many workers is not simply the amount of time spent at work but *when* those hours are worked – that is, how the agreed working time is scheduled or *arranged* within the 24 hours of the day and across the seven days of the week. Longer opening times and economic pressures to operate plant and equipment more intensively are two of the factors acting to increase employers' demands for extending the working period. Third, as well as questions of duration and arrangement, the relationship between work time and overall work experience is influenced by the extent to which working time is actually spent in productive activity – that is, the degree to which working time is *utilised*. The utilisation of working time may be changed either by altering the pace of work or by changes in the length and frequency of non-productive periods. Integral to this issue of work-time utilisation is the question of whether or not work is becoming a more intensified activity over time. Evidence on this is reviewed later in the chapter.

These three interrelated elements – the duration, arrangement and utilisation of working time, or what Adam (1990) calls the time, timing and tempo of work – combine to shape workers' overall experience of their working time. In turn, these temporal aspects form a key element in the broader experience of work itself. Yet, issues of time have in fact been the focus of comparatively little research enquiry. The ubiquitous nature of time in human existence has probably acted against it being addressed directly as a research topic. Further, the subjective nature of working time has been particularly under-recognised, with too common a tendency to view work time in terms of 'clock time' – regular, unerring and unidimensional – rather than an aspect of social existence which is experienced in a variety of ways. What is more, despite the overall character of working time being the outcome of the interplay of elements of duration, arrangement and utilisation, there has been a tendency for those campaigning for change to address themselves to only one of these aspects, such as the length of the working day, the hazards of night work, or the need in certain activities for additional rest periods. At times, the result of this over-focused attention has been that changes introduced to one aspect of working time have been accompanied by unforeseen (and from the worker's point of view, potentially disadvantageous) changes in another: for example, reductions in the working period being secured only by conceding an increased tempo of work, or a greater spread of working time across the week. Although the complexity of working time has suffered from insufficient attention, however, leading writers on the world of work such as Karl Marx and F. W. Taylor recognised the centrality of work time to capitalism and to efficient work organisation. While Marx (1976) analysed the particular relationship between the working period and the creation of surplus value, Taylor (1911) was concerned with the most efficient ways in which an individual's work time could be utilised: a concern which subsequently gave rise to generations of 'time and motion' study.

The remaining sections of this chapter are concerned with developments in, and the implications of, managerial approaches to working time, together with the ways in which workers subjectively experience working time and attempt to mitigate the perceived negative aspects of managerially defined time patterns, through the development of their own, alternative time-reckoning systems. The chapter begins, however, with the question of workers' internalised attitudes towards working time. For it can be argued that, if the development of more closely controlled and co-ordinated time schedules marks out capitalist industral organisation from its predecessors, employer efforts to assert control over workers' time have been much facilitated by the sense of time consciousness and time-discipline which the majority of workers typically bring to their job – a sense of the importance of punctuality, regularity and what constitutes a 'fair day's work'.

THE (PARTIAL) GROWTH OF TIME-DISCIPLINE

The Making of a Capitalist Time Consciousness

It has been persuasively argued, particularly by E.P. Thompson (1967), that the creation of a time-discipline among the workforce represented a key feature in the development of an urbanised, industrialised economy. For Thompson, developments such as the spread of the school system, with its emphasis on punctuality and its daily diet of bells and whistles, helped to embed an increased time consciousness and time-discipline into the labouring classes (see also Lazonick, 1978). The importance of time-keeping taught in schools was reinforced by the moral edicts emanating from church and chapel about the degradation associated with idleness, the duty to view time as a scarce resource, and the importance of exercising time thrift by employing all time, including working time, to its greatest effect (see also discussion of the work ethic in

Chapter 3). Other significant factors for Thompson include the spread of clocks and other time-pieces which heightened general awareness of the time, and probably more importantly, the emergence of an acquisitiveness among the labouring classes. This latter factor reflects the argument that, prior to the development of capitalism, the lack of available goods for purchase and the general absence of opportunities for workers to progress beyond their existing material position, resulted in most people holding a view of work as something necessary for subsistence, but that once a subsistence level had been reached, any desire to continue working, rather than spend time in other activities, diminished. Hence weavers, for example, might 'play frequently all day on Monday, and the greater part of Tuesday, and work very late on Thursday night and frequently all night on Friday' in order to make a sufficient wage (quoted in Pollard, 1965: 214). In this way, while the weavers could not avoid the necessity of earning an income, they retained a measure of control over the timing of their work. An aspect of this control over working time which extended beyond the textile districts was the honouring of 'Saint' Monday: whilst Sunday was the rest day from work each week, large numbers of workers also habitually took many Mondays as unofficial holidays (or 'holy-day' – hence 'Saint' Monday) to extend their weekend (Reid, 1976). With the growth of capitalism and larger-scale production, however, E.P. Thompson (1967) argues that there was more for workers to spend their wages on. As a result, bourgeois values relating to ambition, hard work and thrift became increasingly reflected among a working class desirous of improving their lot. Aspirations towards greater material comfort no longer remained the preserve of the middle and landed classes, but also (and in however small a way) the ambition of much poorer workers. According to Thompson, the overall effect of these various influences was to create a different attitude among workers towards time, leisure and income, increasing their propensity for regular time-keeping, in order to maximise their wages and thus their purchasing power.

Pollard (1963 and 1965) similarly emphasises the importance of time-discipline and regular attendance for the development of the nineteenth-century factory system. However, unlike Thompson, who focuses particularly on the development of an internalised self-discipline towards time-keeping, Pollard places greater emphasis on the role of external factors, particularly the actions taken by employers to impose a greater time-discipline. For Pollard (1965: 213) the developing factory system required 'regularity and steady intensity in place of irregular spurts of work'. This did not come easily to the new factory operatives, however, and had to be reinforced by systems of rules, backed by punishments. For example, many nineteenth-century employers sought to control lateness by imposing fines or by locking the factory gates after the start of the work period, thereby forcing anyone arriving late to lose a whole day's pay (Pollard, 1965: 215). These attempts to establish regular attendance and punctuality were part of a broader employer effort to enforce a strict factory discipline towards work habits, standards of cleanliness and drinking.

Enforcement took the forms of close supervision, elaborate rules, corporal punishment, fines and summary dismissals for even minor transgressions. Despite their distinct emphases on internal and external influences on the development of time-discipline, however, Thompson and Pollard reach the same conclusion that gradually the industrial workforce came to exhibit a greater time-discipline.

Yet, while a reading of Thompson and Pollard might encourage the belief that the question of workers' time-discipline was settled some time in the nineteenth century, with workers abandoning their previous lackadaisical approach to time-keeping in the face of opposition from school, church and employer, on closer inspection it is clear that the employers' victory was never complete, and that in several important respects workers' time-discipline has continued to remain partial and problematic (Whipp, 1987). In practice, working time remains a contested 'frontier of control' between management and labour, with each seeking ways to exert greater influence over different aspects of the working peri-od. Insights into workers' attitudes towards time-discipline can be gained through examining issues relating to the extent to which people turn up for work (their attendance and absence patterns) and what time-related practices they engage in while at work.

Attendance at Work

'Most workers', as Edwards and Scullion (1982: 107) point out, 'attend work for most of the time'. Nicholson (1977: 242) has made a similar point: 'Most people, most of the time, are on "automatic pilot" to attend [work] regularly'. Whether the driving force is internalised values, habit, economic necessity or fear of employer sanctions, employees' attendance at work is characterised far more by regularity than by absence. Yet, although workers' time-discipline towards attendance is high, it is rarely complete: many workers occasionally absent themselves even when they are able to go to work. In a study of attendance and absence in Britain in the late 1980s, for example, Edwards and Whitston (1993) found that, on average, workers had been absent from work on over 16 days during the previous year. Studies undertaken in parts of Western Europe indicate that countries such as the former West Germany and the Netherlands may have absence levels up to twice this rate (Prins and de Graaf, 1986, cited in Edwards and Whitston, 1993: 220). Of course, absence from work (and its related time-keeping aspects of lateness and leaving work early) may be due to illness and thus be involuntary and unavoidable. However, it is also clear that a proportion of total absence is voluntary and avoidable. Voluntary absence goes by different names at different times and in different regions – 'skiving', 'having one off', 'taking a sicky', 'swinging the lead', 'on the hop' and 'wagging' are a few such expressions. For obvious reasons, precise data on voluntary absence are difficult to obtain (admitting to being voluntarily absent could cost workers their jobs). However, evidence from different periods indicates a persistent tendency for some workers to 'skive off' from work occasionally. McClelland (1987) for example, identifies the continued practice of Saint Monday throughout the latter half of the nineteenth century in the north-east engineering industry, even though it was under attack from employers. A graphic description also exists of the tendency for boilermakers before the First World War to extend their holidays. As Pollitt (1940: 59) recounts,

> It was at Tinker's boiler-shop in Hyde that I first learnt the custom of the brick in the air. The first day after a holiday we would all... make a ring in the yard, and the oldest boilermaker... would pick up a brick, advance to the centre of the ring, and announce "Now lads. If t'brick stops i' th' air, we start; if t' brick cooms down, we go whoam". I do not remember any occasion on which we did not "go whoam".

Likewise, in the 1920s, an estimate for the dock-working industry indicates that on average over nine million man hours a year were lost through bad time-keeping (D.F. Wilson, 1972: 77). Some industries, such as coal-mining, have long been characterised by comparatively high levels of absence, with unauthorised absence frequently higher before or after annual or statutory holidays, particularly among younger age work groups (McCormick, 1979: 146–7). More generally, absence levels in different industries and organisations have shown a considerable resistance to decline (indeed many have risen) despite increased managerial attention. There is no indication either that attendance patterns of white-collar workers are any less subject to the taking of voluntary absence than the manual worker examples cited above.

Many organisations seek to control lateness and absenteeism by different means of time-recording and by a variety of punishments and incentives, including disciplinary action (ultimately ending in dismissal) for those persistently absent and, less frequently, bonuses for those attending punctually every day in a given period. Nevertheless, for some employees, going absent from work clearly represents a way of fulfilling family or other responsibilities, or gaining a respite from excessive work pressures. For others, taking occasional days off acts as a way of coping with 'the routine frustrations of going to work' (Edwards and Scullion, 1982: 110), an escape from the continuous daily repetition of work, eat and sleep. As one woman in Edwards and Scullion's study put it, 'It's not really boredom with the job. It's just that things get too much for you and you need a rest; you feel generally fed up' (1982: 110). In this way, workers occasionally relax the moral pressure of time-discipline.

The gap between a 'complete' and the 'actual' time-discipline of workers is also reflected in attitudes toward the legitimacy of voluntary absence. In their study of attendance in four organisations, Edwards and Whitston (1993) sought opinions on three hypothetical situations: a worker taking an extra day off having recovered from an illness; a working parent taking time off to look after a child who is ill; and a worker staying at home to get away from work pressures. Over four-fifths (84 per cent) of the male and female workers interviewed accepted the legitimacy of going absent in at least one of these hypothetical cases – a pattern of response which the authors concluded reflected 'a widespread acceptance of the need for workers to go absent in situations which management might see as voluntary or illegitimate absence' (1993: 45).

Whilst much voluntary absence is unorganised, in the sense that it is an action taken by an individual without the involvement of others in a work group, by no means all absence is unorganised. In some situations, for example, work groups are able to arrange their work in such a way as to enable individuals to take turns in having some time off. Historically, in the dock-working industry, for example, dockers employed a system known as 'welting' (also referred to in some areas as 'spelling') whereby half a gang absented itself from work for an hour or more, with the other half of the gang leaving off the work when the first half returned. The development of this informal arrangement appears to have been widespread; D.F. Wilson (1972: 215), for example, identifies a similar arrangement operating in dock work in many different parts of the world. Such an arrangement not only provides an easier work regime for those involved, but may also extend jobs over a longer period of time and could even result in an increase in earnings if, as a result of the 'welt', work was carried over into (premium-paid) overtime.

Just as dockers engaged in welting would be highly unlikely to be recorded by management as absent, Edwards and Scullion (1982: 102) identified a similar pattern operating in a metals factory, where workers with a relatively high degree of control over their work organisation had developed a working pattern which enabled individuals to take it in turns to leave the factory for up to half a day, without being recorded as absent. It is important to note that such time-keeping arrangements stem not only from the way that workers have organised their work, but also from management's unwillingness (or inability) to enforce their control over the work organisation to ensure that all the workforce are engaged in productive activity for the whole of the work period; as discussed later, this issue of work-time utilisation is one which, in recent years, has been subject to increased managerial scrutiny. Further, it is important to note that, just as work group norms may encourage absence as an informal element in the effort–reward bargain, work group norms and peer pressure can also act in the opposite direction. For example, where there exist high work loads and tight staffing levels, voluntary absence may be viewed very negatively by the group, since one person's absence is likely to put significantly greater pressure on those attending (Nicholson and Johns, 1985). Similarly, in a context where the norm is very high levels of attendance, someone taking more absence than the rest of the group may incur peer pressure to conform with the group attendance norm. As well as acting to encourage or suppress voluntary absence, attitudes held by the work group may also influence perceptions of what constitutes 'legitimate' reasons for voluntary absence. For instance, a work group of female employees may acknowledge the 'legitimacy' of voluntary absence to care for a sick child, irrespective of the work pressure implications for the remainder of the group attending work.

Accounts of work organisation in general, and studies of absence behaviour in particular, suggest there exists a widespread tendency for managers to tolerate a degree of voluntary absence without making concerted efforts to suppress it. In part, this probably reflects the difficulties management typically face in trying to establish whether individual, short-term absences are voluntary or involuntary. Absences are likely to attract greater management attention, however, where they exceed a level judged to be 'acceptable', or where production systems are so highly interdependent and/or where staffing levels have been created which contain so little spare capacity, that ensuring cover for absent individuals is far more difficult. As noted earlier, managerial efforts to control absence can range from giving bonus payments for unblemished attendance records to holding interviews with those whose absence or lateness exceeds a certain level, and ultimately invoking disciplinary procedures ending in dismissal for those persistently absent or late. Clearly, the existence of such sanctions and the ultimate threat of dismissal will affect many people's decisions over whether or not to go absent voluntarily, and how frequently. Besides this threat of sanctions, an additional discouragement to frequent absence for many (particularly those engaged in manual work) is that being absent from work can incur a significant loss of income where sick pay benefits are lower than earnings levels.

These instrumental reasons (fear of job loss and desire to maintain income) are important factors in controlling levels of voluntary absence. Yet, at the same time, the persistence of voluntary absence underlines the fact that employers have so far failed in their endeavour to instil into their workforce a complete time-discipline, with many workers continuing to exhibit some measure of discretion over their level of attendance. In other words, management's continued need to monitor attendance, and their lack of success in totally suppressing voluntary absence, indicates a continuing tension between two temporal rationalities. On the one hand, there is the managerial rationality based on the twin notions of the definition of the working period and the requirement for workers to utilise the whole of that period in productive activity. On the other hand, there exists an employees' counter-rationality which emphasises such needs as breaking up the monotony of work or reducing work pressures by occasional absence or lateness. The tension between these two rationalities represents a continuing source of conflict and accommodation in the overall employment relationship. It is a tension which is also relevant when assessing recent efforts by management to impose greater control over employees' opportunities for operating alternative time schedules, and considering in what ways (and how effectively) workers are able to resist these efforts and maintain a counter-rationality relating to their working time.

TEMPORAL COPING STRATEGIES

'Making' Time and 'Fiddling' Time

If one frontier of control over working time is whether or not workers attend the workplace, rather than voluntarily absenting themselves, another involves control over the working period itself: the extent to which the working period, as defined by management, is actually spent working. Production problems, such as shortage of materials and production bottlenecks, are among several possible causes of non-productive periods (White, 1987). In addition, however, sources of non-productive time are those fashioned by workers themselves to achieve an easier work regime (and as a result, a more favourable effort–reward bargain). As Ditton (1979) and others have pointed out, such time manipulation by workers can be achieved in a number of ways. Two of those ways, however, are particularly worthy of comment – what Ditton terms 'making' time and 'fiddling' time. Making time involves arranging work in such a way as to produce breaks which would not occur otherwise. Traditionally, an apparently widespread means of achieving this is by what Blauner (1964: 100) terms 'working up the line' – a pattern of accelerated working which results in workers building up a 'bank' or 'kitty' of finished output, which can then be drawn upon to create a break, or an easier work period (see also Burawoy, 1979; and Ditton, 1979 on this practice). As Blauner's reference to a 'line' suggests, this practice has been associated with assembly-line operations, but in many other situations too, in both manual and non-manual settings, scope has existed for workers to alter their tempo of work by building up banks of finished output in this way. In Edwards and Whitston's (1993: 301) study, this practice was known in one plant as 'using the back of the book', referring to workers carrying out tasks, but not immediately recording them.

In addition to making time, managerially defined work-time structures can also be 'fiddled' in various ways. At their simplest, such fiddles can take the form of employees delaying the start of work, covertly extending the length of meal breaks or leaving off work before the official end of the working period. In situations where work time is recorded by clocking equipment, time fiddles can also involve manipulating the clocking procedures, so that time officially recorded as having been spent working is greater than the time actually spent at work (a fiddle which may involve, for example, workers being clocked-out by others, the former having already left; see Ditton, 1979; also Scott, 1994). In addition, other ways that time might be fiddled include sabotaging equipment or otherwise causing a machine breakdown, resulting in a pause in work while repairs are carried out (see also the discussion of sabotage in Chapter 8).

Mars (1982) argues that in jobs which are dominated by repetitive, short-cycle activities, workers' ability to control time is likely to be exercised particularly through their ability to slow a job down. An example of how this can be effected is by employees seeking to manipulate the way that jobs are timed by work study engineers. If employees can convince those timing the jobs that they actually take longer to perform than is really the case, then any resulting 'standard' times established will allow employees to complete the required work with a reduced tempo of work, than would have been the case if the tasks had been allotted a shorter standard time.

Where jobs have more of a linear than a short-cycle character, however, such as the tasks of refuse collecting or bus driving, which involve travelling along a route, Mars (1982) argues that the source of workers' time control is more likely to lie in speeding up the work process. By so doing, this will potentially create unofficial free time at the end of the task. As an example of this latter working-time strategy, Mars quotes Blackpool tram crews who, if they succeed in making the journey along the designated route in a faster time than is timetabled, secure an additional unofficial break period.

> The main aim of being a tram conductor is to control the job and to stop it controlling you. This is why tram crews will go to all sorts of extremes to get a tram from A to B ten minutes earlier than it should get there so that they can get a ten-minute break the other end. The times are so worked out that if you follow the route properly you'll never get any tea-break at all and you'll be working your guts out for the whole shift. So the main aim of the job as I see it is to fiddle time. (Blackpool tram conductor quoted by Mars, 1982: 82.)

Notable in this conductor's comment is the importance given to wresting some control of time away from the managerially defined timetable, and that without this, the latter's time-reckoning system would be overly burdensome. We return to this issue again, below.

Coping with Monotony

In accounts of workers seeking to manipulate working time, a commonly referred-to objective is to counter the effects of monotony and boredom. Altering the otherwise unceasing tempo of repetitive tasks represents an attempt to introduce greater variety and thereby assist workers to 'get through' their working day (see Chapter 8). One means of achieving this is by breaking up the day into different temporal segments. A particularly vivid account of workers breaking up a monotonous working day by punctuating it with differently characterised time periods, remains that by Roy (1960) and his description of 'banana time'. While observing a work group in a US garment factory engaged in the repetition of very simple operations over a long (12-hour) work day, Roy was particularly interested in how workers dealt with the 'beast of monotony' without 'going nuts' (1960: 156). Central to the workers' coping strategies was the division of the day into different elements (over and above the formally recognised mealtimes and coffee breaks). These additional interruptions occurred almost hourly and were very short in duration. The breaks were designated as different 'times' and normally featured not only the consumption of some food or drink, but importantly were also a focus for a period of interactive banter between the members of the work group. 'Peach time', for example, occurred when one member of the work group produced some peaches to share, invariably accompanied by verbal banter from the others about the (poor) quality of the fruit. An hour later came 'banana time', which routinely involved one member of the group stealing (and eating) a banana from another's lunch box, again to the accompaniment of much verbal banter. 'Window time' came next, followed by 'pick up time' and later 'fish time' and 'Coke time'. These different times punctuated the day, acting as a focus of jokes and other social interaction, and capturing the attention of members of the group, giving them something to think about as they resumed work. The combined effect was to make an otherwise monotonous work day pass more easily.

> The major significance of the interactional interruptions lay in... a carryover of interest. The physical interplay which momentarily halted work activity would initiate verbal exchanges and thought processes to occupy group members until the next interruption. The group interactions thus not only marked off the time; they gave it content and hurried it along. (Roy, 1960: 161.)

Thus, just as some workers may seek to modify an unchanging work period by 'working up the line', so too Roy's portrayal of the 'banana time' group highlights another means by which a work group has introduced greater temporal variation into an otherwise uniform work period. In both cases, the effect has been to introduce not only temporal variety, but also a degree of counter-rationality into the formal (managerially defined) working-time rationality. This interplay of managers' and workers' rationalities over working time is far from static. Indeed, significant developments in the arrangement and utilisation of working time have been evident in recent years, many of which have potentially important implications for workers' overall experience of working time, and the extent to which they are able to influence and modify management's formal work-time rationality. As the next section examines, changes (and notable areas where there has been an absence of change) are also evident in relation to the duration of work time.

RECENT DEVELOPMENTS IN THE WORKING PERIOD

The total time people spend at work is determined by a number of variables including their age of entry into, and exit from the labour market, whether they work full- or part-time, whether or not they work overtime and/or experience short-time working, the amount they are absent from work, the length of paid holidays, their experience of unemployment, and whether they are involved in single, dual or multiple job-holding: clearly, the influencing factors are many and diverse. Historically, however, two aspects of working-time duration – the length of the working day and working week – have periodically acted as a prime focus of contest and dispute between employers and employees. Just as workers have sought improvements in remuneration for their work, so too they have also periodically campaigned for reductions in work hours. Typically, these calls for shorter hours have met with opposition from employers, the latter claiming that cuts in working time would damage their competitiveness. Yet, as a result of several factors – not least, continued increases in labour productivity and employers' periodic preference for reductions in hours rather than conceding higher wage settlements – the length of the basic working week has fallen considerably over the past century and a half, typically from over 60 hours to less than 40 hours per week (Blyton, 1985 and 1994).

Yet, despite this reduction in basic weekly hours, many workers in practice continue to work far longer than this, as a result of high levels of overtime working (and in some cases, multiple job-holding). A complete picture of overtime working is difficult to establish since available data generally relate only to paid overtime, whereas in reality a significant amount of overtime worked (and disproportionately that undertaken by higher levels of non-manual workers) is not paid for specifically. Likewise, the long hours worked by some family members in small businesses, and work carried out in the hidden work sector (see Chapter 10) do not appear in the working-time statistics. Hence, actual levels of overtime worked far exceed those recorded in the official statistics. However, it is clear even from the partial information available on weekly work hours that among some groups a high level of overtime working is the norm. In Britain in 1995, for example, among the 55 per cent of male manual workers who were working overtime in the period surveyed in the *New Earnings Survey* (NES), well over a third (38 per cent) worked more than 10 hours overtime a week, and a significant minority (11.4 per cent) worked over 20 hours overtime. Overall, male manual workers in Britain worked an average of 5.7 overtime hours per week in 1995, adding over 14 per cent to the average basic work week (*New Earnings Survey*, 1995). Later, there is a discussion of whether or not work has become more intensive over time; these high levels of overtime working, however, indicate that, for many, work is also characterised by its *extensiveness*, the long work days of a significant proportion of the workforce resulting in work occupying a large part of individuals' total waking hours.

Within Europe, the level of overtime working in Britain is particularly high. Among EU member states, for example, the UK has the highest proportion of workers working in excess of 48 hours – the maximum length of the working week specified in the EU Directive on Working Time (for a discussion of the Directive, see Incomes Data Services, 1996). Further, primarily as a result of the high levels of overtime, the average working week of full-time workers in the UK is some three hours longer than the EU average (EIRR, 1995; Keen, 1995). Several factors may account for this high level of overtime working in the UK, including the absence of any statutory controls on the maximum number of work hours an individual is permitted to work. Also significant for many workers is the importance of overtime earnings for supplementing (low) basic wage levels. Groups such as postal workers, for example, are often reliant on high levels of overtime earnings to boost a relatively low basic wage. Further, although overtime is often paid at a premium rate (e.g. time-and-a-half, or double time) it represents a preferable option for many employers, compared with introducing shiftworking and hiring additional staff. Overtime potentially offers not only a more flexible means of extending the working period, but may also reduce any pressure on employers to raise basic wage levels, since the availability of overtime work is offered as an incentive to attract and retain staff in otherwise low-paying jobs. For the employees involved, however, it means that the overall experience of work is coloured by the long hours spent at work and the resulting diminished opportunity for pursuing non-work activities. In a number of (mainly manual) occupations, the requirement to undertake overtime is a contractual obligation. In others (among many white-collar, managerial and professional occupations, for example) there is a widespread expectation that additional hours (paid or unpaid) should be worked to complete tasks which are outstanding. In such situations, working long hours is often taken by management as a sign of commitment, whilst an unwillingness to work extra hours may be viewed as an indication of a lack of commitment. This may raise particular difficulties for those with outside commitments, in particular those women employees carrying substantial domestic responsibilities, whose situation prevents them from working additional hours.

The duration of the contemporary working week is characterised not only by some working very long hours, but also by a growing diversity of working-time schedules, including a significant proportion of the workforce working very few hours. The overall growth of part-time working, and the fact that most part-time jobs are held by women, has already been noted (see Chapter 2). An important aspect of part-time working is that the hours of many part-time jobs are very small indeed. As Table 4.1 indicates, in Britain approaching half of part-time male workers and around two-fifths of female part-time workers work fewer than 16 hours per week, while one in five of the men and approximately one in eight of the women work fewer than 8 hours. The trend is also towards an increase in these shorter part-time schedules. A survey of changes in average hours in Britain between 1983 and 1993, for example, found that average hours of part-time workers had fallen by almost 5 per cent over this period, while among their full-time counterparts, there was little discernible change (Butcher and Hart, 1995: 215). For employers, part-time working in general, and the use of short schedules in particular, allows the concentration of workers at

Table 4.1　　*Distribution of work hours of those working less than 30 hours*
　　　　　　　　per week, Great Britain, 1995

Percentage with normal basic hours in the range	Male Part-timers	Female Part-timers	
		Manual	Non-manual
	(%)	(%)	(%)
8 or less	19.5	11.0	13.2
8 – 16	27.8	32.1	24.7
16 – 21	18.5	24.4	29.1
21 – 30	34.1	32.5	33.0

Source: *New Earnings Survey*, 1995, *Part A: Streamlined and Summary Analysis*, London: HMSO, Table A 28.2

times when work pressures are at their highest. For many employees, however, jobs comprising only a few hours per week yield only very limited income, often leading to the necessity for multiple job-holding.

If some jobs are characterised by their short duration, others operate on the basis of no guaranteed duration at all. 'Zero hour' contracts (also known as 'reservism' and 'on call' arrangements) involve employers guaranteeing no definite hours, but simply calling on workers specifically when, and in the amount, required – for example, to cover for unforeseen absence. There is little aggregate information on this form of working, though one national study in Britain suggested that around 5 per cent of employees (4 per cent of men and 6 per cent of women) were subject to this form of contract (Wareing, 1992). Such contracts provide employers with both a very high degree of temporal flexibility, and at the same time, extend only minimal contractual commitment to those employed under such arrangements. The workers hired on such contracts are typically afforded no job security, and no guarantee of earnings or hours; yet, these contracts are restrictive in that employees need to keep themselves available ('on call') which acts to reduce their opportunities for pursuing other activities.

CHANGES IN THE ARRANGEMENT OF WORKING TIME

There have been several factors in recent years encouraging employers to increase their total operating hours. In the service sector, this reflects partly the general increase in opening hours which has taken place as a result, for example, of the liberalisation of Sunday trading, changes in licensing hours, extension of banking hours, and evening opening of retail and other service activities. In manufacturing, increased investment in technology, coupled with a faster rate of technological obsolescence, has forced employers to consider more ways to increase capital utilisation in order to maximise returns on investment. The result of a gradually declining basic work week and the pressures to maintain or increase operating times, has been greater de-coupling of individual work hours from operating hours. This means that instead of an organisation's operating time being the same as the employees' work period (for example, 9 a.m. to 5.30 p.m.) the operating time is lengthened (for example, to 10 p.m.) with the additional time being covered for example, by a part-time shift. Such de-coupling is, of course, not new. Those industries where shiftworking has been common practice, such as hospitals, hotels, continuous process operations, transport services, postal services and parts of the engineering sector, have long been used to a distinction between the length of the operating period and individual work hours. What *is* new in more recent years, however, is the spread of this arrangement into areas where traditionally shiftworking has been comparatively rare, such as in retailing and financial services. The pressure to extend hours affects not only weekdays but also weekends, nowhere more so than in the banking sector, where Saturday opening has become a norm, and in retailing, with the increase in Sunday trading. Thus, when viewed in combination with the greater use of a wide range of part-time schedules, an effect of this extension of operating/opening hours has been to create an overall working-time pattern which is diverse, not only in terms of the number of hours which people work, but also in terms of when they work those hours. A popular belief, for example, is that a majority of people still work Monday to Friday, from 9 a.m. to 5 p.m. or thereabouts. In practice, however, this is far from the actual experience of the majority of employees. In Britain, for example, only around a third of employed men and women operate such a working-time pattern (Table 4.2).

Table 4.2 *The timing of work weeks for men and women in Britain*

	%
Full time, Monday to Friday, starting between 8–10 a.m., finishing between 4–6 p.m.	34
Full-time, Monday to Friday, other hours	7
Part-time, Monday to Friday	11
6- or 7-day week	23
1–5 days, some weekend work	11
1–4 days, no weekend work	14

Source: P. Hewitt, *About Time: The Revolution in Work and Family Life*, London: Rivers Oram, 1993, p.23.

There are various ways that an employer may schedule working hours to create a longer working period. The use of overtime for this purpose has already been noted. In addition, a long-established means of lengthening the working period is by shiftworking; a simple definition of shiftwork is 'a situation in which one worker replaces another on the same job within a 24-hour period' (Ingram and Sloane, 1984: 168). Various shiftwork patterns exist, some extending across the whole day and week (e.g. continuous three-shift working, with shifts starting for example, at 6 a.m., 2 p.m. and 10 p.m.), with others extending the productive period but not across the entire day or week (e.g. 'double day' shifts, for example 6 a.m. – 2 p.m. and 2 p.m. – 10 p.m.). In 1993, just under one in five workers in Britain worked shifts (G. Watson, 1994), with shiftwork particularly evident in such sectors as metal manufacturing, chemicals, paper-making, food and drink industries, textiles and vehicle production (Bosworth, 1994: 619). One reason why the proportion of employees working shifts has not gone even higher is the replacement of formal shiftwork systems with alternative working-time arrangements which extend the productive period but do not incur the wage premia usually paid to workers on shifts. One example of these arrangements is that of 'compressed' work weeks, whereby employees work their total weekly hours in longer work periods but for fewer than the normal number of days (for example, working for twelve hours a day for three days rather than seven and a half hours for five days). Across a workforce as a whole, the effect of this can be to create longer work periods without the use of a formal shiftwork system (Poor, 1972).

Attempts by employers to extend the length of the productive work period have also been accompanied, in a growing number of instances, by attempts to redefine what constitutes normal work hours, in order to reduce the amount of time attracting (premium paid) overtime rates. Recent examples of negotiations over the redefinition of normal and overtime periods are widespread, occurring, for example, in Australia (see discussion in Deery and Mahony, 1994: 333–5) and Germany, where extensive negotiations over working time during the 1990s have included discussions on payments for Saturday working, and temporary increases in weekly hours without incurring overtime payments (Blyton and Trinczek, 1995). In the UK and elsewhere, an example of managerial efforts to reduce reliance on overtime during busy periods has been the introduction of 'seasonal hours' working, whereby the normal work week is lengthened during busy periods and reduced during slacker times. A number of consumer electronic firms in the UK, for example, operate this pattern, with longer work weeks (up to 44 hours) in the months prior to the busy Christmas period, with shorter hours in the following months to bring the average work week back to 39 hours. For the employer this arrangement both reduces overtime payments during the busy months, and also reduces excess labour capacity in the quieter periods (Blyton, 1994: 517–18). For employees, however, this seasonality of the working period can be more problematic, since it is likely to entail both a loss of overtime earnings, and eliminate any discretion they may have enjoyed over whether or not to work overtime. An extension of seasonal hours arrangements are 'annual hours' contracts, under which employees work an agreed number of hours per year, with working time schedules (including holidays) determined at the beginning of 12 month cycles. Such arrangements usually build in flexibility for employers either by establishing a schedule where more hours are worked during busy periods, or by leaving some of the agreed total hours as non-rostered work time, for which employees are effectively 'on-call' and can be brought into work to cover unforeseen circumstances (Blyton, 1995; Pickard, 1991).

Seasonal and annual hours arrangements not only create the potential for reducing overtime costs, but coupled with this, enable a closer matching of available labour with levels of output demand. Together with arranging hours to cover longer operating periods, this desire for a closer matching of work schedules with output demand has become a second major focus for employers. In some sectors, demand fluctuates considerably over the working day and week. In parts of the retailing industry, for example, demand rises significantly during lunchtime periods and towards the end of the week. One of the ways working-time schedules have been arranged to reflect this is via the introduction of various part-time schedules which increase the volume of available labour during busy periods. Hence, it has become common practice in retailing to schedule part-time workers to work during lunch periods and/or at weekends.

Thus, in various ways, employers are increasingly concerned to arrange working time in such a way as to maximise labour coverage and flexibility, and minimise labour cost. However, two ways in which employees also exert some influence over how work hours are arranged are through flexible working hours systems and via informal working-time arrangements. According to G. Watson (1994), around one in eight employees in Britain (10 per cent of men and 14 per cent of women) work flexible working hours or 'flexitime'. Typically, such schemes provide employees with a degree of choice over start and finish times provided that agreed 'core' hours are worked, and that over a certain period the number of contractually agreed hours are completed (though many schemes also allow some degree of carry-over of credit/debit hours from one settlement period to another). Flexitime working remains far more common among non-manual workers, particularly in larger public (and recently privatised) service sector organisations, than among their manual counterparts and others located in manufacturing and smaller establishments in the private sector (Wareing, 1992). Beyond formal flexitime systems, however, it is evident that a proportion of employees operate less formalised systems which provide an element of choice over start and finish times. Those in higher level jobs typically enjoy greater access to this informal flexibility: for example, in Wareing's (1992) study, half the employees in professional occupations had a measure of flexibility over their start and finish times, compared to less than one in ten of those in semi-skilled occupations. At other levels too, however, it is evident that many employees (and management) secure a degree of flexibility over working hours by reaching informal 'understandings' with other workers and with management in relation, for example, to start and finish times. Such informal agreements are also reflected in much of the overtime that is worked. As noted above, for a proportion of workers, overtime working is a contractual obligation. However, in a large-scale study in Britain, Marsh (1991) found that, in the period immediately prior to her survey, more than three male full-time workers in every ten and over a quarter of full-time female workers had agreed to work extra time at short notice – a far higher proportion than the 6 per cent who indicated that they were required by their contract to work overtime (see also Horrell and Rubery, 1991).

THE UTILISATION OF WORKING TIME

Just as increased attention has been given to arranging working time to cover longer opening/operating periods, and to concentrating labour time at periods of highest work pressure, greater attention has also been paid in recent years to increasing the extent to which labour time is effectively utilised. In the 1980s, White (1987: 51) estimated that in engineering between 20 and 40 per cent of paid time was non-productive. As noted earlier, part of the explanation for this will lie in scheduling and production problems such as shortages of materials, equipment breakdown, and a lack of orders, together with possible poor managerial organisation and instruction concerning the tasks to be completed. As we have seen, however, non-productive time can also be fashioned by workers themselves to create an easier or more varied work tempo. In this context, three recent developments relating to work time utilisation are particularly noteworthy. The first is the introduction of practices designed to define the working period exclusive of, rather than inclusive of, preparatory activities such as changing into and out of work clothes and walking to and from the actual work area. Efforts to tighten the definition of the working period have centred on practices such as 'bell to bell' working, which refers to the bells or buzzers announcing the start and finish of working periods, with employees required to be in position to commence working when the bell for the start of the shift sounds, and only terminating work after the bell which signals the end of the shift (Blyton, 1994: 520). Such managerial attempts to impose a time-reckoning system which minimises non-productive time, together with responses by workers to operate a counter-system which creates or extends additional rest periods, have been a feature of capitalist industrial development throughout its history. Karl Marx (1976) for example, remarked on employers' continual efforts to maximise 'surplus labour time' – that is, that part of working hours creating surplus value – by seeking to extend the working period and by efforts to minimise the 'porosity' of the working day: the number of holes or 'pores' in the working day when workers are not actually working. Marx (1976: 352) characterises employers as continually 'nibbling and cribbling' at workers' mealtimes and other breaks in an attempt to maximise the quantity of labour effort in the working day. As current managerial interest in bell-to-bell working and similar practices illustrates, this issue of non-productive work time continues to be significant for late twentieth-century management as was the case for their nineteenth-century counterparts.

A second area of change with potentially important implications for work-time utilisation, concerns the introduction of just-in-time (JIT), *kanban*, and similar process systems whose development has been facilitated by advances in information technology, and which form a major element in the development of so-called 'lean' manufacturing systems. Under a JIT regime, emphasis is placed on work 'flowing' continuously through the different stages of production, with components arriving 'just-in-time' to be incorporated into the manufacturing process, with only minimum stocks held of materials, work-in-progress and finished articles (Turnbull, 1988). Among other implications, this method of organising production potentially undermines any ability workers may have to build up 'banks' of finished work which, as discussed earlier, could then be used to create an additional break or an easier work pace later in the working period.

The growth of task flexibility during the 1980s and 1990s represents a third area of workplace change with potentially important implications for time utilisation. The issue of labour flexibility has been much debated over the last decade and it is clear that actual developments in flexibility have not necessarily been in the ways, or to the extent, that many of the early predictions and prescriptions suggested (see, for example, Atkinson, 1984; see also Blyton, 1992; Cross, 1988; Pollert, 1988). Nevertheless, it is also evident that, cumulatively over the period since the early 1980s, developments in work organisation based on broader job definitions, reduced skill demarcations and enlarged jobs, have led to significant changes in the way that individual tasks and work groups are organised. Some blurring of skill boundaries and widespread development of greater flexibility among less-skilled workers have increased the mobility of labour between tasks within workplaces and been part of a shift towards more tasks being covered by fewer workers, as organisations seek cost cutting through staff reductions. In a study of trade unionists in more than 4000 workplaces, Waddington and Whitson (1996: 158–9) identified developments in flexibility as the most prominent in a series of work reorganisation measures, with much of the development in flexibility occurring in the recent period: over a fifth (23 per cent) of respondents indicated that management had introduced significant levels of task flexibility, most of this over the previous three years. Levels of multi-skilling were lower, with 16 per cent indicating significant development. While developments in multi-skilling were most pronounced in the private sector, task flexibility was more marked in public services, such as in the health service where, for example, general assistant grades have replaced former, more specialist, grades (Waddington and Whitson, 1996: 164). Related to the growth of flexibility in some settings, has been the introduction of teamworking. Waddington and Whitston (1996: 158) found a lower incidence and growth of teamworking compared to flexibility. Nevertheless, as management attempts not only to locate more responsibility for performance within work groups themselves, but also to increase flexibility through greater worker interchange-ability and to reduce the number of supervisory posts, it may be anticipated that interest in teamworking is likely to expand in coming years. In some contexts, working in teams has proved only marginally different from prior systems of work organisation based around less formal (but nonetheless important) work group arrangements. However, the circumstances under which teamworking has been adopted (often in contexts of job reductions, lower staffing levels and increased emphasis on quality assurance, for example) means that, for many, teamworking is part of a significant change from what has gone before, not least in the additional responsibilities held by the team over such areas as quality and task allocation.

These aspects of workplace change, coupled with evidence that levels of productivity rose considerably in the UK during the 1980s (manufacturing productivity, for example, rose by over 5 per cent per year during the 1980s) have prompted writers such as Elger (1990 and 1991) to consider the extent to which this productive gain has been the result of work becoming more intensive (see also Guest, 1990; Metcalf, 1989; and Nolan, 1989). The question of whether or not workers are working harder is, in practice, difficult to answer with any degree of accuracy, for it is complicated by various factors, not least the lack of any systematic study of effort. Other factors, too, complicate comparisons of effort: for example, the experience of working harder can be the result of a faster work pace and/or reductions in the extent of non-work time (Elger, 1990). Further, effort may comprise the expenditure of either (or both) manual and mental energy; hence, identifying a decline (or increase) in one may not give an accurate picture of what has happened to levels of effort overall. Thus, it is frequently argued that automation and the other technological changes have reduced the degree of physical effort required to perform many jobs. The decline in employment in manufacturing in general, and in heavy industry such as iron-and steel-making, shipbuilding and coal-mining in particular, has also been adduced to argue that the number of jobs in the labour force as a whole requiring high expenditure of (physical) effort, is likely to have declined. Yet, at the same time, various attitude studies show that despite the decline of heavy industry, many workers have experienced an *increase* in effort over recent years, both physical and mental. A prominent argument here is that the increases in productivity during the 1980s were primarily accounted for by workers working harder, either because of a fear of losing their jobs in a period of extreme uncertainty, or due to an increase in managerial power, forcing workers to work harder. This argument is supported by various studies of worker and trade union perceptions of effort (for example, Batstone and Gourlay, 1986; and Edwards and Whitston, 1991). Clearly there are potential bias problems if relying on asking workers whether or not they are working harder than they used to. However, the strength of worker opinions on questions of effort suggest support for the argument that effort levels have indeed gone up. In a survey of worker attitudes in a steel plant conducted by one of the authors, for example, almost seven out of ten of the 450 workers who took part felt that significant amounts of change had occurred in their jobs in recent years. Among those experiencing change, the majority thought that the degrees of physical and mental effort required by their jobs had changed, and of these, *four times* as many thought the job had become more rather than less physically tiring and *nine out of ten* thought the job had become more rather than less mentally tiring (Blyton *et al.*, 1996).

It is possible that as expectations over work performance have risen – as a result, for example of higher output targets, more exacting quality levels, reduced levels of waste and using more highly complex equipment – so levels of mental effort required to perform many jobs are likely to have also risen. Further, Elger (1991) argues that the drive for greater flexibility has contributed to labour intensification because reductions in workforce numbers, with the fewer remaining workers covering more tasks, has resulted in more intensified work regimes. This is echoed in the study by Edwards and Whitston (1991: 597) where, for example, one of the factors affecting the perceived increase in effort levels among British Rail platform staff was that the standard labour allocation had been cut from three workers per railway platform to two. Similarly, in the steel study cited above, a prominent characteristic of the plant under investigation was continued cuts in workforce numbers, with those remaining required to cover a broader range of tasks. Further, just as competitive pressures in the private sector have fuelled a search for lower labour costs (and thus potentially stimulated labour intensification), so too political demands for more efficient public services have led to a corresponding search for reductions in labour costs, as in-house groups have been forced to compete with external providers of similar services. This was one of the factors affecting the hospital ancillary workers in Edwards and Whitston's (1991: 597) study, where competitive tendering had led to work remaining in-house, but only through cuts in labour costs and the need for remaining workers to work harder to complete the tasks.

CONCLUSION

Time is a central factor shaping the experience of work. What this chapter has underlined is the diversity of time schedules: a diversity reflected in the different lengths of working hours, the ways those hours are variously arranged across the day and week, and the degrees to which working hours are actually utilised in productive activity. What has also been stressed are the different ways that management and workers perceive working time. On the one hand, a managerial rationality emphasises the linear quality of time, the importance of regularity for the co-ordination of different time schedules, and the importance of maximising the productive use of working time. On the other hand, however, there is a workers' counter-rationality seeking, in part, to mitigate the negative aspects of an unchanging work tempo. These two rationalities exist in a state of mutual influence, with the result that the formal time regime defined by management typically bears only partial resemblance to actual working-time patterns performed by their employees.

These twin rationalities also reflect a tension between the objective and subjective nature of time. The managerial rationality is essentially based on a linear view of time as 'clock time': time as a scarce resource, and a commodity capable of being 'spent' , 'wasted', or 'lost' – its objective character summed up in the classic temporal cliché of capitalism, 'time is money'. On the other hand, however, workers experience time at work subjectively: it can pass quickly or slowly, can be varied or monotonous, and for many will be experienced as a cyclical (rather than a linear) phenomenon, with one day more or less repeating the cycle of the previous day; or even one hour repeating the pattern of the previous. As has been noted, the creation of circumstances to improve the way time is experienced can take various forms, ranging from occasional absence to escape the routines of work, to the creation of different 'times' within the working day, when the tempo of work is altered and the regularity of time is suppressed.

The relationship between the objective and subjective character of time, and between a managerial rationality and a workers' counter-rationality towards time, represents an on-going tension in the employment relationship. On the one hand, for example, continuing levels of voluntary absence indicate workers' ability to ward off managerial attempts to impose a comprehensive time-discipline on its work force. On the other hand, management's introduction of tighter staffing levels and practices such as bell-to-bell working, signals their pursuit of higher levels of working-time utilisation. Moreover, the tension between the two rationalities may be expected to continue for the foreseeable future, and manifest itself within particular aspects of working time. For example, management's efforts to cut labour costs by restricting the periods defined as overtime (via arrangements such as seasonal and annual hours contracts, and varied part-time schedules) are likely to be countered, to a degree at least, by workers seeking to establish an easier pace of work which allows, among other things, unfinished work to be carried over into (premium paid) overtime hours. Such a carry-over of work into overtime remains particularly important in those low-paying jobs where workers rely heavily on overtime earnings. Of course, an obvious cost to those working long hours is the reduced time available for non-work activities and responsibilities. In broader societal terms, the cost is also that while many are working very long hours to earn an acceptable wage, others remain unemployed for want of available work. Overall, it is a situation satisfactory to neither group. However, despite an on-going debate over work-sharing and the reorganisation of working time, to date this has remained an issue lacking the political will to bring about any significant change.

5 Work Skills

EXPLORING THE CONCEPT OF SKILL

Of all the concepts we come across when studying work and employment, 'skill' stands out as the most difficult to pin down. Yet, strangely enough it is perhaps one of the few topics that most people might claim to have an understanding about. If you ask someone about a job, they would more than likely be able to tell you whether it is skilled or not, and they would probably be able to give a reasonable explanation as to why they considered it skilled. The problem, however, is that we all stress different aspects of a job in evaluating whether it is skilled or not.

In a survey (Francis and Penn, 1994) respondents came up with over 16 different definitions when asked the question 'What do you think is meant by the term *skilled job*?', although there was some convergence around five main characteristics: training, qualifications, apprenticeship, experience and high

Table 5.1 *Various meanings of the term 'skilled job'*

Feature of skilled work identified as important	Characteristics of respondents (statistically significant)
Apprenticeship	Older, male, manual workers (particularly those possessing apprenticeship qualifications)
Training	Younger, female, public-sector service employees (particularly those possessing higher level qualifications)
Qualifications	Women (particularly in retail distribution) Younger respondents People with lower-level qualifications
High abilities	Men People with higher level qualifications
Experience	No statistically significant relationships

Based on B. Francis and R. Penn 'Towards a phenomenology of skills' in R. Penn, M. Rose and J. Rubery (eds), *Skills and Occupational Change*, Oxford: Oxford University Press, 1994, pp.223–43. The survey comprised 987 adults aged between 20 and 60, and was undertaken in Rochdale, UK, in 1986.

abilities. Interestingly (although not surprisingly) the researchers found that responses to the question differed between types of employees: they emphasised different features of skill (see Table 5.1). Francis and Penn conclude that different occupational groups will categorise skill in different ways, which suggests that a person's conception of skill is largely based on his or her own experiences of employment.

In extreme cases, the lack of consensus over what constitutes a skilled job is less important because the job attributes are diverse enough for people to reach general, if not specific agreement – for example, most people would probably agree that the surgeon's job is more skilled than the hospital porter's job, or that the teacher is more skilled than the school caretaker. But what about the hotel receptionist compared with the security guard? The cleaner and the car-park attendant? The insurance broker and the travel agent? The police officer and the social worker? To come to an agreement on such comparisons, it is necessary to achieve consensus on what is meant by the term 'skill'. This is not an easy task: skill is a definitional minefield. However, in this chapter we are going to enter this dangerous territory and explore the theoretical concept and its empirical expression.

But why worry about defining skill at all? This is a reasonable question, but, as explained later, the concept of skill is fundamental to the status people attach to different occupations, and is frequently linked to the level of economic reward. Moreover, skill is a key factor in the structure of employment, most notably in the way it act to reinforce the gender division of labour in society.

The first puzzle that needs to be solved is the problem of where skill resides. Is it part of the person, the job or the setting? Cockburn (1983: 113) suggests all three aspects need to be taken into account. In her study of (male) printworkers she argues that:

> There is the skill that resides in the man himself, accumulated over time, each new experience adding something to a total ability. There is the skill demanded by the job – which may or may not match the skill in the worker. And there is the political definition of skill: that which a group of workers or a trade union can successfully defend against the challenge of employers and other groups of workers.

A closer consideration of Cockburn's research will be undertaken later in the chapter, but it is worth pausing to give some thought to her three categories because each suggests a different approach to examining skill. An analysis that concentrates on the *person* is likely to attempt to identify individual attributes and qualities, and seek to measure them through, for example, an aptitude test under experimental conditions; typically this approach has been taken by psychologists. Similarly, a questionnaire might be administered to assess the individual's education, training and experience, which could then be used as a proxy for skill – a method employed by economists. Alternatively, if the analytical focus is the *job* then the concern is less with the person performing the task than with the requirements embedded in the task itself. In this case, attention would be turned towards the complexity of the tasks required to perform the job competently – an approach typically taken by management theorists. Finally, if the focus is on the political and historical *setting*, an analysis would be assessing the way skill is constructed over time by different interest groups, rather than being a facticity of the person or the job – an approach pursued by some sociologists, but most typically by historians.

These differences in approach to analysing skill are summarised in Table 5.2. It illustrates how the focus tends to be associated with different methods of analysis and shows how academic disciplines have tended to address different aspects of skill. Consequently, it is possible for several theorists to arrive at contrasting conclusions about skilled work because they are focusing on different features and using different methods of analysis.

Figure 5.2 *Approaches to the analysis of skill*

Focus	Principal area of concern	Typical method of analysis	Typically adopted by:
Person	Individual attributes acquired through: • education • qualifications • training • experience	Questionnaire surveys Aptitude tests/experiments	Economists Psychologists
Job	Task requirements • complexity • discretion	Job analysis Job evaluation	Occupational psychologists Management theorists Industrial relations theorists
Setting	Social Relations	Case studies of industries and occupations Ethnographic studies of workplaces	Social historians Sociologists

Having charted the terrain, it is necessary to explore each of these areas in closer detail. To do this the chapter has been divided into three sections, each analysing a different aspect of skill: the person, the job and the setting. Each section draws out the strengths and weaknesses of the particular approaches, thereby demonstrating that there is no simple way of assessing skill. Following this, a final section illustrates the contemporary importance of the concept of skill by examining how it perpetuates the gender division of labour.

SKILL IN THE PERSON

In this first approach, skill is generally considered to be a possession of the individual. It can take numerous forms – for example, knowledge, dexterity, judgement, linguistic ability – but the assumption is that it is accrued by the individual as a product of accumulated education, training and experience. At first sight, this is an attractive conception of skill because it is relatively easy to measure, and produces quantifiable data that can be incorporated into statistical analyses. For example, a person can be asked to complete a questionnaire listing their years in formal education, number of qualifications, amount of training undertaken, and on-the-job experience. It is not surprising, therefore, that many labour economists are satisfied with these measures as a proxy for skill. This is typified by the approach of human capital theorists (for example, G. Becker, 1964) who argue that, in a market economy, a person's human capital will determine their value as employees. From this perspective it is argued that people can choose, as individuals, to increase their human capital through taking advantage of educational opportunities and training; or conversely, they can choose to ignore these opportunities, with the consequence of lowering their relative value in the labour market. For human capital theorists, responsibility for success in work clearly lies with the individual; they invoke the notion of a meritocratic society, where individual endeavour is rewarded.

Three problems are immediately apparent with this approach, however. The first is that it assumes that everyone has the same opportunity of access to the activities which improve human capital. Yet this is clearly not the case. For example, private education generally provides children with better facilities, smaller class sizes and a more intense learning environment, but such education is only available to the minority of children whose parents can afford it, and a small number who are awarded scholarships. Similarly, take the example of experience: in order to get work experience, a person has to be offered a job, but when there are high rates of unemployment allowing managers to pick and choose, a person needs previous experience in order to get the job. It is a classic Catch-22. So, the fundamental problem is that people do not compete on equal terms, because, to use the well-worn metaphor, there is not a level playing field to begin with.

A second, more general, problem is whether the variables of education, training and experience are valid measures of skill. The number of years a person spends in formal education is linked to qualifications attained, but even then it does not necessarily imply that the skills learned will be appropriate or transferable to the work setting. Similarly, whilst the measurement of training may be a better indicator of industry-specific knowledge and aptitude, it does not take into account the applicability of the training to the current context. For example, an apprenticeship in printing to acquire the skill of hot metal composition has not permanently added to the human capital of the printworker because this skill has subsequently been made redundant by new technology. The skill may remain in the person, but it is the economic and technical context that determines the value of the skill. The same is true of experience. Forty years' experience of mending mechanical typewriters represents a huge amount of diagnostic skill and understanding of the machines, but the word-processor has made much of this accumulated experience valueless in a very short time.

This leads on to a third problem: should measurement include only those attributes which have a current value – in other words the measurement of 'skills in use' rather than skills possessed? For example, if a person learns to speak Welsh and gains a qualification proving their competence, does this constitute a skill? If it has some market value, human capital theorists would say yes, but if few employers require Welsh speakers, its value is severely reduced. In other words, skill is not a fixed concept, but is relative to its market value. In this sense, all knowledge and abilities can be seen as potential skills, but it is the demand for them and their supply that gives them value. Therefore, measuring the skills possessed by the person can be misleading without exploring the labour market context.

One way around some of these problems of measurement is to associate education, training and experience with the individual's job. Using this method, the amount of relevant education, training and experience needed to perform the job competently is set as a skill benchmark. A good example of this approach can be found in the Social Change and Economic Life Initiative (SCELI) – a large-scale research programme conducted in the UK during the late 1980s. The researchers use five different indicators of skill:

> first, people's reports about the qualifications that somebody would need to get their type of job if they were applying for it now; second, the length of training that people received for their kind of work after completing full-time education; third, the amount of time that it had taken them, after they first started the type of job, to learn to do it well; fourth, whether or not they had direct responsibility for supervising the work of others, and fifth, whether they themselves considered their work to be skilled (Gallie, 1991: 325).

The first three of these indicators reflect qualifications, training and experience (common quantitative measures of skills), whilst the fourth indicator seeks to measure one aspect of job content (responsibility for others). In contrast, the fifth indicator is an attitudinal measure, revealing the respondent's perception of their job. (Further findings from this study will be examined in Chapter 6.) This approach is still ostensibly focused on the individual, but it begins to acknowledge the importance of the job setting.

Similarly, occupational psychologists have tended to focus their attention on the individual whose 'skills' are measured by the use of aptitude tests, often administered under experimental conditions. Typically, this approach is used to match the person to the job; thus skills assessments can be used as part of a selection process – for example, by work sampling, such as asking a machinist to assemble part of a garment. Whilst a full discussion of the pros and cons of the occupational psychologists' approach to skill measurement is beyond our immediate concern, it is worth noting that psychologists themselves disagree about how skills should be measured. For some, it is only under controlled experimental conditions that skill can be assessed (for example, Seymour, 1966) whilst others argue that skills can only be assessed in the specific context in which they are used (for example, Rogoff and Lave, 1984). In this sense, some occupational psychologists are bridging a gap by arguing that it is possible and desirable to have two foci: the individual *and* the job setting. It is to the second of these that the discussion now turns.

SKILL IN THE JOB

In this section the focus is adjusted to bring 'the job' into sharp relief. Two different aspects of skill are considered: complexity and discretion.

Skill as Complexity

It seems reasonable to suppose that the more complex the tasks required by the job, then the more skilled the job is. This indicates that all one has to do is measure the extent of complexity and thereby arrive at a skill level. The assumption is that it is possible to derive an *objective* measure of complexity. This is a seductive idea because it would mean that different jobs could be compared and ranked according to their complexity, and that this in turn could be reflected in systems of status and remuneration. Indeed, this has been attempted through job evaluation schemes (Thomason, 1980). On paper this seems a feasible and logical exercise: however, in practice it is notoriously difficult because evaluating job content is essentially a *subjective* experience. Imagine being in the position of observing a job and assessing its complexity: it might appear complex if it is unfamiliar. For example, to the observer who cannot drive, driving is likely to seem a very complex activity involving physical co-ordination, spacial awareness, concentration and quick decision-making. Yet for the seasoned driver it might not be viewed as a complex skill at all, not least because it is a widely shared ability. This presents a paradox: a fair evaluation would necessitate the observer having a familiarity with the task, but this familiarity may lead the observer to undervalue the task. In other words there are problems with relying on observation because of the subjectivity of the observer.

A possible alternative approach is to ask the person doing the job to identify its complexity. But this also poses problems for similar reasons: familiarity and adeptness may lead a person to undervalue a task. As Attewell (1990: 430) argues:

[Mundane activities] become socially invisible to both the actors performing them and to observers familiar with them... They become buried within their practitioners – either psychologically in the form of habits and non-conscious information-processing or somatically in muscles and neurons (knack, deftness and cunning).

This suggests that both observation and self-assessment would lead to a general conclusion that much of human activity in work (as well as outside) is not complex, and, by implication, requires little skill. But, as Attewell points out, this is particularly ironic because when a person achieves a high level of competence, they have internalised procedures and routines such that they can accomplish the task 'without thinking'. For the novice, each situation and each problem is unique and uncertain and so he or she must apply conscious thought, but 'the maestro has been there before and has more (nonconscious) routines to apply' (Attewell, 1990: 433). To put this another way, beginners rely on abstract rules which have been derived by others, and they use these to guide their progress and accumulate experience; experts rely on context-bound knowledge that they have developed through experience, and are therefore less conscious of the decision-rules they are using.

In a similar vein, Manwaring and Wood (1985) identify the importance of considering 'tacit skills' (based upon the analysis of Polanyi and Prosch, 1975; Koestler, 1976; and Kusterer, 1978) to suggest that work necessarily involves the internalisation of learning so that tasks can be performed successfully by drawing on unconscious thought, and that different degrees of awareness are required both within and between jobs. The greater the frequency of unfamiliar situations, the less likely the adequacy of the existing routine, and so the greater the awareness required. From this perspective, it might be argued that skill is embedded in *all* jobs but that tacit skills are taken for granted rather than being formally recognised.

A further illustration of this is the extent to which social skills generally remain unrecognised unless the job specifically requires direct social interaction with clients and customers (see Chapter 7 on emotion work). This is well illustrated by Burchell *et al.* (1994) who used a questionnaire survey to compare the perceptions of employees and managers regarding the skill content of a range of job categories. They found that the greatest divergence occurred over the perceptions of social and organisational skills needed for production and service jobs: managers rated the importance of these skills considerably lower than the employees who were actually doing the jobs. Findings such as these have an important contemporary relevance because although communication and cooperation have always been demanded by most work processes, social and organisational skills are increasing in importance through new employee relations policies such as teamworking, quality and empowerment. Employees may therefore be required increasingly to use tacit skills which have traditionally lain outside the wage – effort bargain.

Skill as Discretion

An alternative (although not necessarily mutually exclusive) way of assessing skill is to examine it in relation to the *discretion* the employee can exercise and hence, the amount of control over his or her work. As shall be explored in Chapter 6, this approach to the analysis of skill has been most closely associated with a perspective that argues that there is a general tendency under capitalism towards the deskilling of jobs (Braverman, 1974); but this debate can be postponed for the time being, because there are still a number of definitional problems to address.

Discretion is about choosing between alternative courses of action. The greater the amount of decisions required by an activity, then the greater the skill level. So the more an employee can exercise his or her judgement, then the more skilled a task may be said to be. In this way skill levels might be assessed by examining the amount of rules employees are obliged to follow: the more rules, the less scope for discretion and the lower their skill will be judged to be. This distinction between prescribed (rule-dominated) and discretionary (choice-dominated) work was first conceptualised by Jaques (1956 and 1967). Whilst it is a useful schema, it must be treated with caution, as Fox points out:

> It is easy to accept... that no work role can be totally discretionary. The occupant of the most elevated post has to operate within prescribed limits, usually a great many. It may be more difficult, however, to accept that all jobs contain discretionary as well as prescriptive elements. Surely many jobs in our kind of industrial society are *totally* prescribed; totally without discretion? Such a view cannot be sustained. However elaborate the external controlling structure of mechanical, administrative, technical or policy prescriptions, some residual element of discretion always remains. (Fox, 1974: 19–20, emphasis in original).

This resonates with our earlier discussion about tacit skills, which suggested that all jobs require discretion to be exercised, even though such discretion may not be identified by the job description or acknowledged in the reward system. The problem of using discretion as an indicator of skill is that we are focusing on the visible when many of the choices and judgements exercised in the work process remain invisible.

A second concept identified by Jaques (1967) is the 'time-span of discretion'. This is the length of time that a person is allowed to exercise their discretion free from surveillance by superiors: the longer a person's period of autonomy, the higher their skill level. Again, however, this is somewhat limited in its usefulness as far as defining skill is concerned. A major problem with the time-span of discretion is that it fails to take into account the significance of the task and the consequences of making a mistake. For example, a gardener may be allocated a patch of land to tend and be left completely alone for long periods. He has few rules to follow and could work incompetently for weeks before it came to anyone's notice. Conversely, the anaesthetist exercises her judgement within a strict frame-work of rules and even a slight error of judgement will come to the attention of her work colleagues within minutes.

Discretion is also a misleading indicator because it fails to take into account fully the interdependence of many jobs in advanced industrial systems. The notion of discretion tends to evoke an image of a romanticised past reminiscent of the craft worker, and use this as a benchmark for current jobs. Consequently, as Attewell (1990: 443) argues, 'the ideal of the artisan conceiving an object, choosing tools and procedures unconstrained by external rules or routines, and fabricating the object from first to last step is so at odds with the reality of modern work that everyone today, from managers down, appears deskilled'.

The common theme that links the two notions of skill as complexity or discretion is that both approaches emphasise skill as being principally about the requirements of the job. Skill therefore is seen as an objective feature of work which is measurable through an analysis of job content, both in terms of technical complexity and discretionary requirements. Consequently, researchers tend to view skill as consisting of sub-components, each of which can be measured. This can be illustrated with a study of skill by Rolfe (1986 and 1990) who devised a model of skill consisting of six 'substructural' measures (see Table 5.3). These are used as a framework to explore skill changes brought about by new technology for different occupational groups. Rolfe's analysis is qualitative in approach; she does not develop quantitative measures of skill for the components, but instead uses the model to help direct her analysis and interpretation.

Table 5.3 *Rolfe's model of skill*

Technical complexity	1. Complexity of tasks
	2. Knowledge
	3. Range and variety of tasks
Discretion	4. Decision-making and judgement over product/process
	5. Control over the organisation of work
	6. Supervision

Source: based on H. Rolfe, 'In the name of progress? Skill and attitudes towards technological change', *New Technology, Work and Employment*, (1990), 52, pp.107–21.

An assumption underpinning both 'skill in the job' models and the approach of 'skills in the person' researchers (examined in the previous section) is that the concept of skill can be objectively defined, and in this sense both approaches are overly rational, often ignoring the historical development of skill. Conceptions of skill are not dispassionately developed on blank pieces of paper; they are socially and politically negotiated over time, and reflect power and influence of diverse interest groups. This has been the case because, as noted above, skill is a measure of worth (both social and economic). As Sadler (1970: 23) has observed, skill is 'to a considerable extent determined by social factors present in the work situation and in the occupational culture at large.. [and therefore includes] the evaluations placed on particular kinds of activity and on particular classes of individual and the actions of organised pressure groups directed at safeguarding the earnings and job security of particular trades and professions.' Consequently, to understand skill it is important to examine the setting in which the valuation of skill is negotiated.

SKILL IN THE SETTING

Here the focus of enquiry shifts to the employment relationship itself. As a starting point, it is important to consider one of the fundamental concepts of sociology as defined by Weber (1947) and elaborated by Parkin (1979) and Kreckel (1980). This is the notion of 'social closure' whereby people with a shared interest protect themselves by acting collectively to form a group which is in some way demarcated. Entry to the group is regulated by the existing members, thus they may choose to exclude or include outsiders depending on whether it serves their interests.

> Whether a relationship is open or closed may be determined traditionally, affectually, or rationally in terms of values or of expediency. It is especially likely to be closed, for rational reasons, in the following type of situation: a social relationship may provide the parties to it with opportunities for the satisfaction of various interests, whether the satisfactions be spiritual or material, whether the interest be in the end of the relationship as such or in some ulterior consequence of participation, or whether it is achieved through co-operative action or by a compromise of interests. If the participants expect that the admission of others will lead to an improvement of their situation, and improvement in degree, in kind, in the security or the value of the satisfaction, their interest will be in keeping the relationship open. If, on the other hand, their expectations are of improving their position by monopolistic tactics, their interest is in a closed relationship. (Weber, 1947: 127–8.)

In the case of an occupational group, social closure provides the means of establishing a position at least partially autonomous of labour market competition. Instead of being exposed to the vagaries of the free market, the group is protected by three inter-related components: control of the labour supply, internal self-regulation, and the development of a 'consciousness of difference' (Weber, 1947: 127) through language and symbols. Each of these warrants a closer analysis in relation to the attainment of skilled status.

Social Closure and Skilled Status

To explore the impact of social closure on skill, the following discussion examines the three components in turn, illustrating their impact by focusing on the the role of trade unions. (A similar analysis could be undertaken for professional associations; for example, see Crompton, 1987 and 1990; and Witz, 1992.)

1 Control of the labour supply

Control over the supply of labour is important if the members of an occupational group wish to create a premium price for their work. In normal circumstances the scarcity of appropriately 'skilled' employees will push up the wage that an employer is willing to pay to secure their labour power. Restricting the availability of labour is therefore in the interest of an occupational group.

The control of supply has traditionally occurred through the regulation of entry into the occupation. To regulate entry, for example, a trade union typically sought to establish a closed shop which obliged employers to offer work only to workers who held union cards and were therefore deemed appropriately skilled to be able to accomplish the work safely and with competence. By limiting membership to those who were appropriately qualified, the union could control the labour supply. It could also impose sanctions on members who broke union rules or acted against the interest of co-workers by suspending their membership, and consequently preventing their continued employment.

Overall, the control of supply helps to build skilled status by restricting the size of the occupation, thereby conferring on it the notion that only those with special ability can do the job. Coupled with this is the increased price of labour which suggests work of special value, thus reinforcing the status of the job.

2 Internal regulation

Internal regulation was often (although not exclusively) achieved where the training was controlled through a lengthy apprenticeship system which had the twin effects of slowing entry and socialising the newcomers. As H.A. Turner (1962) noted, this was often an artificially long period of training which acted to give the impression that the job involved a vast accumulation of knowledge and technical ability, thus helping to enhance the claim to skilled status.

Skilled workers were prominent in the early trade union movement in mid-nineteenth-century Britain. At a time of expansion in semi- and unskilled machine-minding jobs, skilled workers saw unionism as a way of protecting their position by reinforcing their claims to skilled status. Key to this were attempts to ensure that employers filled jobs defined as skilled only with workers who had 'served their time' as apprentices. These early skilled-worker unions adopted an approach in line with their position as labour's 'aristocracy': the unions emphasised craft and exclusiveness, rather than militancy and solidarity with the growing numbers of non-skilled workers. These craft unions had more in common with earlier guild organisations than subsequent mass unions, and were more concerned to prevent changes which would reduce their members' status, than to win better terms and conditions.

Subsequently, the growth of closed shop agreements created a strong vehicle for internal self-regulation whereby tasks became clearly demarcated, overtime was regulated via the union – typically through seniority criteria – and changes to working practices were negotiated through formal agreements between the union and management. In return, quality of work and unbroken productivity were assured.

This form of regulation of the labour market by the trade unions was especially condemned in the UK by the Conservative Governments of the 1980s which were ideologically committed to the supremacy of the market, unfettered by the interests of organised labour. The 'distortion' of the labour market was anathema to the Government, and legislation was introduced which had the effect of virtually outlawing the closed shop – indeed, Millward *et al.* (1992) estimate that whilst the closed shop covered around 3.5 million manual workers in 1984, this had fallen dramatically to possibly as few as a third of a million by 1990. This, along with other measures of deregulation and the restructuring of trade union powers, theoretically opened up the labour market to free competition (some of the consequences of which have already been explored Chapter 2).

3 Language and symbols

The third component of social closure is through the manipulation of occupational language and symbols. It can be argued that such features are characteristic of any sub-culture seeking to establish and ring-fence its separate identity (B.A. Turner, 1971). For a group wishing to lay claim to skilled status, it allows opportunity to mystify the work, obscure the mundane activities and portray an image of complexity. Language is a particularly important regulatory device because it can be used both to exclude and include. In this sense it demarcates the in-group from the out-group – it draws a line between 'us' and 'them'. Thus, being able to talk in occupational argot and jargon symbolises membership of the group by identifying those who have accrued enough experience and familiarity with the occupation to speak and understand the exclusive language (see for example the impenetrable occupational argot of rail workers cited by Miller and Form, 1963: 264). In particular, new entrants to an occupation are quickly reminded by language that they are on the periphery. For example, newcomers in an engineering plant might be sent for the 'long stand', the 'long weight'(wait) or the left-handed screwdriver – thereby exposing their naivety and lack of familiarity with the setting. Symbolic regulation is similarly enacted through rituals, rites of passage, initiation ceremonies, humour and other forms of social control (particularly gossip; see Noon and Delbridge, 1993) – examples of these are explored in Chapter 8.

There is also the symbolism embedded in the 'tools of the trade' which further differentiate an occupational group and allow claims to skilled status. This is particularly well illustrated by the case of construction workers discussed by Steiger (1993). Combining his findings with the work of Riemer (1977) and Applebaum, (1981) he argues that owning and being able to use the 'tools of the trade' properly is an important feature of defining skill not least because the tools – and by definition the skills one possesses – are in full view. Common tools, such as the shovel used by the labourer, are looked down upon whereas more specialised tools carry skill status. 'Rarity is important because... only "rare" specialised tools are emblematic of skill. That rarity is important should be of no surprise in a capitalist economy' (Steiger, 1993: 555).

Interestingly, Steiger also cites the example of plumbers for whom technological advances (such as the advent of plastic piping) have reduced the need for specialist tools. The plumbers' response has been to shift the emphasis away from the tools on to their ingenuity and ability to improvise. In this sense, their occupational closure has become symbolised not through the visibility of tools (which are readily available to anyone) but through the invisible 'know-how' which only the 'skilled' plumber has acquired. This is particularly noteworthy because it takes us back to our earlier discussion of tacit skills. The plumbers are elevating the importance of their embedded knowledge that cannot be appropriated by others, or replaced by new technologies.

Consequently, the overall process of occupational social closure is composed of three interacting sub-processes (see Figure 5.1). First there is an *ideological* process, whereby individuals recognise a shared set of values and beliefs, and

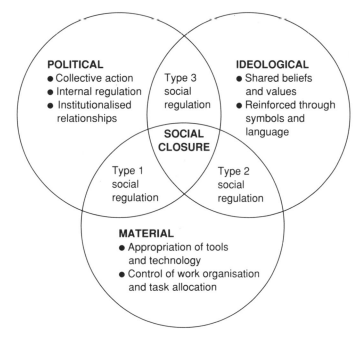

Figure 5.1 *The processes of social closure*

reinforce these symbolically. Second, a *political* process exists, whereby group members act collectively, combining their resources in pursuit of common goals. There will remain a plurality of interests within the group, but they have a mutual interest in combining together and institutionalising their relationship (for example, in the membership of a trade union). Third, there is a *material* process, whereby members of the group seek to appropriate the tools and technology of the work process and (at best) control over or (at least) influence over the work organisation.

The three processes operate concurrently and are mutually reinforcing, but social closure is achieved only when *all three* processes are enacted. Moreover, social closure is a continuing dynamic of interaction. Just as groups can build upon the ideological, political and material processes to construct closure, they can also lose closure through the neglect or undermining of one or more of the processes. In other words, groups may display forms of social regulation which fall short of social closure (illustrated by the intersections in Figure 5.1). Thus, a group may lose or fail to attain (1) its ideological base (by for example, the input of new and heterogeneous ideas through generational changes in membership, the amalgamation of several unions, internal fragmentation or the development of sub-cultures) or (2) its political base (by for example, the attack on the closed shop, the non-recognition of a union, the deregulation of a professional association) or (3) its material base (for example, through the introduction of new technology, the relocation of a factory, the closure of a dockyard). It is upon full social closure that a group bases its claim to skilled status, although social regulation provides opportunities for constructing difference on which claims to a skilled identity can then be built.

The Social Construction of Skill

To summarise the argument so far: in order for an occupational group to lay claim to skilled status it must establish its separateness and distinctiveness. It can achieve this through engaging in the three processes of social closure outlined above – ideological, political and material. In this way skill is socially constructed. This raises a puzzle, however, that cannot be ignored: is the way that skilled status is attributed in industrial society *solely* a product of social construction, or do objective (technical) factors also have an effect? In addressing this question, Littler (1982) argues that the social construction theory of skill can occur in a weak or strong form. In the *strong* form, skilled status can be achieved through social closure without necessarily any inherent task complexity or knowledge (a position originally put forward by H.A. Turner, 1962). In such a scenario, the power of the workgroup and the ability to act collectively is more important than their technical knowledge. The 'talking up' of the skilled nature of the work is therefore crucial to its construction as a skilled job. In the *weak* form (exemplified by More, 1980 and 1982) technical skill (complexity and knowledge) is a necessary basis for socially constructing skilled status. However, this does not guarantee the attainment of skilled status, so the occupational group must enact social closure and develop a collective power base. In other words, technical skill is simply the starting point.

Attewell (1990) identifies a third form which accepts that skilled status can be achieved with or without technical skills being present (in this sense it combines the strong and weak forms). However, there is an important caveat which points to the dynamics of the process: if skilled status is achieved in the absence of technical skill, the status itself provides the opportunity over a period of time for the occupational group to appropriate technical skill and thereby strengthen its claim to skilled status.

So far, the discussion has focused upon how skill definitions are constructed by occupational groups. However, there is a far more pervasive impact of social construction which raises some serious issues concerning fairness and equality.

GENDER AND SKILL: THE SOCIAL CONSTRUCTION OF DISADVANTAGE

It is possible to argue that a form of social closure exists which centres not on occupational group, but on gender. The evidence suggests that just as an occupational group may seek to construct a notion of skill in its own interest, so too have men acted as a social group; they have constructed skill in such a way as to benefit their own gender and to disadvantage women. To substantiate such a statement, we need to examine the evidence built up over recent years by academics who argue that all analysis of work must explore gender as a central and integral factor (see in particular, Bradley, 1989; Walby, 1986). As a framework to locate our arguments, we will use the three interlinking processes discussed above: the ideological, political and material processes of social closure.

Gender and the Ideological Process

Underpinning the concept of skill is an ideology of gender which labels certain attitudes and forms of behaviour as masculine and others as feminine. These identities are perpetuated not just in the workplace, but throughout the whole of society (although they may vary slightly from culture to culture) and result in the stereotypes we hold about what constitutes being a man or being a woman. It is not surprising, therefore, that work is a domain which similarly reinforces these images. It has already been suggested in Chapter 3 that work provides people with a social identity – thus it can be a domain for the expression of gender. As Matthaei (1982: 194) found, 'a basic force behind sex-typing of jobs was the workers' desires to assert and reaffirm their manhood or womanhood and hence their difference from the opposite sex'.

Jobs therefore tend to be associated with attributes of gender stereotypes which reflect (and reinforce) dominant cultural beliefs about male and female. For example, jobs requiring physical strength, stamina, or logical thought have traditionally been considered men's jobs, because those are attributes supposedly possessed by men, whilst women, allegedly being innately sensitive, patient and dextrous, have been cast as suitable for caring, boring, repetitive or fiddly work.

The source of this belief is the view that a work role is a reflection of a 'natural' ability, in other words, determined by and constrained by biology. For example, in Cockburn's study of printworkers, the men argued that their job was not suitable for a woman and rallied a number of commonly held views as to why women could not and should not do their work: women lacked the strength; there was too much standing involved; they lacked the mental ability; they did not have the right temperament (aversion to technical work); they were too temperamental (emotional, bursting into tears); they were unreliable (because of menstruation); they would be exposed to bad moral influences (swearing, horseplay, vulgarity); and they would force men to behave differently (see Cockburn, 1983: 171–90). For the printworkers, women represented a threat because their entry into the occupation challenged the ideology of what constituted male work:

> It's man's work. If you hear of a man secretary, a lot of people raise a few eye brows. Well, it's the same with a woman working alongside a man doing *his* job... if I said to my mates I was working with a woman, they would feel, say, oh, he's doing a woman's job – because they can see that a woman *can* do it. (A compositor quoted by Cockburn, 1983: 180, emphasis in original.)

Similarly, a Transport and General Workers Union shop steward at an electrical components factory is quoted by Charles (1986: 163):

> There's been a great increase in humdrum jobs like the jobs here, that you wouldn't get a man doing... But the women can sit at a bench eight hours and pick up little fiddly screws and put them in. I think it's fantastic, and they can go for week in week out, you know – but you'll never get a man doing it, so that's why you need... women working.

But such opinions are not exclusive to men. Consider, for example, the views of these women quoted by Pollert (1981: 99) in her study of a tobacco factory:

> *Kate (stripping room):* I can't imagine a man doing my work. It's too boring for a man. Women have much more patience.

> *Gale:* Men'd go mad. It'd kill them with boredom! Girls are expected to do that kind of thing. Girls are thought to be the weaker sex.

In white-collar work, there is similar evidence of sex stereotyping of skill. A vivid example of this is provided by Collinson and Knights (1986) whose case study of an insurance company reveals how the male managers manipulated the setting (the work organisation), the recruitment process, selection criteria, and rationale for promotion to segregate the office according to gender, and to justify this in terms of business rationale. The effect is to produce a subordinate situation for women, which is then used against them and rationalised as being a product of their gender. To illustrate this, consider the quotes below (taken from Collinson and Knights, 1986: 155, 158, 162, 165).

Branch manager: Women aren't taken seriously in the insurance world. It can be a soul destroying job. Inspectors have to advise our professional clients who recommend insurance and pensions to their clients and we want them to recommend us. Yes, it can be a soul-destroying job, and women are either not hard-bitten enough to ride off insults or those that can are pretty unpleasant people.

Office manager: My job is to keep them [the female clerical staff] as busy as possible... You can't keep all six happy at the same time. With some you can tell their monthly changes, even the other girls say so. Sometimes when they're having a good chunner [moan] about the inspectors I have to impress on the girls that if it was not for the men, there'd be no jobs for them, if the blokes don't go out and sell insurance.

Personnel officer, head office: The door is always open to move into the career structure, but we've found by and large, they're girls who are not particularly ambitious, looking forward to getting married, leaving and having a family and that's about the measure of it.

Senior pensions clerk [female]: I'm very temperamental, you see. This is another thing Mr Brown [the branch manager] drew to my attention. I can get annoyed very easily and I also get strong moods. He said 'There's no way you could go out to a broker with some of the moods you have'.

The assumption frequently made is that work is not a central life interest for women. Research evidence reported in Chapter 3 suggests this is a false assumption when comparing the work orientations of men and women in *full-time* work. However, the view persists that the central life interest for all women is the family (either their existing one or the prospect of one), and hence they are considered more willing to tolerate boring, repetitive jobs with low career prospects and little responsibility. But we should not overlook the circularity of this argument: are women allocated tedious work because they are perceived to have a lower work orientation than men, or might it be that they have a lower work orientation *because* they only have access to boring, repetitive, low paid, undervalued jobs? Further, not only does stereotyping of men's work and women's work preordain the type and range of jobs that either gender are supposedly able to do competently, it also disadvantages women in terms of the valuation of 'women's work'. The argument is summed up by Jenson (1989) who identifies the way work performed by women tends to be seen as involving some natural female 'talent', whereas work done by men is viewed as involving a learned skill.

The critical importance of gender in defining skill was first explored in a keynote article by Phillips and Taylor (1986). Their conclusion was that, 'it is the sex of those who do the work, rather than its content, which leads to its identification as skilled or unskilled' (1986: 63). In arriving at this position they bring out two important issues which help to identify the importance of the ideological process of social closure. First, where men and women work in similar workplaces, doing jobs of similar content, men are more likely to achieve skilled status. The research of Rubery and Wilkinson (1979) into box and carton manufacture is used to illustrate this point. The production of cartons and paper boxes involves a similar process except that whilst box production involves exclusively female labour, carton manufacture is undertaken by men and women. The latter is recognised as semi-skilled, the former as unskilled. Similarly, Spradley and Mann (1975) reveal that the work of waitresses is equally as demanding of a range of abilities as the work of bartenders, yet, unlike the (male) bartenders, the waitresses do not enjoy skilled status.

Second, where new work processes were introduced allowing employers to deem some jobs 'female' from the outset, the work tended to be classified as low-skilled, 'not simply by virtue of the skills required for it but by virtue of the "inferior" status of the women who came to perform it' (Phillips and Taylor, 1986: 61). In an excellent analysis of women's work in a range of industries, Bradley (1989) argues that the hosiery industry provides the best example of the feminisation of an occupation, whereby women are brought in not directly to take over the work of men, but to work on newly reorganised and degraded work processes. Thus, women are at a disadvantage from the outset:

> The work of women is often deemed inferior simply because it is women who do it. Women workers carry into the workplace their status as subordinate individuals, and this status comes to define the value of the work they do. (Phillips and Taylor, 1986: 55.)

The contemporary pattern in the occupational structure is a general under-valuation of jobs where women predominate, with this disadvantage frequently institutionalised and consolidated by job evaluation schemes that either fail to recognise all the attributes of jobs mainly performed by women, or else value such attributes lower than comparable work mainly performed by men (Horrell *et al.*, 1994; Neathey, 1992; Steinberg, 1990). The overall effect is a relatively lower pay rate for jobs where women predominate. For example, job evaluation schemes typically rate fiscal responsibility (for example, devising budgets or counting cash) higher than social responsibility (for example, caring for the sick or minding young children). Indeed, we will explore later (Chapter 7) how social skills are often taken for granted and frequently undervalued by employers. Another example: physical strength (a supposed male natural ability) is often rated higher than dexterity (a supposed female natural ability). The danger is that the evaluation process is widely considered to be fair because it is seen as an *objective* measure of skill – but, as noted earlier in this chapter, such an assumption is naive.

So, in Steinberg's words, 'job evaluation systems... have been constructed to embed cultural assumptions about what constitutes skilled and responsible work in a way that significantly benefits men through the work they have historically performed' (1990: 454). They institutionalise and perpetuate the ideology of masculine and feminine work, and in this way assist in the ideological process of social closure.

Gender and the Political Process

In many settings men have been proactive in seeking to protect and differentiate their skills from those of women. The situation is summed up well by Steinberg (1990: 476):

> Skill determinations are socially constructed in highly political contexts, in which males – whether employers or employees – exert considerably more power to maintain their definitions of skill... Struggles over the meaning of skill between employers and (primarily male) employees have been frequent, bitter, and hard fought. When employees have won, males have maintained their skill designations and wage rates, even in the face of the deterioration of job content. When employees have lost... skill designations are lowered, wage rates deteriorate, and male employees exit to be replaced by women.

As work processes have changed, men have sought to hold on to their skilled status. Often this has been to the detriment of women (as we elaborate below) such that 'skill has been increasingly defined against women – skilled work is work that women don't do' (Phillips and Taylor, 1986: 63).

Trade unions have played an important role in this political process in providing the means by which male workers can organise and exclude women from their trades (Hartmann, 1979). At no time was this more evident than during and after the First World War. In the period leading up to the war, government officials secured an agreement with union leaders to allow a temporary dilution of skilled labour in munitions and other industries related to the war effort ('dilution of skill' referring to workers who had not served apprenticeships undertaking tasks previously performed by skilled workers). With so many men having volunteered, and later been conscripted into the army, this skill dilution opened up opportunities for women to undertake work formerly the preserve of male skilled workers, and at pay rates comparable to the skilled rates. However, as part of this agreement between Government and unions, it was also agreed that customary practices over the hiring of skilled workers would be restored after the war – thus, the skill dilution and the opportunities this provided for many women was, for the vast majority, short-lived (Ursell and Blyton, 1988: 109).

The historical analysis of gender relations in employment by Walby leads her to conclude that 'from the last quarter of the nineteenth century an increasing proportion of trade unions used grading and segregation as their response to women's employment, rather than the exclusionary strategy... It is almost never the case that a union which included men did not follow one of these two patriarchal strategies' (1986: 244). Thus the political process of organising through trade unions has acted to the detriment of women in terms of both access to 'skilled' work, and the attainment of skilled status for jobs where women predominate. Furthermore, research shows that the domination of the male agenda persists within trade unions, and that 'a wide gap exists between what the unions claim for women and what they deliver, but more to the point, between what they claim and what they *attempt* to deliver' (Cunnison and Stageman, 1995: 237–8, emphasis in original).

Gender and the Material Process

Cockburn (1983, 1985 and 1986) explores the importance of material aspects of male domination. Through this she is able to identify the way men appropriate the tools and technology which give them an advantage in constructing notions of what constitutes skilled work. The first part of her argument is that the physical differences between men and women are often exaggerated to the benefit of men. Obviously there are biological differences between men and women but these limit either gender in only a very small range of tasks – most of which are not work based. Similarly, there are physical differences in average height and body weight, but again these are not necessarily impediments to most jobs. Gender differences are encouraged through childhood and socialisation – men being expected to participate in physical activities, women in sedentary endeavours. As a consequence, men, on average, attain physical effectivity to a greater extent than women.

The second part of Cockburn's argument concerns the appropriation of technical effectivity: familiarity with and control over machinery and tools. As noted above, such control is important in constructing a skill identity. Cockburn argues that men have historically acquired control over the design of technology and work processes, and as a consequence this perpetuates existing patterns of dominance. As Wajcman (1991: 41) puts it, 'men selectively design tools and machinery to match their technical skills. Machinery is designed by men with men in mind. Industrial technology thus reflects male power as well as capitalist domination.' This does not necessarily imply an organised conspiracy against women by men, but it certainly reflects a gender-centricity often resulting in machinery and tools being too bulky or heavy for the 'average' woman. There are exceptions to this which prove that alternative approaches are available. Clarke (1989), for example, shows how the increased availability of female labour in Sweden prompted Volvo to invest in the design of tools ergonomically suited for the 'average' woman, and to develop hydraulic lifting devices to lessen the physical requirements of vehicle assembly. But such examples remain rare.

Generally, technical effectivity is sustained through an ideology that perpetuates the notion that men are technically more competent than women. Nowhere is this more evident than the division of labour in the home (see for example, Oakley, 1974 and 1982; Pahl, 1984). Cockburn vividly portrays this in a chapter entitled 'The kitchen, the tool shed' (1985: 198–224) – essential reading to fully appreciate the subtlety of her argument. She illustrates how men not only acquire technical effectivity through work but can use this to improve their social standing in the community, through, for example, being the person who can fix cars or do some rewiring. Women, on the other hand, are discouraged from transporting any technical skills into the home. A woman may use pliers, screwdrivers, Allen keys and a soldering iron at work, but at home these are almost invariably kept for the exclusive use of men, and are locked in the toolshed. Acutely aware of the advantage of technical effectivity in constructing advantage, men jealously guard their knowledge.

> Men's know-how is seldom passed by men to women as a cost-free gift, taught in a serious, generous and genuine way. Often it is hoarded behind a cachet of professional knowledge or craft skill and handed out sparingly, reluctantly. Sometimes it is dispensed from a great height and purposefully used to put women down. (Cockburn, 1985: 202–3.)

Overall, the two components of physical and technical effectivity constitute the material of male power. As Cockburn (1986: 97–8) argues, 'the process... involves several converging practices: accumulation of bodily capabilities, the definition of tasks to match them and the selective design of tools and machines'. It is an important argument because it demonstrates how the material power base, constructed historically, is perpetuated to the benefit of men. It is no coincidence, therefore, that we began our exploration of skill in this chapter by alluding to the work of Cockburn: her analysis demonstrates the way men have appropriated technology and used it to define their own work as skilled and women's work as unskilled. In this sense, there is an on-going process of gendered social closure. This is embedded in the power of occupational groups and their institutions, and the patriarchal structures of management.

CONCLUSION

The controversy surrounding skill is likely to continue as long as there remain different theoretical perspectives from which to look at the problem of what skill is and how (or if) it can be measured. Once again, it demonstrates the importance of acknowledging the plurality of approaches to a particular problem. By exploring the diversity of meanings, this chapter has been able to explain the principal competing interpretations of skill. Instead of suggesting there is one way of looking, the analysis has explored different angles and produced a more complex picture with greater depth. As the different viewpoints have been brought into focus, so new aspects of the notion of skill come into sharp relief.

As has been shown, the social construction of skill can be used to integrate the different approaches because it provides a framework for understanding the way both technical (objective) measures and social (subjective) meanings of skill can be negotiated. In other words, skill is constructed by drawing on meanings which incorporate all three foci explored above: the person, the job and the setting. These provide the resources that allow the claim to skilled status to be made. Attainment of this claim, however, depends on the successful enactment of the political, ideological and material processes of social closure.

The concept of skill is important because it has wide ramifications. It has been shown how it has been used by different interest groups to lay claim to status, special treatment and higher rewards. In particular, it was noted how this has impacted on the gender division of labour with a dramatic undervaluing of the work of women. Yet there is a further issue that remains unanswered: to what extent might there be a general historical shift in nature of skill? Might skill be hard to define because work is continually changing and demanding different abilities? And if such a change can be detected, in which direction is it heading? Are people becoming less skilled or more skilled? These are the questions at the heart of the next chapter.

6 Work Routines

INTRODUCTION

The aim of this chapter is to address a puzzle that has occupied the minds of researchers and theorists for decades: whether there is a fundamental shift in the overall nature of work causing people to experience either deskilling and degrading, or upskilling and enrichment, of their working lives. We have already noted some of the structural changes occurring in patterns of employment (see Chapter 2); this chapter assesses the impact of these broader employment dynamics by focusing on the nature of work tasks. To explore these issues, the chapter is divided into five sections. The first examines two dominant traditions in work organisation – Taylorism and Fordism – using contemporary examples to illustrate the central principles of each. This provides the basis for the next three sections, each of which examines a different perspective on how work is changing: the deskilling thesis, the upskilling antithesis, and the attempts to synthesise these contrasting approaches. The fifth section of the chapter develops a conceptual framework to integrate the analysis.

THE DOMINANT TRADITIONS OF WORK ORGANISATION

The Service Sector – Burgers and Taylor

Imagine the scene: you are in the centre of a city you are visiting for the first time; it is lunchtime and you are feeling hungry; you do not have much money to spend on food; and you only have 30 minutes before your train leaves. As you look along the busy, unfamiliar street you recognise a sign in the distance: a large yellow letter 'M'. A sense of relief overwhelms you as you head for that emporium of American pulp cuisine: McDonald's. Any uncertainty and anxiety has been replaced by the predictability that is the McDonald's experience: no matter where you are, you will get the standard tasting burger, covered with the same relish, lodged in the same bun, served in the same packaging for consumption in the familiar decor of the restaurant. Consistency is McDonald's strong selling point – you know exactly what you are going to get when you order your Big Mac, large fries and McDonald's cola, in any one of McDonald's 14,000 outlets in 70 countries across 6 continents. Of course, to guarantee that standardised product, the work processes as well as the food have all been standardised. So leaving aside the issue of the product itself, how can we characterise and understand work at organisations like McDonald's?

If we use a metaphor, we can describe McDonald's as a well-maintained machine in almost every aspect of its operations, from the customer interface to the centralised planning and financial control (Morgan, 1986). Employees at McDonald's (or 'crew members' as they are called) are treated as components of this machine. Each receive simple training to perform a number of tasks which require little judgement and leave little room for discretion. Crew members are given precise instructions on what to say, what to do, and how to do it. They are the necessary 'living' labour joining the precisely timed, computer-controlled equipment that cook the burgers, fry the potatoes, dispense the drinks, heat the pies, record the order and calculate the customer's change.

> Much of the food prepared at McDonald's arrives at the restaurant pre-formed, pre-cut, pre-sliced and pre-prepared, often by non-human technologies. This serves to drastically limit what employees need to do... McDonald's has developed a variety of machines to control its employees. When a worker must decide when a glass is full and the soft-drink dispenser needs to be shut off, there is always the risk that the worker may be distracted and allow the glass to overflow. Thus a sensor has been developed that automatically shuts off the soft-drink dispenser when the glass is full. (Ritzer, 1993: 105–6.)

This logic of automation is extended to all the processes, with the consequence that the employees push buttons, respond to bleeps and buzzers and repeat stock phrases to customers like subjects in a bizarre Pavlovian experiment. The dehumanising effects can often be seen in the glazed expressions of the young people who serve. But the most poignant, if not ironic, aspect of all this is that one of the world's most successful multinational corporations at the end of the twentieth century relies on labour management techniques that were developed at the beginning of the century. Indeed, the pioneer of 'scientific management', F.W. Taylor, would have certainly recognised and endorsed the principles of rationality upon which McDonald's is organised.

The ideas of Taylor have been well documented elsewhere (see for example, Kelly, 1982; Littler, 1982; M. Rose, 1988) so it is necessary here only to reiterate the central principles to see how closely aligned the contemporary work processes at McDonald's are to concepts that were originally published in 1911. Efficiency was Taylor's guiding obsession. His own work experience as an engineer led him to believe there was an optimum way of performing any job: the 'one best way'. It was the task of management to discover this through the application of rigorous scientific testing which involved breaking all activities down into the smallest components, and systematically analysing each step. No activity was too complex or too mundane to be subjected to this scientific analysis, argued Taylor. Thus, in front of a special committee of the House of Representatives in the USA, he extolled the principles of developing a science of pig-iron handling and shovelling.

Probably the most important element in the science of shoveling is this: There must be some shovel load at which a first-class shoveler will do his biggest day's work. What is that load? ... . Under scientific management the answer to this question is not a matter of anyone's opinion; it is a question for accurate, careful, scientific investigation. Under the old system you would call in a first-rate shoveler and say, 'See here, Pat, how much ought you to take on at one shovel load?' And if a couple of fellows agreed, you would say that's about the right load and let it go at that. But under scientific management absolutely every element in the work of every man in your establishment, sooner or later, becomes the subject of exact, precise, scientific investigation and knowledge to replace the old, 'I believe so,' and 'I guess so.' Every motion, every small fact becomes the subject of careful, scientific investigtion. (Taylor, 1911: 51–2, reprinted 1972.)

Having discovered the 'one best way' of performing the task, management's responsibility was to allocate tasks to employees, attempting to fit the right person to each job. The employee should have the requisite skills, acquired through systematic training, to complete the task at hand, and no more than those required by the job.

Now one of the very first requirements for a man who is fit to handle pig iron as a regular occupation is that he shall be so stupid and so phlegmatic that he more nearly resembles in his mental make-up the ox than any other type. The man who is mentally alert and intelligent is for this reason entirely unsuited to what would, for him, be the grinding monotony of work of this character. Therefore the workman who is best suited to handling pig iron is unable to understand the real science of doing this class of work. He is so stupid that the word 'percentage' has no meaning to him, and he must consequently be trained by a man more intelligent than himself into the habit of working in accordance with the laws of this science before he can be successful. (Taylor, 1911: 59, reprinted 1972.)

Emerging from Taylor's principles of organising the work process is a distinctive managerial ideology in which four themes dominate. First, there is the division of manual and mental labour: the separation of those who 'do' from those who 'think'. By removing from the employee any discretion over the organisation and execution of work, management are able to secure control over the method and pace of working. As we shall see, this can have important consequences for determining the skill definition of a work activity. Second is the notion that managers play an important role in planning each activity to ensure that it is in line with business objectives. In pursuit of these objectives, employees are to be used dispassionately, along with capital equipment and raw materials, in the search for greater efficiency, productivity and profitability. As a consequence, rigorous selection and training of people (to inculcate required behaviours) become critical management functions. Third is the concept of surveillance. At its base is the belief that people cannot be trusted to perform their jobs diligently, thus there needs to be control through close supervision and monitoring of all work activities. Hierarchies of authority are constructed, giving legitimacy to surveillance, and simultaneously constructing a 'division of management' (Littler, 1982: 53). Finally, Taylor's deeply entrenched belief was that people were essentially instrumental, and so money could be used as a powerful motivator providing it was linked directly to the productivity of the individual: a linkage achieved by piece-rate payment systems.

Whilst the logic of Taylorism is impeccable, the conditions of work it produces are often dehumanising and bleak: a set of highly segmented work activities, with no opportunity for employees to use their discretion, and a system of close supervision to monitor their work performance. However, the practice of Taylorism has not necessarily followed the theory as closely as its original protagonist would have wished, leading some commentators (notably, R. Edwards, 1979; and Palmer, 1975) to argue that Taylor's influence has been over-stated because the practical impact of his ideas was limited – not least due to the collective resistance exerted by employees through trade unions. It is certainly the case that in Taylor's own lifetime the diffusion of the principles of scientific management was modest. Many managers remained unconvinced about the possibility of planning and measuring activities sufficiently accurately to enable the 'science' to work. There were also competing ideas about the nature of job design from the human relations movement (starting with the famous Hawthorne experiments in the 1920s) which brought out the importance of the social factors at work, thus challenging the rational-economic assumptions underlying Taylor's theory of work design (for a full analysis see Schein, 1965). Notwithstanding these reservations, Taylor's ideas *have made* (and continue to make) a crucial impact on the thinking about job design and the division of labour. Indeed, as Littler (1982) argues, we must be cautious of assuming a linear progression of management theory where each neatly supersedes the previous. The persistence of Taylorist principles in organisations like McDonald's are testimony to the resilience of Taylorism. Moreover, it demonstrates how service organisations can use features of 'classic' Taylorism in a similar way to manufacturing industry; indeed, one is left pondering whether shovelling chips into a paper cone is the 1990s equivalent of shovelling pig iron into a furnace which Taylor described a century earlier.

Recently, the pervasiveness of a Tayloristic division of labour in the expanding service sector has been noted by Ritzer (1993). He contends that McDonald's represents the archetypal rational organisation in search of four goals: efficiency, calculability, predictability and control. McDonald's is a contemporary symbol of a relentless process of rationalisation, where the employee is simply treated as a factor of production. Ritzer's thesis (rather pessimistically) is that both theoretically and empirically this constitutes a general process of 'McDonaldisation' which extends beyond work into the culture of society. His conclusion suggests there is an inevitable tendency towards a dehumanisation of work – a theme that echoes the work of the deskilling theorists, which are explored after considering a second key actor in the design of jobs in the twentieth century.

The Assembly-Line – Chickens and Ford

If asked to visualise an assembly-line, many people would probably have an image of a car plant, with a steady procession of partly-finished vehicles passing groups of workers (or robots) who are rapidly attaching windscreens, wheels, trim and so on. This has been the pervasive image of assembly-line work, not least because its innovative form was developed and exploited by the Ford Motor Company – an issue which we return to below. First, though, imagine a different contemporary work setting. You are in a massive room dominated by the sound of humming and churning machinery, whilst intermittently the voices of the all-female workforce can be heard. The room is cool and the air laden with the smell of blood. Overhead, weaving around the factory is a conveyor from which hooks are suspended, and hanging from each hook is the carcass of a dead bird. It is a chicken factory, composed of a variety of 'assembly-lines' which convert live birds into the cellophane-wrapped ready-for-roasting meat displayed in super-market freezers. The work is Tayloristic in the sense that it is segmented into simple, repetitive operations. For example, 'packing' involves four distinct tasks each performed by different employees: inserting the giblets and tucking the legs in; bagging the chicken; weighing it; and securing the top of the bag. But not only are these and similar tasks around the factory simple and repetitive, the pace of the work is also relentless. This was vividly portrayed by an employee on 'inspection' in such a chicken factory, interviewed for a television programme, *Dangerous Lives*, in 1989.

Employee:	The line was coming 'round with about four and a half thousand birds an hour and you used to have to check the chickens for livers, hearts or anything, by putting your hand in the backside of a chicken, feeling around and then bringing anything out, dropping it in the bin, and then going on to the next. Used to be, sort of, every other chicken.
Interviewer:	You were doing two chickens at a time?
Employee:	Yes, both hands in chickens together. You hadn't got time to wipe your nose or do anything really.
Interviewer:	Did that line ever stop?
Employee:	Only if they had a breakdown, you know, a pin went in the line, or there was a breakdown or anything.
Interviewer:	So you were doing over two thousand chickens an hour?
Employee:	Yes.

Interviewer: Fourteen thousand chickens a day?
Employee: Yes.
Interviewer: What did you think about that?
Employee: Hard work. Real hard work!

Similar experiences of unremitting 'hard work' have been found by researchers studying the harsh realities of factory life in different industries, for example, Pollert (1981) in the tobacco industry, Westwood (1984) in hosiery, Cavendish (1982) in motor components, Beynon (1973) and Linhart (1981) in cars. In Chapter 8 the experiences of employees are explored in closer detail, but for now the concern is with the work organisation principles which give rise to the assembly-line.

The name most commonly associated with the development of the assembly-line is Henry Ford, whose unique contribution was in adapting Taylorist principles to a factory setting geared to the mass production of standardised products. Ford established a production method benchmark against which assembly-line work has since been assessed, and the term 'Fordist' has come to be used to describe the combination of linear work sequencing, the interdependence of tasks, a moving assembly-line, the use and refinement of dedicated machinery and specialised machine tools (for a detailed discussion, see Meyer, 1981). It has been argued that Fordism is therefore distinguishable from Taylorism in that it constitutes a form of work organisation designed for efficient mass production (Wood, 1989). The success of Ford, however, can only be fully understood if seen as part of a system of industrial organisation that also sought to create, perpetuate and satisfy mass consumption. The development of mass markets provided the demand for large numbers of rapidly produced standardised products, epitomised by the output at the Highland Park factory which rose from 13,941 Model-T Fords in 1909 to 585,400 by 1916 (Williams *et al.*, 1992: 550). This volume of mass production was only possible because of the development of capital equipment capable of producing on a large scale and the development of an efficient electricity supply to drive the machinery; in other words mass production, mass consumption, technological innovation and segmented work organisation were all ingredients in Ford's recipe for success. Consequently, as Littler (1985) has argued, Fordism came to predominate as the appropriate form of organising work for mass production. It spread to Ford's main competitor in the US – General Motors – to its European rivals – Austin, Morris and Citroën – and then transferred to other, newer, industries such as electrical engineering and chemicals.

However, whilst a widely accepted view is that Fordism is synonymous with mass production, rigidity and standardisation, and that the impact of the ideas pioneered by Ford has been widespread, there remain certain voices of dissent. Notable among these are Williams and colleagues (1987 and 1992), who contend that Fordism has become a stereotype, distorted over time by British and US academics who are keen to attribute failing industrial performance to the persistence of an outdated form of production. Williams *et al.*'s (1992) detailed analysis of Ford's production operations at Highland Park (1909–19) certainly reveals a picture of greater flexibility and less standardisation of the product than most texts on the subject would suggest. Overall, however, such findings do little to dispel the picture of an authoritarian work regime with closely monitored, machine-paced, short-cycle and unremitting tasks.

As the chicken factory example illustrates, Fordist principles persist in contemporary work settings and these are not restricted to factory work. It can be argued that the assembly-line has been transposed into the service sector; for example, McDonald's might be interpreted as displaying Fordist elements in terms of its mass production of standardised products for mass consumption. Similarly, the supermarket in general, and check-out operations in particular, epitomise a Fordist approach to retailing: the customer's items pass along the conveyor and are swept across the bar-code reader by an operator who performs a monotonous series of repetitive actions. The flow-line, the dedicated machinery and the segmented work tasks are evidence of Fordist principles of work organisation. Thus the chicken, as an object for consumption, is typically reared through (Ford-like) battery farming, is slaughtered and processed in a Fordist factory, and is sold through a Fordist retail outlet (the supermarket) or even consumed as Chicken McNuggets in a Fordist restaurant.

The significance of Taylor, Ford and mass production for the way work came to be organised is profound because it changed the work process by introducing greater amounts of rigidity and regulation, which, in turn, has important consequences for the skill content of jobs. In particular, it raises the question of whether work, in general, is becoming less or more skilled. The evaluation of the different attempts to answer this question begins with the deskilling thesis.

THESIS: THE DESKILLING OF WORK

1974 saw the publication of one of the most influential books concerned with the study of work: Harry Braverman's *Labor and Monopoly Capital*. Braverman's thesis is that an inevitable tendency towards the degradation and deskilling of work takes place as capitalists search for profits in increasingly competitive economic environments. His contribution to the study of work must not be under-estimated. Although his thesis has since been subjected to a great deal of criticism, it played a fundamental role in injecting adrenaline into the lethargic 1970s body of industrial sociology. This revitalisation of labour process theory is expertly examined by Thompson (1989) and the subtleties of the debate are meticulously assessed in Knights and Willmott (1990). The discussion below draws from this rich vein of theory, but does not attempt to do full justice to the various complexities of the debate.

At the risk over over-simplifying, Braverman's argument runs as follows. Managers perpetually seek to control the process by which a workforce's labour power (its ability to work) is directed towards the production of commodities (goods and services) that can be sold for a profit. The control of this labour process is essential because profit is accumulated through two stages: first, through the extraction of the surplus value of labour (the price of a commodity greater than the costs incurred in its production); and second, through the realisation of that value when the commodities are actually sold. These two stages are frequently referred to as 'valorisation'. In other words, managers are seeking to control the way work is organised, the pace of work and the duration of work, because these affect profitability. Thus control of labour is the link between the purchase of labour power and valorisation. In Braverman's analysis, the managerial obsession with labour control is key to understanding capitalism and leads managers to seek ways of reducing the discretion exercised by the workforce in performing their jobs.

In order to exert their own control over the workforce and limit the control and influence of the employees, managers are seen to pursue a general strategy of deskilling which, according to Braverman, can be identified in two forms: organisational and technological. First, *organisational deskilling* is embedded in the Tayloristic principle of the separation of the conception and execution of work: the conceptual tasks (the more challenging and interesting parts of the job, such as planning, diagnosing problems and developing new working methods) get transferred to technical and managerial staff, whilst the execution of the work (often the mundane, less challenging part of the job) remains in the hands of the shopfloor worker. Theoretically, this process allows managers both to limit the discretion of the shopfloor workers and to secure a monopoly over technical knowledge about the work, which can then be used to exercise greater direct control over the activities of the workforce.

> A necessary consequence of the separation of conception and execution is that the labor process is now divided between separate sites and separate bodies of workers. In one location, the physical processes of production are executed. In another are concentrated the design, planning, calculation and record-keeping.... The physical processes of production are now carried out more or less blindly, not only by the workers who perform them, but often by lower ranks of supervisory employees as well. The production units operate like a hand, watched, corrected, and controlled by a distant brain. (Braverman, 1974:124–5.)

Second, *technological deskilling* occurs when automation is used to transfer discretion and autonomy from the shopfloor to the office (from blue-collar to white-collar workers) and to eliminate the need for some direct labour. Braverman focuses on the example of the operation of machines by numerical control (NC) – a process whereby the planning and programming of the machines was undertaken away from the shopfloor by technical staff, who prepared punched paper tapes that contained the information for the machine to run automatically. Prior to NC, the machinists would use their own judgement and discretion to set and operate the machines, but they have subsequently been left with only the relatively simple tasks of loading and switching the machine. In other words, a technological development (NC) has allowed the separation of task conception from task execution. Numerical control has more recently been superceded by computer numerical control (CNC) which works on the same principle of separation of programming and operation, but is controlled through a microprocessor. This sort of new technology does not *inevitably* lead to a deskilling of work, but Braverman argues that managers selectively use automation to this end, in order to secure their central objective of exerting control over labour.

> In reality, machinery embraces a host of possibilities, many of which are systematically thwarted, rather than developed, by capital. An automatic system of machinery opens up the possibility of the true control over a highly productive factory by a relatively small corps of workers, providing these workers attain the level of mastery over the machinery offered by engineering knowledge, and providing they then share out among themselves the routines of the operation, from the most technically advanced to the most routine... [But such a possibility] is frustrated by the capitalist effort to reconstitute and even deepen the division of labor in all its worst aspects, despite the fact that this division of labor becomes more archaic with every passing day... The 'progress' of capitalism seems only to deepen the gulf between workers and machine and to subordinate the worker ever more decisively to the yoke of the machine.... The chief advantage of the industrial assembly-line is the control it affords over the pace of labor, and as such it is supremely useful to owners and managers whose interests are at loggerheads with those of their workers. (Braverman, 1974: 230–2.)

Braverman's critics have been plentiful. McLoughlin and Clark (1994) divide these into 'agnostics' and 'sympathisers' (see Table 6.1). Among the latter, the most persuasive defence of Braverman comes from Armstrong (1988) who argues for a more subtle reading of Braverman and in particular that:

> any sensitive reading of his work should reveal that Braverman actually regarded the deskilling tendencies of technical change as a system-wide dynamic or 'law of motion' in capitalist economies which could, temporarily and locally, be interrupted or reversed by a variety of factors, many of which have been rediscovered by his critics as supposed refutations (Armstrong, 1988: 157).

This is an important point because, like all meta-theory, Braverman's thesis will never be able to explain all contingencies, yet this does not necessarily mean its analytical thrust is worthless. Indeed, as Armstrong suggests, many of the 'critics' are in practice offering revisions and amendments to the theory, rather than rejecting it. Although it has been suggested that Braverman's thesis has 'died the death of a thousand qualifications' (Eldridge, 1983, quoted in McLoughlin and Clark, 1994: 45) metamorphosis seems a better metaphor to describe the development and survival of the notion of a general trend of deskilling. To explore this, the key criticisms of Braverman's work are summarised, whilst the arguments of those who reject the thesis are explored in second part of the chapter.

Table 6.1   *The key critics of Braverman's thesis*

Sympathisers	Agnostics
Accept the general approach but offer some refinement.	Acknowledge some value in the approach, but consider it inadequate.
Friedman, 1977a, 1990	Littler, 1982
Burawoy, 1979	Wood, 1982
R. Edwards, 1979	Littler and Salaman, 1982
Zimbalist, 1979	Knights *et al.*, 1985
Armstrong, 1988	Knights and Willmott, 1986, 1990
M. Rose, 1988	T.J. Watson, 1986
P. Thompson, 1989	

Source: based on I. McLoughlin and J. Clark, *Technical Change at Work*, 2nd edn, Milton Keynes: Open University Press, 1994.

Six Common Criticisms Levelled at Braverman

First, the deskilling thesis ignores alternative management strategies. Friedman (1977a, 1977b and 1990) argues that it is false to assume a single trend towards deskilling, since this fails to acknowledge the occasions when it is in the interest of managers to pursue other strategies which leave some discretion in the hands of the employees: a strategy of 'responsible autonomy' rather than the 'direct control' which Braverman described. Friedman had in mind job enrichment and quality circles, but a contemporary expression of responsible autonomy is the notion of empowerment, whereby individual employees are expected to take responsibility for their own actions and initiate improvements in the way they work for the benefit of the organisation as a whole. Under responsible autonomy, the employees are not deskilled but management continue to control the labour process. Thus, the argument here is that there is a wider choice in the mechanisms employed by management for the accumulation of capital than Braverman suggests.

Second, the deskilling thesis overstates management's objective of controlling labour. The control of the labour process is not an end in itself, but a means to achieving profit. To concentrate solely on labour-control objectives ignores the importance of valorisation.

It is not simply the *extraction* of surplus value in the labour process which is problematic for capital, but the *realisation* of that surplus through the sale of commodities in markets.... In other words we need to consider the *full circuit* of industrial capital as the starting point for analyses of changes in the division of labour: purchase of labour power; extraction of surplus value with in the labour process; realisation of surplus value within product markets. There is no sound theoretical reason for privileging one moment in this circuit – the labour–capital relation within the labour process – if our objective is to account for changes (or variations) in the division of labour. (Kelly, 1985: 32, emphasis in original.)

Moreover, the assumption that labour issues (rather than, for example, product development, marketing, or investment) are the central concern of management during strategy formation, is highly questionable (Purcell, 1989 and 1995). Thus, as Littler and Salaman (1982: 257) contend, the process of capital accumulation acts beyond the labour process:

The firm is primarily a capital fund with a legal corporate personality, linked to a production process.... Whilst the production process results in a flow of income to the firm, this does not preclude alternative sources playing a major role or even a predominant one e.g. currency speculation, cumulative acquisition and asset stripping, commodity speculation, and credit manipulation of various kinds.

Child (1972, 1984 and 1985) has highlighted the importance of the political manoeuvring of managers in an organisation who, as key decision-makers, are making 'strategic choices' that reflect their own values and vested interests. Thus, the argument here is that the internal politics of the organisation have a greater impact on deciding how the work is organised and the associated skill requirements than Braverman implies. The logic of capitalist accumulation may remain the predominant tendency, but this can be mitigated by managers at all levels who are defending their vested interests.

Consequently, the criticism is that Braverman's thesis underestimates the diversity and complexity of management objectives. The assumption that there is a single shared objective by management – that of labour control – ignores the plurality of interests within management, and the diverse and sometimes competing objectives (Batstone *et al.*, 1987; Buchanan and Boddy, 1983; Buchanan, 1986; Child, 1985). For example, in research into technological change in the UK provincial newspaper industry undertaken by one of the authors (Noon, 1994) it was found that when managers were questioned about the objectives for introducing new technology, they stressed different reasons which seemed to reflect their own functional responsibilities. In other words, the objective of increased control over labour was not the primary focus for most managers; instead, they said technological change provided new opportunities in terms of product quality, product development, production control, efficiency and flexibility, together with a reduction in labour cost. This suggests that whilst labour control objectives may be relevant, they must be placed within the context of broader business objectives. As Armstrong (1989 and 1995) argues, the pervasive influence of management accountants at board level in UK companies tends to lead to more strategic thinking based on financial concerns rather than human resource matters.

Third, the deskilling thesis treats labour as passive. Employees have not been totally compliant, and have resisted change towards deskilling through both trade union collective action and individual action. Indeed, R. Edwards (1979) argues that management has sought more sophisticated forms of control as a direct response to (and as a way to suppress) worker resistance. He argues there has been a shifting reliance from the 'simple control' typified by the methods of direct supervision that Taylor advocated, to the 'technical control' of the mechanised assembly-line (and more recent developments in computer technology) and the 'bureaucratic control' of workplace rules, procedures and a regulated internal labour market.

Fourth, the deskilling thesis understates the degree of consent and accommodation by employees. The work of Burawoy (1979) stands as an important counterpoint to Braverman in that it explores the extent to which the workforce *consents* to its own subordination. In part this contrasts also with the previous criticism, because it suggests that rather than challenging management control of the labour process, the workforce may develop an informal culture that offers alternative definitions of the work situation and provides the opportunity for meaningful activity. The labour process is thereby redefined as a type of game through which the employees can derive satisfaction (for example, by beating the clock, outwitting the supervisor, or manipulating the machinery). These games act as powerful means of social regulation (self-control) amongst the work groups, and obscure the exploitative nature of the labour process. In so doing, they unwittingly provide alternative additional sources of control for management. Such a brief summary hardly does justice to the subtleties of Burawoy's work, but these issues will be analysed in more detail in Chapter 8.

Fifth, the deskilling thesis ignores gender. Beechey (1982) has argued that several problems emerge from the gender-blind nature of Braverman's argument. First, he fails to appreciate the importance of women's distinct role as domestic labourers because of his 'conceptual isolation of the family from the labour process and of both the family and the labour process from an analysis of the capitalist mode of production as a whole' (Beechey, 1982: 71). Second, his discussion of the pre-industrial family can be criticised for romanticising the past and ignoring the existence of patriarchal structures. Third, his concept of skill fails to explore gender dimensions; an issue already analysed in detail in Chapter 5, where it was noted that the social construction of skill is particularly important in creating 'gendered jobs', resulting in the undervaluation of women's labour power and skills.

Sixth, the deskilling thesis overlooks skill transfer possibilities. The failure of Braverman to recognise that deskilling in one area of work may be compensated by enskilling in another, is most forcefully argued by Penn (1983 and 1990) whose ideas are examined in some detail later. However, it might be argued that this constitutes one of the most unfair criticisms of Braverman. As Armstrong (1988) points out, Braverman explicitly recognised that change would occur unevenly across industries, and that in some instances new skills and technical specialities might be temporarily created within the workforce. It is this last point that constitutes the heart of Armstrong's defence of Braverman. He argues:

> Braverman does *not* propound a universal law of deskilling. What he *does* claim is that there exists a general tendency for deskilling to occur in capitalist economies which will become actual where products and processes make this possible and where its effects are not masked by initiatives aimed at changing technology for other reasons. (Armstrong, 1988: 147, emphasis in original.)

Whilst some commentators (for example, Lewis, 1995) are unconvinced by Armstrong's defence of Braverman, a re-reading of the original text does reveal that Braverman had a less deterministic approach than is frequently attributed to him. Therefore, the deskilling thesis needs to be seen as an overall tendency, rather than a universal law applying in all cases. If Braverman's thesis is to be countered, it should be (and can be) challenged on comparable terms: rather than a tendency towards deskilling, there is an opposite trend towards upskilling occurring within capitalist economies. It is to this antithesis that the discussion now turns.

ANTITHESIS: THE UPSKILLING OF WORK

Whereas the deskilling thesis drew on Marxist economic theory and the crisis of capitalism in industrial societies, the upskilling thesis is based on the economics of human capital theory within a new era of capitalism: the post-industrial society. Human capital theorists (Becker, 1964; Fuchs, 1968) suggest that, increasingly, firms are investing in their workforce through greater training provision; thus the emphasis is shifted to 'human capital' as a central means of accumulating profit. It is held that rapid advances in technology require a more educated, better trained workforce in order to cope with the increasing complexity of work tasks (Kerr *et al.*, 1960; Blauner 1964). In turn, this is linked to an ever-reducing demand for manual/physical labour as western capitalist economies undergo a structural shift away from manufacturing towards service sector activities (Fuchs, 1968). This shift in the economic base of advanced industrial societies is considered by commentators such as Daniel Bell (whose ideas are summarised in Chapter 3) to signal a fundamental transformation to the post-industrial society, in which theoretical knowledge becomes 'the axis around which new technology, economic growth and the stratification of society will be organized' (Bell, 1973: 112). In other words, the upskilling thesis suggests that the general tendency is towards more complex work requiring higher levels of skill. As a consequence, the shift in the pattern of work organisation will not be towards degradation (as Braverman suggested) but to an enrichment of work.

The upskilling thesis has more recently found expression in the concept of 'flexible specialisation' propounded by Piore and Sabel (1984). They argue that the crisis of accumulation under capitalism is leading to an important shift away from Fordism towards more craft-based, flexible, innovation-led, and customer-focused work organisation. Thus, just as the move from traditional craft production to mass production constituted 'the first industrial divide', the move from mass production to flexible specialisation is described by Piore and Sabel as 'the second industrial divide'. The new emphasis lies on flexible production systems which can meet the demands for customised products in increasingly diversified markets. In particular, developments in microelectronic technology allow for more flexibility in the use of capital equipment: machinery no longer needs to be dedicated to specific tasks but can be re-programmed to perform a variety of tasks. More traditional production methods typically involve long set-up times for the machinery which means that large production runs are necessary to recover the cost; short production runs for small batches are an inefficient use of the equipment. In contrast, computerised machinery requiring shorter set-up times enables greater diversity of (small batch) production without incurring the inefficiencies. In other words, economies of *scale* are now complimented by economies of *scope*. This is important because customers are supposedly becoming increasingly discerning and want a greater variety of goods which allow them to express their individual identity (Sabel, 1982). Therefore, economies of scope become a necessity in a dynamic, competitive market. Computerised production and information processing capabilities provide the technological infrastructure, and allegedly bring with them a demand for upskilled rather than deskilled labour.

Five Criticisms of the Upskilling Thesis

Generally, the upskilling thesis has failed to stimulate as vigorous a debate as the deskilling thesis – indeed it might be argued that it has been greatly neglected as a theoretical proposition of general skill change, and consequently remains underdeveloped. However, the related flexible specialisation thesis has provoked considerable academic discussion (see for example, Hyman, 1991; C. Smith, 1989; Williams *et al.*, 1987; Wood, 1989). Consequently, it is possible to identify five major criticisms of the general upskilling thesis.

First, Lee (1982) argues that the drawing of a causal relationship between technical change and rising skill must be seen as a simple technicist generalisation. Like the deskilling thesis, it fails 'to consider the institutional "filters" which complicate the relationship between production methods, skill levels and class' (Lee, 1982: 147).

Second, advanced technology does not always require high skill levels on the shopfloor. Indeed, the upskilling thesis is as vulnerable as its deskilling counterpart to the criticism that there are numerous managerial objectives which reflect vested interests and political manoeuvring, and the design of work will be based on these just as much as 'technical' decisions about skill requirements. For example, in their study of United Biscuits, Buchanan and Boddy (1983) show that even within one company there can be a mixture of skill changes associated with the introduction of advanced technology, which makes any generalisation of upskilling or deskilling difficult to substantiate. Similarly, Sorge *et al.* (1983) reveal how computer numerical control (CNC) technology was used by British managers to deskill the shopfloor workers and turn them into mere machine minders, whilst in Germany the same technology was implemented in such a way as to integrate the (skilled) programming into the work of the operators, thereby enhancing their skill.

Third, there is an implicit tendency within the upskilling thesis to assume that the growth of the service sector will create skilled jobs. Empirical evidence however reveals this to be a gross oversimplification; companies like McDonald's, for instance, epitomise the success of service sector expansion whilst embodying some of the worst elements of monotonous, routinised, low-discretion work.

Fourth, the upskilling thesis in general, and flexible specialisation in particular, assumes that a radical break with Fordism is taking place, but this understates the resilience of mass production for mass markets. For example, the almost insatiable demand for consumer electronics over the past two decades typically has been met by the supply of goods manufactured using production systems that are labour intensive and low skilled (see for example, Delbridge *et al.*, 1992; Sewell and Wilkinson, 1992). Similarly, the flexible specialisation thesis overstates the extent to which small-batch production will create upskilled and multiskilled workers. As Pollert (1991) and C. Smith (1989) point out, small-batch production can and has adopted low-skilled, short cycle assembly-line techniques. Hence, the criticism here is that the upskilling thesis relies on a false dichotomy between mass and craft production.

Fifth, the upskilling thesis needs to be put into a global perspective. With the rise of the multinational organisation it is no longer sufficient to consider change simply in a national context. For example, a shift in the manufacture of consumer electronics from Western Europe to South East Asia removes the demand for low-skilled work in one country, only to increase the demand in another. As a result, it becomes problematic to try to interpret a fall in the demand for low-skilled labour in one national context as a sign of general upskilling – equally it may indicate a global redistribution of demand for skills, reflecting the mobility of capital in the search for lower labour costs and the pursuit of greater profitability.

Overall, the upskilling thesis is as ambitious as the deskilling thesis in attempting to arrive at a theoretical framework that reflects a general tendency of skill change in one direction. However, in both cases the unidirectional argument needs to be qualified. Indeed, the question of whether the dynamics of skill change can be simplified in such a way is highly problematic; a more robust theoretical approach might be to hypothesise multi-directional change within different sectors, industries, occupations and tasks. Three approaches which address such a synthesis are examined in the next section.

SYNTHESES: POLARISATION, COMPENSATION AND THE DUAL IMPACT OF AUTOMATING AND INFORMATING

The Polarisation of Skills

One of the most thorough of recent attempts to assess the changing experience of work has been that embodied in the Social Change and Economic Life Initiative (SCELI) research project. Part of this research focused on the changing nature of skill (Penn *et al.*, 1994b); some of the findings from the study have already been explored in Chapter 5. Importantly for our present discussion, the researchers specifically addressed the question of whether there had been a general trend towards upskilling or deskilling during the 1980s. The conclusion from this survey is that a complex picture of skill change emerges, and neither the upskilling nor deskilling thesis adequately explains skill change in the UK. Table 6.2 provides a summary of the main findings.

The SCELI research suggests there has been a *polarisation* of skill associated with three distinct factors: existing skill differentials, advanced technology and gender. To quote the conclusion of Gallie (1991: 349–50):

> Those that already had relatively higher levels of skill witnessed an increase in their skill levels, while those with low levels of skill saw their skills stagnate.... Those that have been in a position to use advanced technology in their work have seen their skills increase; those that have not had this possibility, have been much more likely to see their skills remain unchanged. Finally, the evidence points to a deep gender divide in skill experiences. It is men above all that have benefited from the progress of skills in the 1980s, while women are much less likely to have seen their skills increase. The central factor connected with this would appear to be the existence of a major sector of part-time female work, in which the existing levels of skill are typically low and which has remained untouched by the processes that have elsewhere contributed to skill enrichment.

Table 6.2 *Patterns of skill change in the UK – summary of the main findings from SCELI*

Skill change within occupational classes
- A higher proportion of employees reported an increase than a decrease in the skill level of their jobs over the last 5 years.
- This trend was less marked for non-skilled manual employees, where a greater proportion reported that their skill levels remained static.
- Those experiencing upward occupational mobility were more likely to report skill increases, the greatest increase being those who moved from manual to service occupations.
- Those who remained in the same job experienced less upskilling.

Skill change within sectors
- The general pattern was upskilling rather than deskilling.
- Non-skilled workers in manufacturing experienced upskilling in greater proportions than their counterparts in the service sector.
- In the service sector, there was a marked difference between public and private organisations, the latter having much greater proportion of low-skilled jobs.

Automation and skill
- The use of advanced technology varies between occupations – only 39 per cent of the respondents were using automated or computerised equipment.
- In every occupational class, work with advanced technology was associated with higher skill demands.

Gender and skill
- The skill requirements of the women's jobs (measured by qualifications needed and training) appeared substantially lower than those of the men. Women and men are doing very different types of work.
- Both men and women were more likely to have increased than decreased their skills, although a greater proportion of men had done so (56 per cent compared with 45 per cent).
- A greater proportion of men than women were working with advanced technology, so consequently benefited more from its positive impact on skill.
- Women in male-dominated occupations were twice as likely as women in feminised occupations to have experienced an increase in their skills.
- Women in part-time employment were in jobs with lower skill requirements than men doing part-time work.
- Much of the difference in the experience of skill change between men and women can be explained by the negative impact of part-time work. When full-time jobs of men and women are compared, the gender differences in terms of skill change virtually disappear.

Overall
- Deskilling was rare.
- The most common experience was upskilling.
- The argument best supported by the evidence is the polarisation of skill.

Source: summarised from D. Gallie, 'Patterns of skill change: upskilling, deskilling or the polarization of skills?', *Work, Employment and Society*, 5 (1991), 3, pp. 319–51.

The findings are unexpected to some extent; in particular the lack of evidence for the deskilling thesis, although this may be hidden by the extent of 'stagnation' of skills. Moreover, it is worth bearing in mind how the research method might have influenced the results: a respondent might be unwilling to say their job has become less skilled because it projects a negative image of their own abilities; similarly, any new aspect to a job, because of its unfamiliarity, may lead the respondent to overstate the skill required (such problems of measuring skill were examined in detail in Chapter 5).

The Compensatory Theory of Skill

The argument put forward by proponents of the compensatory theory (Penn and Scattergood, 1985; Penn, 1990; Penn *et al.*, 1994a) is that the general theories of both upskilling and deskilling are inadequate to explain the complexity of skill change, and that empirically derived, middle-range theory offers a better way forward. As Penn (1990: 25) argues, 'If the dynamics of skill change are essentially dualistic, then both [upskilling and deskilling theories] can find illustrative examples to support their respective, if incompatible, positions without securing any semblance of an adequate overall analysis.'

The compensatory theory is based on the proposition that technological change generates *both* deskilling and upskilling. This can be observed empirically in two respects. First, the effects are international: 'the shift of routine manufacturing from advanced, core economies to less developed, peripheral economies, and the increasing internationalisation of the capital goods (machinery) industry' (Penn, 1990: 25). Second, the effects differ between and within occupations: some groups are advantaged by having a more skilled and central role, whilst others find themselves deskilled and marginalised. More specifically:

> technological changes tend to deskill *direct productive roles* but put an increased premium on a range of *ancillary skilled tasks* that are associated with the installation, maintenance and programming of automated machinery. This is because modern machinery incorporating micro-electronics tends to simplify many production skills but renders maintenance work far more complex.... [However] within maintenance work itself... there is a far greater need for new electronic based maintenance skills than for traditional mechanical maintenance skills. (Penn, 1990: 25, emphasis in original.)

There is a somewhat technologically determinist undertone to part of this argument: the suggestion that microelectronics have tendencies to affect certain jobs, independent of the actions and choices of those who design, commission or purchase the technology. Nevertheless, the general thrust of the argument is of interest since it highlights the importance of acknowledging a broader picture of skill change across occupational groups, industries and national contexts.

Automating and Informating: The Dual Impact on Skill Change

The important role of advanced technology in reconfiguring skills is explored in detail by Zuboff (1988). She argues a distinction must be drawn between the processes of *automating* and *informating*, since they have affected skills in different ways. The process of automating work operations involves the replacement of living labour with technology: thus it is characterised by a deskilling of work and the reassertion of management control over the work process. Increasingly, however, technological developments also provide an opportunity to generate detailed information about the work operations themselves which, if systematically gathered and analysed, increases the visibility of the productive and administrative work undertaken in an organisation. In other words, technology is informating the work process, and the data requires interpretation through the use of cognitive ability. This constitutes an upskilling of work and provides 'a deeper level of transparency to activities that had been either partially or completely opaque' (Zuboff, 1988: 9). Taken together, the processes of automating and informating lead to a reduction in action-centred skills (doing) but an increase in intellective skills (analysing). At the same time, 'these dual capacities of information technology are not opposites; they are hierarchically integrated. Informating derives from and builds upon automation. Automation is a necessary but not sufficient condition for informating.' (Zuboff, 1988: 11.) Moreover, Zuboff argues that although automating displaces human presence, it is not yet clear what the full effects of informating are. Whilst managers can choose either to exploit or to ignore the informating process, her own case-study evidence suggests the tendency has been for managers to stress the automating process and ignore the informating potential. This is not surprising because the informating capacities of advanced technology force managers to rethink traditional structures, work organisation and forms of control.

> The shifting grounds of knowledge invite managers to recognize the emergent demands for intellective skills and develop a learning environment in which such skills can develop. That very recognition contains a threat to managerial authority, which depends in part upon control over the organization's knowledge base.... Managers who must prove and defend their own legitimacy do not easily share knowledge or engage in inquiry. Workers who feel the requirements of subordination are not enthusiastic learners.... Techniques of control that are meant to safeguard authority create suspicion and animosity, which is particularly dysfunctional when an organization needs to apply its human energies to inventing an alternative form of work organization better suited to the new technological context. (Zuboff, 1988: 391–2.)

The analysis presented by Zuboff is detailed, so this summary cannot really do justice to the subtlety of her argument. Nevertheless, it illustrates how both the deskilling and upskilling theses are inadequate as single explanations of skill change because while the former concentrates on the process of automating, the latter is focused on the process of informating. As a result, the dual impact of advanced technology is overlooked by both approaches.

The Common Thread of the Three Approaches

It is notable that the syntheses summarised above are more firmly based on empirical research than either the deskilling or upskilling thesis, and readily address the complexity of skill change. This means that all three syntheses identify the possibility of deskilling and upskilling occurring simultaneously, and therefore they reject the notion of an overall general tendency in one direction only. In moving away from general theorising to context-specific understanding of skill change, they can more easily accommodate the diversity of empirical evidence. In spite of their different methodologies – the quantitative survey approach of Gallie (1991), the historical industry studies of Penn (1990), and the qualitative case studies of Zuboff (1988) – they converge in concluding that the overall picture is one of *differing experiences* of skill change.

DISCUSSION: TOWARDS A CONCEPTUAL FRAMEWORK

The possible trends in work transformation represented by the various approaches explored above can be depicted by developing a simple framework. As with any conceptual schema that seeks to simplify the complexities embedded in work organisation, this is necessarily limited in its explanatory powers, but it does allow us to theorise some analytical distinctions. The framework draws on Fox (1974), Friedmann (1961) and Littler (1982) by proposing that work can be described as varying in terms of its specificity and diffuseness, across two dimensions: the range of work performed and the control over work content (see Figure 6.1). In the case of the first dimension, work can vary according to the range of tasks that the employee performs: at one extreme an employee will perform a single task, thus his or her work role could be described as 'specific', whilst at the other extreme an employee will be expected to perform a multitude of different tasks, and so the work role is more accurately labelled 'diffuse'. The second dimension refers to the extent to which an employee has the ability to exercise choice over how the work is performed. If the work is specifically defined, there will be little opportunity to exercise discretion, but if the work is diffusely defined, the job will require the employee to use discretion. By combining these two dimensions, it is possible to visualise the way jobs may vary and to plot four ideal typical cases:

1. Specialist work: high discretion over a narrow range of work.
2. Specialised work: a narrow range of prescribed tasks.

3. Generalised work: a wide range of prescribed tasks.
4. Generalist work: high discretion over a wide range of work.

The generalist (4) and the specialised worker (2) are polar opposites in as much as their work can be described (respectively) as wholly diffuse or specific. The specialist (1) and the generalised worker (3) have a mix of specificity and diffuseness in their work.

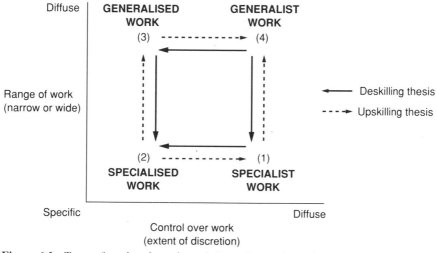

Figure 6.1 *Types of work tasks and trends in work transformation*

The nature of jobs identified above can be used to map the trends proposed by the skill change theses. First, the deskilling thesis is based on the premise that there is a general trend from diffuseness to specificity in work. This manifests itself in the form of a degradation of work along the 'control' dimension, and/ or a simplification of work along the 'range' dimension. These trends are represented by the solid arrows in Figure 6.1. Second, the upskilling thesis identifies an opposite trend towards diffuseness from specificity. Thus, there is an enrichment of work along the control dimension and/or multi-tasking along the 'range' dimension (the broken arrows in Figure 6.1). Those researchers who reject a general tendency would argue that a mixed pattern would emerge, and that the extent of change could occur along any of the paths represented by the arrows, and are likely to vary greatly both between and within countries, sectors, industries, workplaces and workgroups.

Finally, superimposed on the framework in Figure 6.2 are the production paradigms. These represent the dominant form of production associated with the four types of work task (Figure 6.1). Once again it can be seen how skill-change theses suggest very different patterns of work organisation. Deskilling theses suggest that the dominance of craft/artisan production gave way to Fordism, and this paradigm is continually being renewed as the dominant mode of work

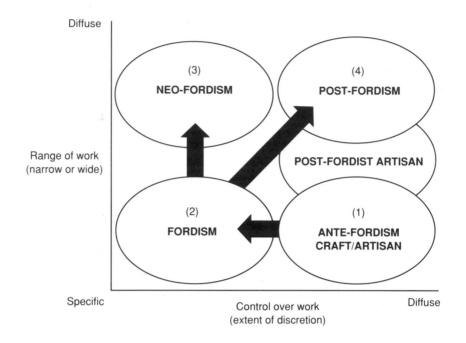

Figure 6.2 *Paradigms of work organiisation*

organisation under capitalism. A variant of this is the notion of neo-Fordism, which represents not so much a dramatic shift to a new paradigm as the evolution of Fordism (see for example, Harvey, 1989; Wood, 1989). This perspective contends that through task restructuring around increasingly automated and internationalised production processes, Fordism enters a new era of capitalism. Proponents of this view stress the importance of recognising continuity with the past, rather than characterising industrial change as a quantum leap into a new dimension of capitalism (for example, Aglietta, 1979). In contrast, whilst advocates of the upskilling theses concur with the historical dominance of Fordism, they argue that a dramatic change *has* taken place in advanced capitalist economies. It is suggested that this constitutes a paradigm shift to post-Fordism based on new concepts of work organisation and an increasingly dominant service-based economy – frequently characterised as the post-industrial society. As noted above, from the perspective of the flexible specialisation thesis, this would encompass a return to the bespoke manufacture reminiscent of the ante-Ford craft-based production paradigm. Further, it would suggest new forms of work associated with fragmented, smaller, high technology organisations operating under increasingly deregulated conditions, perhaps offering the short-term, part-time, employment contracts highlighted in Chapter 2, and thereby making insecurity and vulnerability one of the dominant realities of work.

7 Emotion Work

INTRODUCTION

Whilst it has become commonplace to distinguish between jobs involving mainly physical tasks, and ones that primarily call for mental performance (utilising knowledge and information), a growing proportion of the workforce are in fact also engaged in what might be termed the performance of 'emotion' work. For those acting as airline cabin crew, rescue workers, debt collectors, supermarket check-out operators, waiters, bank staff, health care employees and a host of other occupations, the management of their own – and other people's – emotions represent key aspects of their job. In most service occupations involving direct contact with the public, the *way* in which employees deliver that service has come to represent an increasingly important aspect of the service itself. In some contexts, of course, the significance of social interaction as a vital component of service provision has long been recognised. In the restaurant industry, for example, the diner's experience depends not only on the quality of the food consumed but also on the ambience created in the restaurant, which invariably hinges on the disposition and demeanour of the staff waiting on the tables. Thus, as well as performing tasks such as providing information and advice about the menu, taking down orders accurately, and serving and clearing away food carefully and efficiently, waiters and waitresses are expected to behave in a manner which contributes to a positive and welcoming atmosphere, irrespective of the pressures they are under or the way they are responded to by their customers. Or, as one waiter succinctly put it, 'I always smile at them ... that's part of my uniform' (quoted in Hall, 1993: 460).

In this way, the 'service and its mode of delivery are inextricably combined' (Filby, 1992: 37); or, to put it another way, 'the emotional style of offering the service is part of the service itself' (Hochschild, 1983: 5). It is clear, however, that in recent years the range of activities involving emotion work has grown. Thus, for most supermarket check-out operators, for example, it is no longer sufficient to charge up the goods speedily, and handle cash, cheques and credit cards accurately; this has also to be a service performed 'with a smile', a friendly greeting, gaining eye contact and a farewell. Moreover, these requirements apply, whatever the circumstances:

> The worst thing is that you are on the till trying to go as fast as you can and you can hear them [the customers] moaning that you are slow ... there are times that I just want to look up and say shut up but you have to be busy and

keep smiling. (Supermarket check-out operator, quoted in Ogbonna and Wilkinson, 1990: 12.)

So too, in the high street banks, management now attach greater importance to the warmth and friendliness of the cashier. As the following extract from a customer service questionnaire distributed by a leading UK bank indicates, these are aspects of employee behaviour which are now increasingly monitored by their employers.

Which of the following statements most accurately sums up your impression of branch staff?
1.   Staff are not very friendly and can be rather frosty.
2.   Staff are efficient and business-like.
3.   Staff are always genuinely warm and friendly.

In fact, the questionnaire had ten questions seeking customers' opinions about the cashiers, including the level of staff politeness, appearance, and even the extent to which they looked happy in their work.

Similarly, on an airline flight, the expectation is that cabin crew will always display an air of reassurance, even if they fear otherwise.

Even though I'm a very honest person, I have learned not to allow my face to mirror my alarm or my fright. I feel very protective of my passengers. Above all, I don't want them to be frightened. If we were going down, if we were going to make a ditching in the water, the chances of our surviving are slim, even though we [the flight attendants] know exactly what to do. But I think I would probably – and I think I can say this for most of my fellow flight attendants – be able to keep them from being too worried about it. (Delta Airlines flight attendant quoted in Hochschild, 1983: 107.)

As social actors we all learn through processes of socialisation in families, schools, and elsewhere how to control and 'manage' emotions in different contexts. Many children, for example, are taught not to be overwhelmed by adversity, but rather to persevere by 'putting on a brave face' or 'grinning and bearing it': that is to say, by creating an emotional 'mask' behind which real feelings can be hidden. Similarly, in most work situations, individuals are required to suppress some emotions and, often, to display others. Thus, doctors are taught to control their emotions towards pain and death, to remain neutral and detached. Similarly, people in authority may regard it as prudent to maintain an emotional distance between themselves and their subordinates, so as to avoid any compromising of their ability to exercise discipline over those under them. Likewise, those at lower levels within organisations may continue to 'show respect' for those higher up the hierarchy, even if they regard those at more senior levels as incompetent. Thus, in many situations in both work and non-work life, gaps arise between expressed and felt emotions, or what Snyder (1987: 1) refers to as 'the public appearances and private realities of the self'.

Our particular interest in this chapter lies in those jobs where employees are explicitly required to adopt particular sets of 'emotion rules' which define – often in considerable detail – which emotions they must publicly display, and which to suppress, in the performance of their job. Though, implicitly or explicitly, such rules have long represented important elements in many occupations, the coincidence of three developments in recent years makes this aspect of work behaviour particular worthy of closer attention at this time. First, it is only comparatively recently that researchers have paid specific and detailed attention to emotional aspects of work performance and their wider significance: most of the studies in this area have been published since 1980. The timing of this growing interest is less surprising, however, in the light of the second and third factors stimulating greater interest in the topic. One has been the increase over the last two decades in the proportion of jobs in which employees are 'customer facing', that is, in direct contact with customers of different kinds. In large part, this growth reflects the expansion of the service sector (see Chapter 2). In addition, however, a significant proportion of manufacturing jobs (such as in sales and purchasing) rely heavily on contact with customers and outside suppliers. The other factor is the increased recognition which has been given to 'customer relations' as a vital aspect of competitiveness; this recognition in turn has increased the importance attached to the emotional performance by employees in direct contact with customers. The meanings attached by management to customer relations (so-called 'Customer Care') are examined later in the chapter. So too are the experiences of, and implications for, those delivering that 'care'. Before this, however, it is necessary first to consider briefly what different writers on this subject mean by terms such as emotion and emotional labour.

EMOTION AND EMOTIONAL LABOUR

Puzzling over what constitutes an emotion has a long pedigree. As Rafaeli and Sutton (1989: 4) comment, though it was more than a century ago that writers such as Charles Darwin and William James wrote on the subject of emotion, those currently seeking to define and interpret human emotions remain baffled by a number of unanswered and seemingly intractable questions. The subject of human emotion, just like the range of emotions a person can express, is a very wide one, and it would delay us unduly to explore the many social, psychological and biological avenues of emotion. It is sufficient for the present discussion to note the widespread agreement among those writing on emotions in the workplace that emotions centrally concern an individual's *feelings*. A recent book on the subject, *Emotion in Organization*, for example, describes itself as 'a book about feelings' (Fineman, 1993: 1), while other notable contributions to this area of study similarly make reference in their titles and subtitles to 'feelings' (James, 1989) 'human feeling' (Hochschild, 1983) and 'real feelings' (Van Maanen and Kunda, 1989).

Even when we narrow the focus to emotions or feelings expressed in the work-place, however, it remains apparent that the topic is still a potentially enormous one, not least because the workplace represents an important part of social existence, and encapsulates the range of human feelings – the loves, hatreds, fears, compassions, frustrations, joys, guilt and envies – that develop over time wherever any social group interacts. In addition, large areas of research, such as what makes employees satisfied or motivated, are concerned with exploring the feelings that people have about work. So, in the discussion that follows, the principal focus is narrowed to address those (increasingly common) situations where service employees are required, as part of their job, to display specific sets of emotions (by verbal and/or non-verbal means) with the aim, in turn, of inducing particular feelings and responses among those for whom the service is being provided. This can be summed up as *emotional labour*. Hochschild (1983: 7) coined this term to refer to 'the management of feeling to create a publicly observable facial and bodily display'. This form of labour, like physical labour, is purchased by employers for a wage; its precise performance can be specified in sets of rules, and its adherence monitored by different forms of supervision and control. Subsequent writers in this area have sought to develop Hochschild's pioneering work. Wharton and Erickson (1993) for example, emphasise that emotional labour is not a uniform activity, but varies in both type and degree: a variability which must be taken into account when assessing the consequences of performing this type of work (see below). Ashforth and Humphrey (1993: 90) define emotional labour as 'the display of expected emotions', which concentrates attention more on behaviour, rather than (in Hochschild's definition) any presumed management of feelings underlying behaviour. James (1989), on the other hand, defines emotional labour in a slightly different way, identifying it as the 'labour involved in dealing with other people's feelings' (James, 1989: 15) – the sort of labour, for example, widely performed in hospitals and hospices, where James conducted her research.

On closer inspection, it is evident that these definitional positions are in practice closely related. In Hochschild's approach, for example, the employee's emotional display is specifically designed to induce a particular set of feelings (for example, the 'satisfied customer') in the recipient of the labour. Correspondingly, for the nurses in James' study, one of the main ways in which patients' grief and anger is dealt with is by the nurses regulating their own emotions. Indeed, what these different emphases on the performer or recipient of emotional labour underline is the essentially *interactive* nature of this form of labour. It is work performed by employees in direct contact with others (customers, patients, clients) in which the response of those 'others' has a direct bearing on the experience of employees performing emotional labour, and on the attitudes of employers as to how that labour should be performed.

This raises a key issue: what lies at the heart of emotional labour is not necessarily the expression of real emotions, but *displayed* emotions, which may or may not be truly felt. As the supermarket employee quoted earlier commented, the check-out operators have to smile – and the smile must look authentic – whether or not they feel positively disposed towards the customer. Where employees are required as part of their job to demonstrate feelings they may not share, they are *performing* emotional labour in the sense that the work role involves aspects not unlike those of an actor – for example, adopting the role and the script of the 'happy worker', pleased to be of service (no matter how the customer responds). This has become an influential metaphor not lost on the employee, as demonstrated by the Cathay Pacific flight attendant who commented, 'We say we are all entertainers now because everyone is on stage' (quoted by Linstead, 1995: 198).

A number of sociologists and psychologists have considered social life, including life within work organisations, from a performance or 'dramaturgical' perspective (see for example, Goffman, 1969, 1971; and Mangham and Overington, 1987). This perspective envisages social life as a series of scripted performances in which people act out parts which are consistent with the 'selves' that they wish to present. Individuals are viewed as performing different scripts in different social situations. Goffman (1969: 183) refers to 'the arts of impression management' in relation to how individuals present themselves to the outside world, how different circumstances elicit different performances from the 'actors' involved, and how people 'self-monitor' their performances and adjust these as conditions alter (see also Snyder, 1987, for a discussion of self-monitoring).

The metaphor of the theatre and its component terms such as actor, performance, role, script and being 'on' and 'off' stage, can usefully be applied to an analysis of emotional labour, and the display rules of emotional conduct. At the same time, from a dramaturgical perspective, emotional labour can be seen as a variant of what already occurs in most other social contexts. In jobs requiring emotional labour, employees perform a particular emotion script, just as in other settings individuals perform other emotional displays, some of which are likely to be as inauthentic as those indicated by the check-out operator quoted earlier, who is required to smile even at rude customers. The key difference between these work and other settings, however, lies in the fact that those employees performing emotional labour are *required* to follow what Ekman (1973) and Ashforth and Humphrey (1993: 89) term the 'display rules', as part of their job. Discretion and choice over the nature of displayed feelings is removed or reduced, and the emotional performance forms part of the effort–wage bargain in the same way that physical performance does. As discussed later, for some critics of emotional labour (such as Hochschild, 1983) the problem is that some jobs require employees to undertake 'unacceptable' levels of emotional display, with potentially detrimental effects on the individuals involved. Before examining the effects of emotional labour, however, and the way people learn, experience and cope with this form of labour, it is necessary to consider in a little more detail the factors behind the expansion of this aspect of work.

THE EXPANSION OF EMOTIONAL LABOUR

In Chapter 2, the degree to which advanced industrial economies have experienced a shift in industrial structure was highlighted, with a diminishing proportion of the total workforce engaged in the primary and secondary sectors, and a growing proportion located in the tertiary, service sector. Whilst an important aspect of service activity involves commercial organisations providing services for one another (for example, management consultancy, specialised maintenance work and office cleaning) the growth in the service sector has been particularly notable in the area of personal services – the range of services available to the individual citizen. Few of these services are unique to the recent period. What is evident, however, is a growth in consumer choice, either as a result of the multiplication of similar services (such as a proliferation of leisure facilities, financial institutions, or different restaurants in a particular locality) or because of the extension of existing services, in part as a result of advances in technology (for example, travel agents equipped with computer reservation systems enabling them to provide a much extended service, or libraries with access to much greater information via electronic storage systems).

The growth of services to individuals can be categorised in various ways. Lynch (1992) for example, identifies an expansion in:

- financial services (including banks, building societies and insurance companies);
- travel services (e.g. coach, rail and air services, together with related activities such as car hire);
- leisure services (e.g. hotels, restaurants, cinemas, theatres, pubs, clubs, sporting facilities);
- provisioning services (different types of shops);
- communication services (e.g. telephone, media); and
- convenience services (e.g. hairdressing, travel agents).

In addition, in the public (and increasingly, the privatised) sector there has been a growth in competition in, for example:

- educational services;
- health and welfare services; and
- environmental services.

This expansion in service activities alone would probably have been sufficient to raise awareness of the significance of how employees interact with customers. However, a major reason why attention has come to focus so strongly on the nature of that interaction reflects not only the fact that such interactions have become more numerous, but that they are also occurring in an increasingly competitive environment, and that the *significance* of those interactions on the customer's overall judgement of the service has increasingly been recognised by management and, as a result, given greater emphasis. The increased competitiveness reflects both a general growth in service choices (for example, different leisure services competing for the customer's free time: should we take the kids to a theme park, the zoo, the swimming pool or the cinema today?) and also the multiplication of very similar services within a particular locality (shall we take the kids to eat at McDonald's, Burger King, or Wimpy's?). One effect of this growth of very similar services (and this multiplication is as evident in financial services, supermarkets and a range of other activities as well as in the fast food industry) is a tendency to even out many of the differences in price and quality between those services: overall the hamburgers are very similar, as are the hotel rooms in the different hotel chains, the airline seats and the various products offered by different estate agents, banks, travel agents and supermarkets.

In such an environment, where the actual services being offered for sale are little differentiated, increased significance becomes attached not to the physical nature of the service being offered, but to its *psychological* nature. The facilities at different banks, for example, may be almost identical, but in which one does the customer feel that they have been 'treated' the best? In this situation, the aim of any particular service provider comes to centre on making the customer feel more positively disposed to that service, such that they return to that particular service provider (be it a shop, restaurant, airline or hotel) when a repeat service is sought. It is this psychological element which is of particular significance in the recent expansion of emotional labour. The goal of securing a favourable psychological response from the customer has given rise to a much greater emphasis on 'customer care'. Notions of customer care have long existed of course, embodied in such maxims as 'service with a smile' and 'the customer is always right'. But the growth of a more articulated and extensive customer care philosophy can be traced to the growing importance attributed to customer relations within the 'excellence' movement (Peters and Waterman, 1982; Peters and Austin, 1985) and the spread into the service sector of ideas such as total quality management (TQM) and 'continuous improvement', originally formulated within manufacturing contexts (Deming 1982; Juran, 1979).

In part, customer care involves simply the efficient delivery of a service – a high quality product, delivered on time and to specification. However, with the duplication of very similar services, customer care manuals have also come to emphasise additional means of securing customer satisfaction. For example, the following comment, by a management writer on the psychology of customer care (Lynch, 1992: 29) is implicit in much of the thinking behind customer care:

> Any action which increases the self-esteem of the customer will raise the level of satisfaction .... Conveying in a sincere manner the message 'You are better than you think you are' is a powerful tool for any service provider.

Thus, boosting the customer's self-esteem is seen to be an important aspect of customer care. There are various ways of achieving this esteem or status enhancement; Lynch (1992), for example, cites the importance of using the customer's name. Indeed, the whole manner in which an employee may be required to deliver a service (smiling, gaining eye contact, giving a friendly greeting) can contribute to putting customers at their ease, showing deference to them, making them feel special, even sexually attractive (Hall, 1993; Linstead, 1995). In some situations, attributing status to the customer, and thereby potentially raising their self-esteem, is expressed in ways other than establishing 'friendly' relations. The undertaker's staff, for example, demonstrate a sensitivity to (and thus acknowledge the status of) the bereaved's feelings by performing their duties in a solemn way (at least while in sight of the bereaved). The waiter at a very high class restaurant may also acknowledge a customer's status by being unobtrusive (though remaining attentive and efficient) thereby acknowledging the customer's right to privacy and their status as someone with the ability to eat at such an expensive restaurant (Hall, 1993). In a less expensive restaurant on the other hand, status is still attributed to the customer, but more likely to be in the form of the waiter creating a more openly friendly relationship.

What these various aspects of customer care underline is that in a context of intensifying competition, *how* a service is delivered has come to be defined as central to overall organisational success. As a result, those staff in direct contact with the customer have become increasingly recognised as key representatives of the service organisation. Customer-facing staff are situated in crucial 'boundary-spanning' positions which link the organisation to external individuals or groups. One chief executive of a major airline sums up these interactions between organisational members and customers as key 'moments of truth', on which the latter form lasting judgements about the organisation as a whole (Carlzon, 1987).

Thus, management have come to pay much greater attention to the manner in which employees perform their interactions with customers. In some settings, detailed rules have been established specifying which emotions must be displayed, and which suppressed; these display rules are backed up by sanctions (and less frequently, rewards) in an attempt to secure full compliance. However, the fact that systems of punishment and reward exist at all indicates that compliance with the rules of emotional display remains problematic in many organisations. As the next section examines, in practice many employees experience difficulties in performing this aspect of their job, and resort to various strategies to cope with the exacting demands of emotional labour.

LEARNING AND EXPERIENCING EMOTIONAL LABOUR

While various situations exist where employees are required to present feelings which are solemn (undertakers) disapproving (debt collectors) or even hostile (night-club bouncers or police interrogators) most consideration has been given to the more common contexts where employees' emotional performance is designed to induce or reinforce positive feelings within the customer. In each of these contexts, the required emotional performance typically involves, 'a complex combination of facial expression, body language, spoken words and tone of voice' (Rafaeli and Sutton, 1987: 33). This combination is secured primarily through the processes of selection, training and monitoring of employee behaviour. Non-verbal elements form an important part of many jobs involving emotional labour, and can be prominent criteria in selection decisions. At Disneyland, for example, the (mainly young) people recruited to work in the park are chosen partly on the basis of their ability to exhibit a fresh, clean-cut, honest appearance – the non-verbal embodiment in fact of the values traditionally espoused in Walt Disney films (Van Maanen and Kunda, 1989). Airline companies too emphasise non-verbal aspects of the work of customer-contact staff, including the importance of a high standard of personal grooming, covering such aspects as weight regulation, uniform, and even colour of eye-shadow (Hochschild, 1983; Williams, 1988). Similarly, at most supermarkets, check-out operators are expected to conform to particular patterns of non-verbal behaviour even when not serving. One check-out operator, Denise, for example, (name changed) commented, in an interview with the authors, that at her store not only were the check-outs constantly monitored by closed circuit television equipment, but supervisors regularly patrolled behind the check-outs, preventing any of the operators from turning round to talk to fellow operators by whispering the command 'FF', which meant 'Face the Front'. Denise and her colleagues were required not only to 'FF', but also to sit straight at all times; they were strictly forbidden, for example, to put their elbows on the counter in front of them to relax their backs.

Non-verbal rules of emotional display play an important part in many service organisations, but it is the verbal rules which have been increasingly emphasised in a growing number of settings involving direct contact with customers. While in some contexts, employees receive little or no guidance on the 'correct' verbal behaviour, in others the prescribed verbal repertoire is passed on through detailed training and instruction. At her supermarket, for example, Denise has been instructed to greet the customer, smile and make eye contact, and when the customer pays by cheque or credit card, read the customer's name and return the card using their name ('Thank you Mrs Smith/Mr Jones'). This verbal display of friendliness and deference represents an increasingly common feature not only in supermarkets (Ogbonna and Wilkinson, 1990) but also in other areas of retailing, and service activities involving the public. Those entering the space ride at

Disneyland, for example, are met with the words 'Welcome Voyager' by the ride operator (Van Maanen and Kunda, 1989).

Both verbal and non-verbal emotional labour is prominent in the work of waiters and waitresses (see, for example, Hall, 1993; Mars and Nicod, 1984; and Spradley and Mann, 1975). Those waiting at tables are expected to perform a number of physical tasks but, in addition, a warm, friendly and deferential manner is widely seen by employers as a key element in creating a positive ambience. For the waiters and waitresses, there is an additional instrumental reason for performing their emotional labour effectively, as a significant part of their income derives from tips. Studies have shown that those who smile more do better at attracting larger tips than those who do not (Tidd and Lockard, 1978, cited in Rafaeli and Sutton, 1987). Indeed, one study found that tips to waitresses were higher where the waitress had made physical contact with the (male) customers by, for example, a fleeting touch of the hand when returning change, or touching the customer's shoulder (Crusco and Wetzel, 1984). Such studies appear to underline further the significance of the service provider boosting the customer's self-esteem by making them feel attractive.

It is the airline industry, however, which has given rise to one of the path-breaking studies of emotional labour (Hochschild, 1979 and 1983). In her study of Delta Airlines flight attendants (elsewhere often referred to as cabin crew, formerly as air hostesses or stewardesses) Hochschild explores the development, performance and consequences of emotional labour. Selection and training are shown to play particularly important roles in inculcating particular 'feeling rules' into the recruits. Selection criteria, for example, included both non-verbal and verbal aspects. Not only were physical attributes and overall appearance taken into account in the selection process for flight attendants, but so too was the ability to 'project a warm personality' and display enthusiasm, friendliness and sociability (Hochschild, 1983: 97). However, while the selection process is used to identify those who have the predisposition to perform emotional labour effectively, Hochschild emphasises the training sessions as the place where the flight attendants are given more precise instruction on how to perform their role. As well as training in the technical aspects of their job (such as what procedures to follow in an emergency), instruction is also given on the emotional aspects of the work. At its simplest, the training affirms the importance of smiling.

> Now girls, I want you to go out there and really *smile*. Your smile is your biggest *asset*. I want you to go out there and use it. Smile. *Really* smile. Really *lay it on*. (Pilot speaking at a Delta Airlines Training Centre, quoted in Hochschild, 1983: 4, emphasis in original.)

The employee's smile and accompanying pleasant and helpful manner are given considerable emphasis. Flight attendants are encouraged to think of passengers as 'guests in their own home', for whom no request is too much trouble

(Hochschild, 1983: 105). The cabin crew member's smile is designed not only to convey a welcome (in the way the supermarket operator's smile and restaurant worker's smile endeavours to do) but also to project a confidence and a reassurance that the company in general, and the plane in particular, can be trusted with the customer's life (1983: 4). The emphasis in the training is on fully identifying with the role, in order to generate a more 'genuine' smile – 'smiling from the inside' – rather than a false-looking smile.

It is one thing to be able to smile at friendly, considerate and appreciative customers, but another to smile under pressure such as the bar worker, waitress, or check-out operator faced with large numbers of customers, or service workers in general faced with offensive individuals. It is in these problematic circumstances that management also require compliance with display rules. It seeks to achieve this partly by encouraging employees to interpret the situation differently, to suppress any feelings of anger or frustration, and to respond in the manner prescribed by management. A key aspect in the emotion training of the Delta flight attendants, for example, was the instructions on how to respond positively to awkward, angry or offensive customers ('irates' as they are known in Delta). As Hochschild (1983) explains, a key training device for dealing with such passengers was to re-conceptualise them as people with a problem, who needed sympathy and understanding. Thus, employees were encouraged to think that perhaps the passenger who was drinking too much and being offensive was doing so to mask a fear of flying (or a stressful job, sadness at being away from home, or whatever). Underlying this training is the requirement for attendants to respond positively to such passengers, reflecting the fact that they may be frequent flyers and thus important sources of revenue to the company. Thus, the attendants are required to 'think sales' (1983: 108) no matter how irksome or rude the passenger is being.

It is evident from the studies undertaken that workers perform emotional labour in different ways. Hochschild (1983) for example, distinguishes between those who engage in 'surface' acting and those who perform 'deep' acting. Surface acting involves a behavioural compliance with the display rules (facial expression, verbal comments, and so on) without any attempt being made to internalise these rules: the emotions are feigned or faked. Deep acting on the other hand, involves employees internalising their role more thoroughly in an attempt to *experience* the required emotions. The training programmes described by Hochschild were designed to elicit deep acting – that, by developing a set of inner feelings (towards the company, the customer and the attendant's work role), the outward behaviour would follow as a matter of course. Ashforth and Humphrey (1993: 94) have subsequently pointed out that these two 'routes' to emotional labour should be supplemented by a third, which takes into account the situation where the expected emotional display is fully consistent with an individual's own inner feelings. In such cases, there is no need for the worker to 'act' at all, since the emotion is in harmony with what the individual would have naturally displayed as part of their own identity. An example might be a nurse who has entered that occupation to fulfil a strong desire to care for people who are ill. However, even the person who identifies fully with his or her job will have off-days and the occasional bad mood. At those times they - like their counterparts who identify with their job less strongly – will be required to manage their emotions to hide their true feelings.

REACTIONS TO EMOTIONAL LABOUR

For many employees, for much of the time, performing emotional labour is unproblematic. Smiling at customers often elicits a smile in return, and the creation of a friendly interaction. Further, as just noted, there will be those service employees who are very positively disposed to their work, and to smile while doing it is wholly consistent with their general feelings towards the job and the customer. In these latter cases, there is little or no dissonance or 'gap' between the individual's felt and expressed emotions at work: expectation and actuality are closely aligned.

Other circumstances can arise, however, where the performance of emotional labour becomes much more problematic for the individual. One of these circumstances is where the emotional display is required over long periods of time. Cabin crew members aboard inter-continental flights, for example, not only work long duty times, but also suffer from additional fatigue as a result of jet-lag and interrupted sleep patterns. The strain of prolonged emotional display, particularly where customers are being difficult or offensive (see also below) is illustrated in the following extract from Hochschild (1983: 127).

> A young businessman said to a flight attendant, 'Why aren't you smiling?' She put her tray back on the food cart, looked him in the eye and said, 'I'll tell you what. You smile first, then I'll smile'. The businessman smiled at her. 'Good', she replied. 'Now freeze and hold that for fifteen hours'.

A second problematic circumstance may arise where part of the emotional display is considered to be inappropriate by the worker performing the task. The supermarket employee Denise, quoted earlier, for example, expressed considerable difficulty with using the customer's name when handling cheques or credit cards. To Denise, a shy self-effacing woman, this seemed 'too forward, too familiar' in a situation where she was not acquainted with the individual whose name she was required to use; the result was a continuing unease and embarrassment. A third situation where emotional labour can be problematic for those performing it, is where employees are required to maintain the emotional display towards customers who are being rude or offensive. Examples of objectionable behaviour are evidenced in many studies of emotional labour, and occur in all settings from the supermarket check-out and the hospital to the restaurant and the aircraft cabin. Instances range from verbal abuse to physical assault. To handle these sort of problematic situations, and generally to reduce the stresses of the emotional aspects of the job, it is clear that performers of this kind of labour adopt a variety of coping strategies.

It is one thing for management to issue sets of guidelines and instructions and run training programmes and refresher courses to perfect and sustain various forms of emotional labour; it is another, however, to be confident that, once trained, employees will carry out the emotional labour as specified at all times. That managers recognise the tendency for employees to lapse in their emotional display is reflected in the practices adopted to monitor employee behaviour: disciplining those falling short of the prescribed norms and (less frequently) rewarding unusually high performers. Many of the studies of emotional labour highlight particular supervisory practices, often covertly conducted, to check employee behaviour. Airlines, for example, regularly use 'ghost riders' to check on how employees perform their roles; similarly, supermarkets employ 'mystery shoppers' (people hired by the company and disguised as customers) to monitor performance of check-out operators. At Disneyland, supervisors secrete themselves around the park to check on the behaviour of workers while remaining unobserved themselves (Van Maanen and Kunda, 1989). Further, a growing number of services regularly issue 'customer service' questionnaires (like the one quoted earlier) to gauge reactions to how employees are performing their roles.

Despite this level of surveillance, however, it is clear that those required to perform very frequent repetitions of an emotional display and/or perform emotional labour over long periods use various coping strategies, both in response to the general pressures, and to handle particular situations such as angry or offensive customers. At their simplest these strategies involve employees retiring to places, such as a rest room or canteen ('off-stage' areas where customers are not present) where they can 'let off steam'. Here, employees can express their anger or frustration in ways which are denied them when performing their jobs.

> We do get some very difficult customers ... when you get too angry you just go into the office and have a good swear at them and you come out smiling.
> (Supermarket employee, quoted by Ogbonna and Wilkinson, 1990: 12.)

Other strategies for coping with rude customers include engaging in covert activity which at the same time maintains the mask of emotional display: for example, the waiter who adulterates the offensive customer's food in some way, or the sales assistant who manages to look in all directions except at the loud customer who is demanding their attention. Disneyland ride operators deploy a number of covert activities in response to their situation, and particularly when confronted by offensive customers; these can include the 'break-up-the-party' ploy of separating pairs into different rides (despite there being room for both on the same ride), the 'seat-belt squeeze' in which customers are over-tightened into their seats, and other variants of inflicting physical discomfort (Van Maanen and Kunda, 1989: 67).

A more general defence mechanism for coping with the demands of emotional labour is referred to in several studies by phrases such as 'switching off', 'switching to automatic' or 'going robot'. Filby (1992: 39) for example, refers to emotional labourers' ability to 'switch onto autopilot and go through the e-motions'. These various expressions refer to behaviour involving a continued outward adherence to the basic emotional performance, but an inward escape from the pressures of the job. Many performers of emotional labour, for example, are expected to smile as though they mean it ('smile from the inside') so that customers believe in its sincerity and do not see it as simply part of an act. To switch into automatic mode may involve limiting this expression of 'sincerity'. Employees may have only limited scope for adopting this strategy, however, if 'sincerity' is also monitored. British Airways passengers arriving at London Heathrow, for example, are regularly canvassed about the service they have just received: did the check-in staff at the departure airport use the passenger's name; did they look them in the eye and smile; and did the smile seem genuine or forced – on a scale of one to four? (Blyton and Turnbull, 1994: 63). There are also other coping strategies and ways individual employees protest against the pressure of display rules. Hochschild (1983) for example, notes the use of 'slow-downs' among flight attendants and the way some employees enact minor infringements of uniform and appearance codes as a way of not being fully submissive to management instruction. Overall, what such protests and coping strategies indicate is that, in some cases at least, employees experience difficulties in continually performing their role as laid down in training manuals and management instruction. It is argued by some, however, that in more extreme cases the demands for emotional labour have consequences for the workers involved which go significantly beyond the (relatively) minor irritations of the rude customer. It is to a discussion of these consequences that we now turn, in particular the alienating potential of performing emotional labour and the argument that emotional labour has particular implications for women's position in the labour force.

SOME WIDER IMPLICATIONS OF EMOTIONAL LABOUR

In principle, emotional labour is potentially as significant a source of job dissatisfaction and alienation as other forms of labour (see discussion of alienation in Chapter 8). Indeed, any alienation arising from emotional labour could be particularly acute, since the nature of the task carries the potential for individuals to become self-estranged – detached from their own 'real' feelings – which in turn might threaten their sense of their own identity. Further, where the expressed emotions are not felt, this may cause the individual to feel false and create a sense of strain, which Hochschild (1983: 90) terms 'emotive dissonance'. Other writers too have drawn attention to this 'falseness' potentially leading to poor self-esteem, depression, cynicism and alienation from work (Ashforth and Humphrey, 1993: 97). Emotional labourers have been described as 'suffer[ing] from a sense of being false, mechanical, no longer a whole integrated self' (Ferguson, 1984: 54, cited in Mumby and Putnam, 1992: 472). Prolonged requirement to conform to emotional display rules could also contribute to 'emotion overload', particularly where women have to perform a 'second shift' of emotion management in their domestic sphere, once their first shift of emotional labour at work is completed (Hochschild, 1989; Wharton and Erickson, 1993).

But while in principle there is a potential for emotional labour to be dissatisfying or alienating, how much is this the case in practice? Overall, the evidence on this question remains scant, and what evidence there is does not all point in the same direction. In her study of flight attendants, for example, Hochschild (1983) highlighted a number of negative aspects of the job, leading to 'an estrangement between self and feeling and between self and display' (p. 131). Hochschild identifies such problems as 'feeling phony' (p. 181) with the flight attendants being unable to express genuine feelings or identify their own needs – inabilities which, for some, resulted in problems of establishing and maintaining close relationships in their private lives (ibid: 183).

In reviewing Hochschild's work, however, Wouters (1989) argues that the costs of emotional labour should not obscure more positive aspects. For Wouters, the distinction between true and displayed feelings is not as hard and fast as Hochschild implies, for individuals perform all sorts of emotional scripts, outside as well as inside the work place – a multiplicity which undermines any distinction between the 'displayed' feelings in emotional labour and 'true' feelings expressed elsewhere. Wouters (1989: 116) also argues that the costs of emotional labour must be offset against the positive side of such jobs, including the pleasure which many derive from serving customers and receiving from them a positive response in return. This argument reiterates the point made earlier: that there are individuals who strongly identify with their work roles, and for whom the job, and the emotional display rules entailed in that job, are fully consistent with their personal values and identity. Indeed, for some employees it is this 'fit' between personal values and job demands that has attracted them into the job in the first place: for example, the case of the nurse noted above. For such individuals, the performance of the tasks are likely to enhance, rather than reduce, psychological well-being (Ashforth and Humphrey, 1993: 100–1).

A larger-scale attempt to examine the effects of emotional labour was conducted by Wharton (1993) who studied over 600 banking and health service employees, almost two-thirds of whom were judged to hold jobs which required emotional labour. This study found no simple relationship between emotional labour and variables such as the degree of 'emotional exhaustion': as a whole, workers performing emotional labour were no more likely to suffer from emotional exhaustion than others. There was also no evidence of the expected relationship between emotional labour and job satisfaction; indeed, those performing jobs involving emotional labour were slightly *more* satisfied overall than those performing other jobs. What the study also reveals is the importance of *the conditions under which emotional labour is performed* for the effects on people engaged in this type of labour. In Wharton's sample, for example, people performing emotional labour were less likely to experience emotional exhaustion if they had greater autonomy over how they carried out their work. Such findings indicate the need to take account of other variables when considering the impact of emotional labour. The degree of autonomy is one, but others could include the degree of congruence between the employee's personal characteristics and job requirements, and also the success at which employees can disengage or 'switch off' from the job at the end of the day. As noted earlier, the type and degree of emotional labour required by different jobs is also likely to have an important bearing on its effects on employees: those jobs where emotional labour requirements are minimal, for example, are likely to have less impact than where emotional labour requirements are both extensive and prolonged.

As well as its potential for creating feelings of alienation, several commentators have pointed to the possible negative implications of emotional labour for women's position in the labour force: in particular, that it reinforces certain gender stereotypes which in the past have been detrimental to women (see for example, Hochschild, 1983; James, 1989; Mumby and Putnam, 1992). Three aspects of emotional labour are central to this argument. First, the distribution of emotional labour reflects a gender imbalance: the majority of those doing emotional labour for a living are women. Hochschild (1983) for example, estimates that twice as many women as men occupy jobs which require emotional labour. Secondly, most people performing emotional labour occupy relatively low positions within work hierarchies, with emotional labour rarely being ascribed the status of a skill. Thus, just as women in general are located disproportionately within lower levels of occupational hierarchies, they are similarly disproportionately represented among those lower status jobs requiring emotional labour. For some (see, for example, Ashforth and Humphrey, 1995 and James, 1989) this reflects the status of 'rationalism' within contemporary capitalism, and also the customary association of rationality and masculinity (Pringle, 1989). In combination, these create a contrast between jobs which are seen to be highly 'rational' and as a result are afforded high status (and are disproportionately occupied by men), and jobs which are more 'emotional' and are accorded much lower status (and are filled disproportionately by women). In hospitals, for example, it is the rational skills of the (mainly male) doctors and hospital managers which are accredited the highest status and rewards, while the emotional well-being of the patient – a key ingredient in their return to full health – is borne largely by the (mainly female) nurses and auxiliaries, and tends to be unrecognised and much more poorly rewarded (James, 1989). This practise of attributing status to some jobs rather than others is related to the issue of the social construction of skill, discussed in Chapter 5.

The third element in this argument that emotional labour is deleterious to women's position in the labour force contends that the main emotions displayed in emotional labour – in particular those involving a display of caring – act to reinforce gender stereotypes, and in particular that 'caring' is an emotion which is more 'natural' in women. Women are widely seen to be not only naturally more caring than men, but also more emotional than men, and more used to dealing with other people's feelings, as part of their domestic caring role. Various studies, for example, have indicated that women are the primary providers of emotional support for their partners and children (see discussion in Wharton and Erickson, 1993: 469). The critics of emotional labour argue that, as a result of this greater responsibility for emotion management in the domestic sphere, this comes to be viewed as a 'natural' ability in women, or a 'talent' which they have, rather than a skill which has to be acquired. The effect is for management to treat emotional labour as an extension of this natural talent, not as a learned skill – with the effect that it is not accorded the status of a skill. Thus, just as the skills used (disproportionately by women) in the domestic sphere tend to be under-recognised (see Chapter 10), so too the performance of emotional labour skills in the paid work sphere also tends to go under-recognised and under-rewarded. Filby (1992) correctly points out that it would be misleading to argue that all emotional labour deserves 'skilled' status: indeed, 'much emotion work... is untutored and probably poor' (Filby, 1992: 39). Nevertheless, as the foregoing discussion has illustrated, in a number of different contexts, emotional labour is learned through considerable training, and is performed in far from straight forward circumstances.

An extension of this argument of reinforcing stereotypes is that many front-line service jobs entail the performance of tasks as deferential servants – on the aircraft, in the hotel, and in the restaurant, for example. It may be argued that, since the majority of emotional labour jobs are performed by women, this potentially acts to project an image of women as servants – an image already reinforced by the unpaid and problematic status of domestic activities. This is particularly pertinent to those settings comprising mainly women performing emotional labour for a largely male customer group; it is mostly men, for example, who fly business class on airlines, eat business lunches, and stay at hotels on sales conferences. Further, as well as the nurturing and servant roles, some emotional labour jobs also involve women workers emphasising other aspects of their 'feminine' qualities, in particular applying their sexuality as a way of 'keeping the customers happy'. As Hochschild (1983: 182) describes, flight attendants are required to play these different roles simultaneously: 'those of the supportive mother and those of the sexually desirable mate', manifesting themselves in 'both "motherly" behavior and a "sexy" look'. Similarly, Linstead (1995: 196) argues that through the nature of their advertising, airlines 'make no secret of their wish to entice a predominantly male clientele on board in the lucrative first and business sectors with gently erotic evocations'. In general, this message may be more subtle now than in the 1970s – when airlines used such advertising slogans as 'I'm Cheryl, Fly Me' (quoted in Lessor, 1984: 42) and 'We really move our tails for you to make your every wish come true' (quoted in Hochschild, 1983: 93) – but the message remains, nevertheless. Sexuality is similarly present in other settings of emotional labour. Filby (1992), for example, in his study of women working in betting shops, notes the sexual banter between cashiers and (mostly male) customers, which forms part of the employees' task of building customer relations and customer loyalty to that branch. Likewise, Hall (1993) notes the existence of the 'obligatory job flirt' which occurs in many restaurants, again as part of a broader management requirement to 'keep the customer happy'.

However, the arguments over women and emotional labour are less clear cut than some critics have suggested. First, as noted above, it is not necessarily the case that women performing emotional labour experience a negative reaction. Indeed, Wharton (1993) in her study found that women performing emotional labour were significantly more satisfied than their male counterparts engaged in similar types of work. As a result of patterns of socialisation, for example, 'women may be better equipped than men for the interpersonal demands of frontline service work and thus experience those jobs more positively than their male counterparts' (Wharton, 1993: 225). Further, in the longer term, other factors may act in favour of changing the position of women performing emotional labour. First, the growth of jobs requiring emotional labour is resulting in more men needing to manage their emotions as part of the job. As the number of both women and men performing emotional labour rises, this may affect the way emotional labour is delivered, particularly where the clientele is becoming less male dominated. Linstead (1995: 196) notes, for example, the acknowledged need among airline companies to shift the nature of emotional labour in business and first class to attract the growing market in female business travellers. Second, as the emphasis on effective service increases, employees and groups such as trade unions will potentially be able to use this recognised importance as a lever for improving the status and rewards pertaining to those performing these types of jobs. Taking this point further, emotional display does not render women powerless. Indeed, in certain circumstances the 'emotion' could be used as a source of power. Linstead (1995), for example, writing on a strike among Cathay Pacific (CP) flight attendants, points to the attendants' explicit use of emotional display as a means of attracting media attention and public support. The 'perfumed picket line', as it was dubbed by one of the Hong Kong newspapers, gained much more coverage than the CP 'managers in suits'. While the attendants did not win the strike (not least because management was successful in hiring outside crews to operate a reduced service) the flight attendants nevertheless indicated their potential power in 'turn[ing] the seductive skills which company training had developed into an effective weapon to mobilize public opinion' (Linstead, 1995: 190).

CONCLUSION

Analysing the growth and implications of emotional labour underscores a number of broader developments and issues in contemporary industrial society. It is a growth borne not only out of the expansion of the services available to the general public, but also the competition between those services and the identification of customer relations as a key to business success in a competitive environment. Though long established in various areas of employment, a required emotional display and self-management of feelings has become part of an increasing number of jobs. There is every indication too, that this aspect of work will grow further in coming years, as a public increasingly used to a high level of 'customer care' raises its baseline expectation of what constitutes an appropriate level of that 'care' in an ever-widening range of services.

As well as reflecting a growth of, and increased competition between, service providers and the greater significance attaching to customers, emotional labour also underscores certain other issues raised elsewhere in the book. Most notably, emotional labour is an aspect of work which to date has been performed predominantly by women, often while occupying comparatively low positions within their work organisations. It is an aspect of women's work which has also typically been accorded relatively little status. Hence, just as women in general have not typically been the beneficiaries of how the notion of skill has been socially constructed (see Chapter 5) in a similar way, emotional labour has not been accorded prestige or skilled status. Rather, the performing of emotional labour has tended to be seen as something that women are 'naturally' good at – an innate talent rather than an acquired skill.

At the same time, as has been noted, it is important not to adopt too simplistic a view of emotional labour. It is an aspect of work which varies considerably in its nature and degree. Its impact on employees will depend on the character of the individuals involved, and some will be far more predisposed to the requirements of emotional labour than others. Further, for many, emotional labour represents a relatively minor part of their job, not unpleasant and often helping to create a more friendly working environment: smiling at others often elicits a smile in return. It is in those cases where emotional labour expectations are *excessive* that it becomes problematic, potentially giving rise to feelings of alienation and emotional exploitation. Yet, even in these situations, it is clear that workers employ various coping strategies to mitigate the excesses of emotional labour. In their use of various 'survival' strategies to make their job more bearable, emotional labourers are not alone. Workers in all types of occupations adopt a whole range of survival strategies to help them to get through the working day. It is to a broader consideration of such strategies that we now turn.

8 Survival Strategies

INTRODUCTION

This chapter, perhaps more than any other in the book, illustrates the importance of viewing work as a rich and varied domain of human activity. It is concerned with the way employees get through their working day: how they survive the boredom, tedium, monotony, drudgery and powerlessness that characterise many jobs. In examining this issue, it is necessary to cover a wide range of concepts and research evidence. At the same time, there is one central principle around which the discussion is organised: the notion that in order to 'survive' work, people are obliged to become resourceful and creative in developing strategies that allow them to assert some control over, and construct meanings for, the work activities they are instructed by managers to undertake. In the analysis that follows, we are seeking to access the world of the informal which, although normally hidden from the gaze of the outsider, is no less real for the participants. It is a dynamic world where the subjective experiences of individuals are collectively constructed and reconstructed to create shared understandings and develop norms that guide and pattern behaviour. Yet it is also a regulated world where the structural constraints imposed by power-holders (especially managers) limit the actions of individuals and workgroups. The result is a curious mixture of consent and resistance to work. The analysis begins with a discussion of the extent to which work produces conditions of alienation for employees. This is followed by an examination of the way alienating tendencies may be countered through various creative strategies by employees. From an assessment of the empirical research on informal work behaviour, five survival strategies are explored: 'making out', fiddling, joking, sabotage and escaping. Finally, there is an assessment of whether these strategies can be construed as forms of workplace consent or resistance, or both.

ALIENATION: AN OBJECTIVE STATE OR A SUBJECTIVE EXPERIENCE?

The word 'alienation' is freely used in the media (especially in serious late-night TV talk shows and Sunday newspapers) and arises in everyday conversation; yet it remains one of the most contested terms in the academic study of work. In fact, in attempting to define and explain 'alienation' fully it would be possible to write a whole chapter on the concept. We restrict our discussion in this section to outlining two different perspectives on alienation. The first views alienation as an objective state and emanates from the works of Karl Marx, whilst the second introduces elements of subjectivity into the analysis of alienation and stems from a study by Robert Blauner.

Alienation as an Objective State

Marx argues that alienation is embedded in the capitalist labour process (see Chapter 6 above) and therefore is an unavoidable objective state in which all workers find themselves. It manifests itself because in selling their labour power, employees are relinquishing the right to control their own labour, thus discretion over how and when work should be undertaken becomes the prerogative of employers. This subordination of employees to employers (or to managers as agents of capital) makes the activity of work a degrading and dehumanising activity.

> [Under capitalism] all the means for developing production are transformed into means of domination over and exploitation of the producer; that they mutilate the worker into a fragment of a human being, degrade him to become a mere appurtenance, make his work such a torment that its essential meaning is destroyed. (Marx, 1930: 713, quoted in Fox, 1974: 224.)

Thus, rather than representing a potential source of satisfaction in its own right, work under capitalism functions merely as a means of getting money to satisfy needs outside of working hours. As a consequence, employees experience a sense of 'self-estrangement' because, whilst they are in work undertaking the activities as instructed by their managers, they cannot be themselves. They are separated from their true selves; they experience a sense of alienation.

> [The worker] does not affirm himself but denies himself, does not feel content but unhappy, does not develop freely his physical and mental energy but mortifies his body and ruins his mind. The worker therefore only feels himself outside his work, and in his work feels outside himself. He is at home when he is not working, and when he is working he is not at home. His labour is therefore not voluntary, but coerced; it is *forced labour*. It is therefore not the satisfaction of a need; it is merely a *means* to satisfy needs external to it. Its alien character emerges clearly in the fact that as soon as no physical or other compulsion exists, labour is shunned like the plague. External labour, labour in which man alienates himself, is a labour of self-sacrifice, of ·mortification. Lastly, the external character of labour for the worker appears in the fact that it is not his own, but someone else's, that it does not belong to him, that in it he belongs, not to himself, but to another. Just as in religion the spontaneous activity of the human imagination, of the human brain and the

human heart, operates independently of the individual – that is, operates on him as an alien, divine or diabolical activity – in the same way the worker' activity is not his spontaneous activity. It belongs to another; it is the loss of his self. (Marx, 1969: 99–100, emphasis in original.)

Furthermore, the output (the product or object) of a person's labour is not owned by the employee; it becomes the property of the capitalist. Marx considers this significant because the product of one's labour is the physical expression of the effort that has been undertaken – a process he labels 'objectification'. Under capitalism, employees see the product of their labour as something that is distant and separated from themselves. They become estranged from the product of their labour – in other words, it becomes an alien object.

The *alienation* of the worker in his product means not only that his labour becomes an object, an *external* existence, but that it exists *outside him*, independently, as something alien to him, and that it becomes a power on its own confronting him; it means that the life which he has conferred on the object confronts him as something hostile and alien. (Marx, 1969: 97, emphasis in original.)

This alienation has wider repercussions for humankind. Marx argues that, through work, people express their creativity, produce the means of their own existence and hence realise their humanity. This free, creative endeavour is the very purpose of life, but under capitalism work becomes coercion: forced labour. People become estranged from their very nature; they are left alienated from their species being. And in turn, due to this estrangement from their essential nature, people are left estranged from each other: compounding the condition of alienation under capitalism. Figure 8.1 summarises the above discussion by mapping the relationships between the various concepts in Marx's theory of the labour process and alienation. It also suggests how under non-capitalist conditions the problem of alienation may be avoided.

For Marx, the condition of alienation was an objective state under which all employees within capitalist relations suffered. In many ways, this places the concept of alienation beyond empirical investigation because it matters little whether people feel or say they are alienated since the assumption is that the structures of capitalism determine the objective state of alienation. In other words, subjectivity is not part of the analysis, and Marxists are likely to argue that people who claim to be satisfied and fulfilled at work are merely expressing a 'false consciousness': a failure to appreciate the objective reality of their position of subordination and exploitation. Moreover, the Marxist approach to alienation is linked to the work ethic (see Chapter 3 above) because it rests on the fundamental assumption that work *ought* to be intrinsically rewarding. As Anthony (1977: 141) points out:

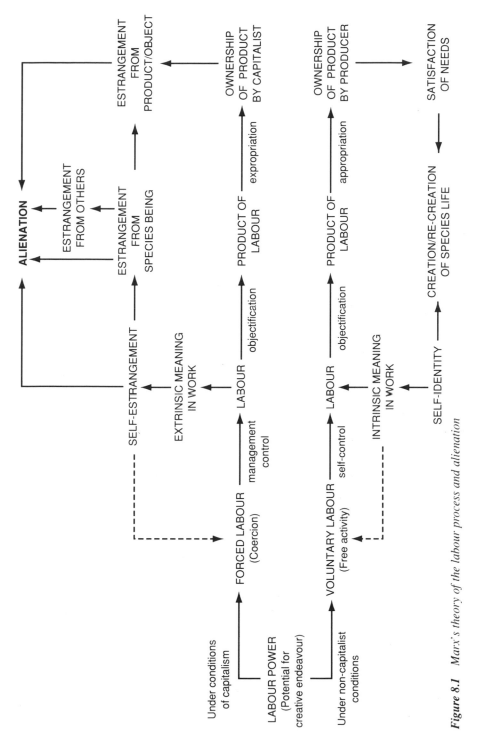

Figure 8.1 *Marx's theory of the labour process and alienation*

For Marx, alienation represents an imperfection in the purity of the ideal of work, which is the only activity that gives man his identity. The essential paradox of alienation is that it is a pathological state of affairs produced in work as the result of an over-emphasis on a work ethic and on work-based values. It becomes possible to speak of man alienated by his work only when he is asked to take work very seriously.

Alienation as a Subjective Experience

To put subjectivity into an analysis of alienation requires the overturning of both assumptions highlighted above: that alienation is not solely an objective state inevitably reproduced under conditions of capitalism, and that work has different meanings for different people. One of the most notable attempts to explore the concept in this manner is that by Blauner (1964). He began from the proposition that 'alienation is a general syndrome made up of a number of different *objective conditions and subjective feelings-states* which emerge from certain relationships between workers and the sociotechnical settings of employment' (Blauner, 1964: 15, emphasis added). He argues that alienation could be broken down into four dimensions, and each of these could be investigated for different workers to enable a profile of alienation to be drawn up. These dimensions are summarised in Table 8.1.

Blauner has been criticised for trivialising Marx's notion of alienation 'by conceptualising it in subjective terms' (T.J. Watson, 1987: 107). However, whilst there are numerous points of criticism that can be levelled at Blauner's work, (not least the degree of thoroughness of the empirical data upon which he based his conclusions; see Eldridge, 1971) the problem of being 'overly subjective' is not one of them. Certainly Blauner was accepting the importance of subjectivity because the implication of his thesis is that different employees will have different alienation profiles. But Blauner was far more interested in using this to generalise about occupational groups, and in particular to assess whether certain types of production technology produced greater alienation than others. In fact, as his analysis progresses, subjectivity disappears from the discussion. If his thesis was truly examining subjectivity, then his focus would have been on individual employees, rather than occupational groups. Moreover, he would probably have been more concerned with exploring whether employees doing similar jobs experience the dimensions of alienation differently, and the extent to which this leads to individual, rather than collective profiles of alienation.

In other words, Blauner, like Marx, was focusing on objective conditions which produced alienation, but rather than generalise about the capitalist system as a whole, he sought to differentiate *between* capitalist enterprises according to their technology, and generalise from this.

There is... no simple answer to the question: Is the factory worker of today an

Table 8.1 Blauner's dimensions of alienation

Alienated state	Definition	Key indicators/measures	Non-alienated state

Powerlessness	Employee is controlled and manipulated by others or by an impersonal system (such as technology) and cannot change or modify this domination.	• Control over conditions of employment
		• Control over immediate work process:
		  - pace of work
		  - method of work
			Freedom and control

Meaninglessness	Employee lacks understanding of the whole work process and lacks a sense of how their own work contributes to the whole.	• Work cycle • Range and variety of tasks • Completeness of task	Purposefulness

Isolation	Employee experiences no sense of belonging in the work situation and is unable or unwilling to identify with the organisation and its goals.	• Type and extent of social interaction
		  - formal
		  - informal
			Belonging

Self-estrangement	Employee gains no sense of identity or personal fulfilment from work, and this detachment means that work is not considered a worthwhile activity in its own right.	• Instrumental attitudes • 'Clock -watching' • Expressions of boredom	Self-expression

Source: Summarised from R. Blauner, *Alienation and Freedom*, University of Chicago Press, 1964, pp. 15–35

alienated worker? Inherent in the techniques of modern manufacturing and the principles of bureaucratic industrial organization are general alienating tendencies. But in some cases the distinctive technology, division of labor, economic structure, and social organization – in other words, the factors that differentiate individual industries – intensify these general tendencies, producing a high degree of alienation; in other cases they minimize and counteract them, resulting instead in control, meaning, and integration. (Blauner, 1964: 166–7.)

Ultimately, this led Blauner to a position of technological determinism: that greater automation would free workers from the drudgery of assembly-lines and machine-minding and would result in decreasing alienation for employees (Blauner, 1964: 182–3). This is an optimistic projection which suggests that the problem of alienation will be resolved within the capitalist framework – a position which, as we have seen in Chapter 6, was vehemently challenged by Braverman (1974) and subsequent labour process theorists.

In spite of these criticisms, Blauner's biggest contribution was to reclaim the concept of alienation from Marxist theorists. In reinterpreting the concept and breaking it down into the four separate dimensions, he provides components of alienation which are potentially variable in their intensity and also measurable (or more accurately, comparable). This shifts alienation from being an absolute to a relative concept, and allows the theoretical possibility of (objective) conditions of alienation producing (subjective) feelings of non-alienation, as well as (objective) non-alienating conditions leading to (subjective) feelings of being alienated. In other words, allowing subjectivity into the discussion of alienation helps to interpret the complexities and dynamics of employee behaviour and orientations to work. Furthermore, it obliges the observer to recognise that there can be multiple meanings and interpretations of behaviour, even though there may be (shared) structural constraints within the work setting.

So, in what ways do employees attempt to combat alienating tendencies at work? As noted above, the central proposition is that employees develop and learn coping strategies which combat alienation by constructing meaning. In some instances the strategies are collectively shared and negotiated, in others they represent individual attempts to survive. As we shall see, the meanings and behaviours are dynamic rather than fixed; plural rather than unitary; and creative rather than mundane. We begin our foray into the domain of the informal by looking at 'making out' on the shopfloor.

'MAKING OUT'

The notion of 'making out' is usually associated with the research undertaken by Michael Burawoy (1979). Like many of the empirical studies discussed in this chapter, Burawoy's method of data collection was based on getting close to the subject under study. It involved participating in the work process in order to experience directly the workplace dynamics and develop an understanding of the meaning and significance of social interaction. With the permission of management, he began work as an employee in the machine shop of an engine plant which was a division of a multinational company in the United States. From this position of participant observer, Burawoy witnessed an elaborate system of informal behaviour by the employees' which regulated the work process and ensured that targets were met, yet provided the opportunity for the workers to reassert some control over their working day. He argues that these unofficial shopfloor activities can be seen as a series of games which employees play. These are games concerned with beating the system, finding the angles, working out the dodges or discovering the loopholes – in other words, 'making out' .

> The game of making out provides a framework for evaluating the productive activities and the social relations that arise out of the organization of work. We can look upon making out, therefore, as comprising a sequence of stages – of encounters between machine operators and the social or non-social objects that regulate the conditions of work. The rules of the game are experienced as a set of externally imposed relationships. The art of making out is to manipulate those relationships with the purpose of advancing as quickly as possible from one stage to the next. (Burawoy, 1979: 51.)

Burawoy builds on the pioneering work of Roy (1952, 1953 and 1955) to explore how the game of making out is typically concerned with ways that employees get around the formal rules and regulations laid down by management. At its simplest, making out can be interpreted as the means through which employees secure themselves higher earnings by creatively manipulating the incentive systems (primarily piece-rate payment schemes). However, Burawoy's research led him to argue that economic gain is not the sole motivator for making out. Rather, he suggests that a range of interlinking motives are at play: the reduction of fatigue; the desire to pass time; the relief of boredom; the social and psychological rewards of making out on a tough job; and the social stigma and frustration of failing to 'make out' on an easy job (Burawoy, 1979: 85).

He describes the elaborate series of informal rules and practices that he and his co-workers engaged in as they joined the game of making out. Yet, in so doing they were adapting to the alienating tendencies in the work; they were manipulating the management's rules for their own ends, but they were not fundamentally *challenging* the rules nor undermining management's prerogative to set the rules. In fact, through playing the game of making out they were *consenting* to the formal rules and structures imposed by management.

> The issue is: which is logically and empirically prior, playing the game or the legitimacy of the rules? Here I am not arguing that playing the games rests on a broad consensus; on the contrary, consent rests upon – is constructed

through – playing the game. The game does not reflect an underlying harmony of interests; on the contrary, it is responsible for and generates that harmony.... . The game becomes an end in itself, overshadowing, masking, and even inverting the conditions out of which it emerges. (Burawoy, 1979: 81–2.)

Burawoy's conclusions are important in overturning the assumptions, previously forwarded by theorists such as Crozier (1964), Mayo (1933) and Roethlisberger and Dickson (1966), that games undermine management objectives because they are the expression of a counter-control by the shopfloor. Burawoy contends that far from representing a threat to capitalism, games 'manufacture consent' towards the extant social relations of production and help secure the creation of surplus value. In this way Burawoy shifts the focus of analysis away from control towards consent. He identifies the way that the labour process under advanced capitalism cannot be explained solely in terms of management's control over employees, but must also take into account the extent to which employees are persuaded to consent to their own subordination (Burawoy, 1985: 126) thereby cooperating with management's overall objectives. This refocusing addresses some of the criticisms levelled at Braverman's (1974) analysis of the labour process which dwelt upon the centrality of the labour control objectives of management (see Chapter 6).

Table 8.2 *Fundamental contradictions in managing the labour process*

Control	vs	Consent
Compliance secured through:		Commitment enlisted through:
Direction		**Initiative**
Monitoring/surveillance		**Autonomy**
Discipline		**Diligence**
Limit discretion	vs	Harness discretion
Close supervision (low trust)	vs	Autonomy (high trust)
Disposable labour (numerical flexibility)	vs	Dependable labour (commitment)
Cohesive workforce	vs	Collective solidarity

The tensions between control and consent have been subsequently brought into sharper focus by Hyman (1987). Figure 8.2 illustrates the four key contradictions embedded in the labour process which emerge from Hyman's discussion (1987: 39-43). The argument starts from the premise that management is faced with two competing pressures: on the one hand, there is a need to control and direct employees to ensure that production and performance targets are met; whilst on the other hand, there is a requirement to enlist the skill and co-operation of employees in meeting those targets. Therefore, the first contradiction is the need for management simultaneously to limit and harness discretion: to limit discretion which employees might apply against management's interests and harness those aspects of their discretion which aid profitable production.

> For even though capital owns (and therefore has the right to 'control') both means of production and the worker, in practice capital must surrender the means of production to the 'control' of the workers for their actual use in the production process. All adequate analysis of the contradictory relationship of labour to capital in the workplace depends on grasping this point. (Cressey and MacInnes, 1980: 14.)

This leads to the second fundamental contradiction in the labour process: the need to impose systems of close supervision, to ensure that management objectives are complied with, versus the need to provide the space and freedom for the employees' creative discretion alluded to above. Friedman (1976) argues that managers are therefore faced with a choice between two broad supervision strategies of either trying to establish 'direct control' (involving the simplification of work and close supervision) or 'responsible autonomy' (wider discretion over how work is completed, with consequently less supervision). These strategies do not resolve the contradiction – not least because they are mutually exclusive. Direct control might be the best way to guarantee compliance, but at the cost of commitment; responsible autonomy may enlist commitment, but does not guarantee compliance with management wishes. So, recognising the two strategies does not resolve the capitalist dilemma, although it may alert some managers to the possibility of placing a different emphasis on control or consent, depending on the group of employees: responsible autonomy for highly skilled core employees in scarce supply, but direct control over low-skilled peripheral workers who are easily replaced. But even responsible autonomy might need to be moderated with some direct control given 'there are few (if any) workers whose voluntary commitment requires no external reinforcement' (Hyman, 1987: 42). More cynically, however, it might be argued that responsible autonomy is a ploy by managers to disguise their dependency on the workforce. By emphasising autonomy, discretion and an absence of close supervision, they can engage in a more subtle attempt to obscure the exploitative nature of the labour process, and particularly the commodity status of labour.

This leads to the third contradiction: whether to treat labour as disposable or dependable. If labour power is considered a commodity to be hired or fired according to the changing requirements of the business (reflecting seasonal, weekly or even daily fluctuations in demand) then managers will seek to maximise the disposability of labour. However, operating a hire-and-fire policy is likely to undermine the commitment of employees to the organisation, and might alert those workers whose skills are in scarce supply, or who are strategically placed, to their centrality to the success of the organisation. Conversely, to implement policies of dependability, such as employment security and the development of an internal labour market, reduces the ability of managers to adapt the labour force to match fluctuations in demand. Indeed, this trade-off between commitment and flexibility has become one of the central problems for contemporary human resource management (for fuller discussion see Noon, 1992: 23–4).

The fourth dilemma for managers lies in the contradiction between cohesion and collectivity amongst the workforce. Managers recognise the need to create a cooperative, cohesive workforce for the benefit of profitable production, but the problem for management is that such a cohesive workforce may develop a collective solidarity that could be used against management's interests. In other words, the workforce cohesion necessary to meet management objectives potentially also provides the conditions for collective solidarity which may lead workers to challenge those objectives. In a similar way, policies aimed at individualising the workforce and controlling the individual worker (through, for example, performance-related pay, appraisal and promotion) potentially undermine the basis of cooperation between employees that management invariably requires to meet performance targets.

Overall, Burawoy's proposition that, within the workplace, 'coercion must be supplemented by the organisation of consent' (1979: 27) helps to synthesise the above contradictions embedded in the capitalist labour process. Essentially, the contradictions reflect the fundamental differences of interest between employers and employees. It is in the employer's interest to secure as much surplus value as possible from the labours of employees, whilst it is in the employees' interest to limit the exploitation and extract full payment for their effort. Consequently, employers and managers seek to obscure the expropriation of surplus value, and it is precisely because the game of making out aids this process of obscuring the exploitation that managers are generally content to go along with it. It is only when making out becomes counter-productive that managers seek to suppress it.

> The participation [of workers] in games has the effect of concealing relations of production while co-ordinating the interests of workers and management.... It is through their common interest in the preservation of work games that the interests of workers and shop management are co-ordinated. The workers are interested in the relative satisfactions games can offer while management, from supervisors to departmental superintendents, is concerned with securing

co-operation and surplus.... The *day-to-day adaptations of workers create their own ideological effects that become focal elements in the operation of capitalist control.* (Burawoy, 1985: 38–9, emphasis in original.)

Whilst Burawoy's analysis is persuasive and helps to explain why alienating work is endured more often than it is challenged, two important criticisms can be levelled at his thesis. The first criticism is that Burawoy's analysis is gender neutral. The workplace he studied was composed entirely of men, so he had no opportunity to explore the importance and effect of gender on the social organisation of production. It could be argued that gender could have an important impact upon several of the features Burawoy characterised as being critical to the manufacture of consent: the shopfloor culture encouraging competition, game playing as an end in itself, the structure of work, the social hierarchy and workgroup dynamics (for a fuller discussion, see Davies, 1990). Of course a similar point may be made about ethnicity and other ways employees are stratified.

The second criticism is that in his eagerness to explain consent, Burawoy tends to overstate it. This blinds him to the possibility that there remains a subversive element in some of the making out he describes. Whilst being incorporated into the system, the employees are still challenging it through constantly subverting the capitalist control of the labour process by continually inventing new ways of making out. As Clawson and Fantasia (1983: 676) comment,

> Over and over again, Burawoy takes some feature of the workplace which had generally been identified as evidence of workers' progressive potential, and argues that it actually serves to reinforce the system. He does not seem to understand that a phenomenon can do both things at the same time, that something can be itself and its opposite. In other words, Burawoy's Marxist argument lacks a dialectical analysis.

This last point needs restating a little more clearly because it has important implications for the analysis in the rest of the chapter. What seems to have happened is that in presenting a case for the importance of consent on the shopfloor, Burawoy has allowed the role of resistance to slip from view. Making out is not just about consent: it may also represent a form of resistance. In other words, in considering making out as a survival strategy we should be aware of its dual impact. Moreover, this is a cautionary note to bear in mind as we turn to the next survival strategy: workplace fiddling.

FIDDLING

Fiddling is not an exceptional activity: almost everyone is at it. Indeed, it has been estimated that between 75 and 92 per cent of people regularly add to their

incomes in ways that are technically against the law (Mars, 1982: 1). As
discussed in Chapter 10, for some people this will entail earning income which
is not declared to the Inland Revenue, thereby attempting to evade tax payments.
For others, fiddling involves adding to their total income by theft from the
workplace, for example, taking office stationery for private use, making private
calls on the office telephone, doing repairs to personal items using the company's
equipment and materials, or artificially inflating expense claims. The list of
fiddles at work is as extensive and varied as human ingenuity, and for many it
represents an important additional (albeit covert) element in their total rewards,
and an important way of altering the balance of the effort–reward bargain.

Various researchers have unearthed the fiddles which are endemic in
particular occupations (see for example, Ditton, 1977, on fiddling among bread
salesmen and a discussion of other studies of fiddling), but it is Mars (1982) who
has perhaps gone furthest in analysing the practice and significance of workplace
fiddles. It is useful to summarise his work briefly here for it reveals not only the
relationship between forms of fiddling and the occupational structure, but also
illustrates how, for many, the motive for fiddling goes far beyond any
anticipated financial benefit – indeed the frequently small financial gain would
often not seem to justify the risks involved unless other contributory factors were
influencing the decision to fiddle.

Mars (1982) has developed a typology of fiddling and linked this to
distinctive characteristics of different occupations, in particular whether or not
jobs are subject to extensive rules and close supervision, and whether or not occupations involve group activity and are characterised by strong workgroup controls. The presence or absence of each of these characteristics translates into four
different occupational categories and, in turn, four different fiddle patterns
(shown in Figure 8.2).

First, 'hawks' are people who work as individuals rather than as part of a

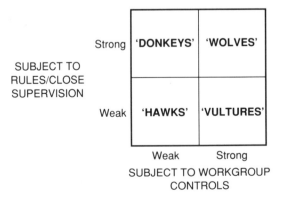

Source: from G. Mars, *Cheats at Work: An Anthropology of Workplace Crime*, London:
Allen & Unwin, 1982, p. 29.

Figure 8.2   *A typology of occupations*

group and also are not subject to close supervision: someone owning and operating a small business would fit into this category. 'Donkeys', in contrast, are those with jobs that are highly constrained by rules and who work in relative isolation from others – such as shop assistants and many assembly-line workers. Third are 'wolves' – people who according to Mars (1982: 2) 'work – and steal – in packs', with groups operating according to clearly defined rules, controls and hierarchies governing their fiddling activity. Examples here might include airport baggage-handlers and dock gangs. Mars (p. 89–92) describes the activities of a dust-cart crew to illustrate the organisation and activities of such a group. Each crew member was allocated a particular kind of discarded item to collect which could later be sold. A clearly defined hierarchy had developed amongst the crew, ranging from the most senior crew member, with rights over collecting scrap metal (the most valuable part of the rubbish) to the newest member of the team collecting deposit-paid bottles (the least valuable of the saleable refuse). The fourth category in Mars' typology are the 'vultures' who need the support of a group in order to fiddle, but who act alone. Mars includes such occupations as travelling salesmen and bread roundsmen in this category where group support may be needed to collude with a fiddle (for example, the delivery drivers who share the knowledge about which places they can deliver short to, where checks are unlikely to be carried out, and where to sell the extra goods afterwards). Such fiddles involve the sharing of knowledge although each person fiddles alone.

In drawing such distinctions, Mars usefully points to the different opportunities and constraints for fiddling which characterise different jobs. Yet, whatever the apparent constraints characterising some jobs, the reality remains that fiddling of one form or another is possible in (and endemic to) almost all occupations. Thus, for a large part of the workforce, the rewards from their job comprise not only the visible element (their wage or salary, paid holidays, pension, and so on) but also an invisible element, reflecting fiddled goods and/or fiddled time. Even in jobs which at first sight appear very highly constrained by close supervision and/or detailed rules governing behaviour, fiddling still takes place. Moreover, it occurs even when penalties are severe and where the possible amounts to be fiddled are small in comparison to the gravity of the sanctions applicable if the person is caught. This leads to the conclusion that any financial benefit from fiddling at work is only one motive, and, for many people, not necessarily the most important one. For some, fiddling provides the only interest in an otherwise monotonous work day – a survival strategy. Indeed, the risk element of getting caught may add a *frisson* of excitement. For others, fiddling may be an expression of frustration or resentment, 'a way of hitting out at the boss, the company, the system or the state' (Mars, 1982: 23). To illustrate this resentment motive, Mars quotes from a supermarket cashier who fiddled the till because she disliked the way she was treated by the shop management, but then stopped fiddling after moving to a different supermarket where she found the atmosphere much friendlier.

Although the types, motives and outcomes of worker-initiated fiddles are many and varied, this picture is made even more complex when management's approach to fiddling is taken into account. One might expect that fiddling is something which is carried out by workers *in spite of* the best endeavours by management to prevent it. In practice, however, it is only in a proportion of cases where management is actively disposed against worker fiddles and assiduously tries to stamp them out. In other cases, management 'turns a blind eye' to fiddling activity, provided that it does not rise above a certain level, and particularly where it involves fiddling a third party (for example, the customer) rather than the employing organisation. Why should management collude with fiddling in this way? There are several possible motives. Partly, it may reflect management's awareness of the near impossibility of stamping out fiddling entirely and if one form of fiddling is suppressed, another is likely to develop to take its place. Also, being indulgent towards fiddling activity may help management maintain a coop-erative workforce – if all fiddling was heavily policed by management this might increase workforce discontent and reduce the degree of worker consent to other management objectives. Partly too, fiddling from third parties may represent for management a form of subsidy for low wages. The availability of fiddles to those working in hotels and restaurants, for example – ranging from not declaring income from tips to the tax authorities to fiddles related to the food and drink served – may enable management to pay lower wages than would otherwise be necessary to recruit and retain staff. Similarly, among Ditton's (1977: 17) bread salesmen (generally low paid and working long hours) morale was sustained by sales supervisors indicating a 'solution' to the threat of the salesmen having to make up shortages in takings: over-charging customers. And partly too, management may ignore employee fiddles because they themselves are also involved in fiddling, either for their own monetary gain or to protect their own position. Mars (1982: 68) for example, recounts the case of a check-out operator in a supermarket where, to balance stocks against stock records, operators were asked to fiddle the customers.

> Every now and then one of the managers will come up to you, usually with a packet of tea, and put it close to the till, near the sweets and chocolates so that it can be taken as a purchase, and say 'put that through a couple of hundred times will you'. There's never any explanation of *why* you're to do it, what it's for – but it's to sort out their stocks. It is usually done just before and just after stock-taking and it'll just be for a day. (Quoted in Mars, 1982: 68, emphasis in original.)

The advent of electronic bar-code readers may give less scope for both management and cashiers to fiddle customers' bills. However, such devices do not make areas 'fiddle-proof' but simply call forth other ways of fiddling (for example, by passing goods of family members or friends through the check-out without reading the code or collecting money for them).

Although a covert activity, fiddling of one form or another appears to be an integral element of most occupations. In terms of a 'survival strategy', fiddling represents a clearer breaking of the rules, whereas making out rather involves working within the rules. But the distinction is not always clear cut. What is clear, however, is that for most people involved in some form of fiddling at work, the monetary value of the fiddling is likely to be small – so much so that the efforts required to prevent it are often not seen to be worthwhile, for reasons noted above. Fiddling can yield additional income, but, for many, a central benefit of fiddling is as a source of other social and psychological gain to individuals responding to aspects of their job, those in authority over them, their co-workers or their customers.

JOKING

The most disappointing aspect of examining the role of humour in work organisations is that when the humour is taken out of the context in which it emerged, it usually ceases to be funny. It is rather like having to explain a joke – it generally ruins it. Consequently, at the risk of ruining some good jokes, this section explores the significance of humour at work. It is important to begin the analysis by acknowledging the pioneering work of the anthropologist Radcliffe-Brown (1952) who identified the significance of the 'joking relationship' between people.

> What is meant by the term 'joking relationship' is a relationship between two persons in which one is by custom permitted, and in some instances, required to tease or to make fun of the other, who, in turn, is required to take no offence... The joking relationship is a peculiar combination of friendliness and antagonism. The behaviour is such that in any other social context it would express and arouse hostility, but it is not meant seriously and must not be taken seriously. There is a pretence of hostility and real friendliness. To put it another way, the relation is one of permitted disrespect. (Radcliffe-Brown, 1952: 90–1)

A primary function of the joking relationship is the prevention or reduction of antagonism; typically it develops between people who are required to be in close contact for long periods of time, yet who have some divergence of interests. Not surprisingly, therefore, the concept can be applied to work settings where teasing and banter are part of the daily routine of organisational life. For example, Bradney (1957) used the concept of the joking relationship to explain how sales staff in a large department store regulated their interpersonal relations. She argued that joking helped to mitigate the intrinsic antagonisms caused by the formal work roles and structures.

There is clearly a divergence of interests among sales assistants... as a result of their formal relationship. Each wants to increase her own sales – to earn both a better living and the approval of her employer – and is in competition with the others to do this. There is also every likelihood of hostility and conflict between them when they interrupt and hinder each other just at a time when this interferes most with selling. (Bradney, 1957: 183.)

The 'joking relationship' provides the employees with an informal structure through which differences of interest and status are negotiated through playful insults and teasing ('permitted disrespect') rather than with open hostility. Bradney concludes:

By means of a tradition of joking behaviour between its members, which is quite unknown to the management, this store is able to avoid considerable tension and disagreement that would be likely to occur as a result of the difficulties inherent in its formal structure. In so doing it gives the employees a source of positive enjoyment in carrying out their routine activities and incidentally, by means of this, renews their energy to cope even more adequately with their routine problems. (Bradney, 1957: 186–7.)

To take another example, Spradley and Mann (1975) used participant observation to explore the working lives of cocktail waitresses, and demonstrate how humour reinforces the gender division of labour within the cocktail bar. The waitresses worked closely with the male bartenders and strong bonds developed between them. Yet there was a clear status differential, with the waitresses in a subordinate position. Waitresses quickly learned that the needs of the bartenders came first because they had the power to make the waitresses' work comfortable or difficult. The joking relationship between the barmen and the waitresses was one means by which any conflict caused by this power imbalance was mediated. The bartenders would use humour to assert their status, cover their own mistakes and to reprimand a waitress. On the other hand, the waitresses employed humour to assert themselves, particularly as a response to feelings of unfairness and powerlessness. Thus, conclude Spradley and Mann (1975: 100):

Anger and frustration are dissipated and feelings of inequality felt by the waitresses are deflected.... It creates a buffer between the waitress and bartender in potential conflict situations and provides a means for handling inadequate role performances that occur in full public view.... But the joking relationship also maintains the status inequality of female waitresses and reinforces masculine values. By providing a kind of 'safety valve' for the frustrations created for women in this small society, joking behaviour insures that the role of female waitresses remains unchanged.

This suggests that humour plays an important role in enabling an employee to cope with the inevitable frustrations and tensions of working life. As a form of safety valve, it allows an individual to let off steam, without challenging the power structures and inequalities that have lead to the frustration in the first instance (C. P. Wilson, 1979). Spradley and Mann's (1975) cocktail waitresses enjoyed moments where they asserted themselves through humour, but the gendered power structure remained intact. Similarly, Boland and Hoffman (1983) in a study of a small machine shop, noted how the machinists would frequently put cartoons into the steel drums containing the finished pieces for the quality inspectors at the customer's plant. The jokes poke fun at the competence of the inspectors and management, compared with the skill and judgement of employees in the machine shop. The jokes display a disrespect for the customer.

Joking at work is a way of challenging authority structures. In other words, jokes are an expression of the informal triumphing over the formal (Douglas, 1975). This raises the question of whether humour may be construed as a subversive activity at work. Empirical studies of humour in fact reveal very few examples where humour is being used in a subversive manner. One such example can be found in Westwood's (1984) study of a clothing factory. As participant observer, she cites a 'prank' that resulted in the end-of-day buzzer being set off ten minutes early and the women fleeing the building with glee, fully aware that it was not the official leaving time.

> The next day management instituted an investigation into what was termed 'the incident'. The shopfloor was absolutely delighted that their speedy exodus had caused such obvious pain to management. Everyone who was asked about it shook their heads wisely, at once 'agreeing' with management's view that this was a very serious matter, while keeping quiet about the identity of the buzzer-pusher. (Westwood, 1984: 91.)

Incidents such as these are few and far between, however, and tend to represent occasions where the humour has 'got out of hand'. What is striking from the case evidence is the extent to which humour is highly regulated and ritualised by the workgroups. Far from subverting authority, humour merely issues mild challenges which seem more about preserving the status quo than overturning it. Indeed, it could be argued that jokes provide an outlet for the expression of frustration and discontent which might otherwise build up unchecked, and eventually become channelled into activities that have more serious consequences for the organisation (see the discussion on sabotage below).

It is also apparent from the examples cited so far that humour seems to be playing a role in establishing a shared group identity. This occurs through a process of social regulation whereby the members of a work-setting use humour as one of a range of cultural devices to establish group norms and perpetuate the group's existing dominant values. Humour thereby reinforces the existing social structure and is performing a boundary function (Linstead, 1985a: 744) by protecting the group from outsiders. For example, in a vivid description of the role of humour amongst engineering workers in a vehicle plant, Collinson (1988) reveals how the supervisors and white-collar staff became the butt of jokes for the engineers: jokes which explicitly denigrated them as being stupid, manipulative and effeminate, and hence different from the hardworking, proudly masculine 'fellas' on the shopfloor. Newcomers and deviants were also controlled by humour. For example, the apprentices were subjected to initiations which range from embarrassing (being sent for a 'long stand') to the degrading: 'Pancake Tuesday is always celebrated by "greasing the bollocks" of the apprentices with emulsion then "locking them in the shithouse, bollock naked"' (Collinson, 1988: 189). These practical jokes 'not only instructed new members on how to act and react, but also constituted a test of the willingness of initiates to be part of the male group and to accept its rules' (Collinson, 1988: 188). It was all about bringing people into line; for example, Collinson was told in reference to a lad who entered the company with 'diplomas galore':

> They had a French letter on his back by ten o'clock. They had him singing and dancing in the loo with the pretext of practising for a pantomime... we soon brought him round to our way of thinking. (Collinson, 1988: 189.)

Whilst undertaking the research, Collinson, as an obvious outsider, also found himself the butt of humour, ranging from walking round with paper flowers on his back to getting a suggested title for his research: 'How I Wasted Twelve Months' (Collinson, 1988: 190). More importantly though, humour was used by the engineers to control their colleagues who were considered not to be working hard enough under the collective bonus scheme. Humour was a way of bringing co-workers into line in order to maximise earnings. The effect of all this was eloquently summed up by the engineer who commented that:

> The men are the gaffers now. They watch each other like hawks. The nature of the blokes is such that they turn on each other.... You're more worried about what the men think than the gaffers.... I'm just as bad if there's someone not working. (Collinson, 1988: 197.)

Conformity and compliance at work can also be encouraged by humour in another way: by obscuring the monotony of the work process. This is vividly demonstrated by Roy's (1960) participant observation as a machine operator in a factory (examined in Chapter 4 above). When Roy first joined the factory he became acutely aware of how tedious the work was, but as he became embroiled in the jokes and pranks on the shopfloor, he found himself distracted from the boredom. Many of the jokes became predictable daily events – 'banana time', 'peach time', 'window time' and so on – and these rituals suppressed some of the drudgery of the 12-hour working day by punctuating it with moments of humour. Indeed, it was only after a serious argument had broken out, causing the social cohesion of the workgroup to break up and all interaction to be 'strictly business', that Roy was reminded of the tedium of the work process and began to experience fatigue. In other words, it was humour that provided a means of coping with boredom.

So far, the analysis has assumed that humour is meaningful. But is this necessarily the case? Can humour be interpreted as merely frivolous activity which does *not* have a serious impact within work organisations. This perspective stems from humour being seen as a taken-for-granted part of everyday life (Linstead, 1985a) and therefore joking at work is considered to have no significance beyond the broader social role it performs in establishing our humanity and individuality. From this point of view, the practical joking and the repartee revealed by the studies cited above are merely examples of employees taking a break from work by indulging in a pleasurable activity. For example, Westwood (1984) notes that a favourite joke of some of the women in the factory she studied was to:

Draw lewd pictures of penises and naked men and women, give them captions and send them around the units hoping that they would embarrass some of the other women and provoke a response.... Written jokes were passed around and sniggered at through the working day. It all added excitement and 'a bit of a laff' to the factory days. Sex, of course, was a crucial ingredient and always managed to spice up the end of the day. (Westwood, 1984: 91.)

Certainly humour allows people to distance themselves from the unpleasant and boring aspects of work (Cohen and Taylor, 1976: 34), as exemplified by Roy's (1960) account or the engineering worker from Collinson's study (1988: 185) who commented that 'Some days it feels like a fortnight.... I had to stop myself getting bored so I increased the number of pranks at work'. However, to disregard all humour at work as insignificant activity would be misguided. As Linstead (1985a: 762–3) points out, in creating a framework for 'non-real' or 'play' activity, humour allows risks to be taken in social exchange, taboo subjects to be broached and sensitive issues to be brought into the open. These are far from frivolous activities, given that they might reinforce or challenge the existing social order. In other words, as theorists of postmodernism are keen to remind us, play is a serious activity.

So what general conclusions can be drawn? A difficulty faced when attempting to generalise about the significance of humour in work organisations is assessing the impact of subjectivity. The meaning of 'a joke' is negotiated by the participants of a setting, but its significance may vary from individual to individual. The same humorous incident can be perceived in various ways and may have alternative meanings for the different participants. However, irrespective of the specific interpretation an individual puts on a humorous event, the empirical evidence suggests a common theme: joking at work plays an important regulatory function by providing a means of expression that assists group cohesion, deflects attention from the dehumanising aspects of work and acts to preserve the existing power hierarchy. In this sense, humour is a vital factor in obscuring the social relations of production, and suppressing the alienating tendencies of work.

SABOTAGE

The notion of sabotage often conjures up the image of people engaged in wilful acts of destruction, as retribution for some felt injustice: from the Luddites in the 1820s who destroyed the machinery that was progressively replacing their jobs, to the more contemporary examples of the sacked accounts clerk whose last act is to reformat the computer's hard disk, erasing all the pay-roll information; or the newspaper sub-editor whose anger with management led him to reword a new story so that the initial letter of each paragraph formed the word 'bollocks' when read vertically. However, studies of sabotage (for example, Dubois, 1979; Edwards and Scullion, 1982; Taylor and Walton, 1971) suggest that this popular image of sabotage fails to account for the complexity and subtlety of motivation and method. In particular, Linstead (1985b) identifies two key problems in the analysis of sabotage: first, the difficulty of trying to interpret the action, especially whether it represented an intentional, malicious attempt to destroy or disrupt the work process or the product. Second, there is the problem of whether or not to designate the action as rational behaviour. Should all acts of sabotage be attributed to a logical cause, even in the absence of a specific declaration of intent? Both these problems highlight the need for specific contextual information before it is possible to understand the meanings and motives of behaviour which, on the surface, may appear to be an act of sabotage.

These problems make any generalisation about sabotage fraught with difficulties, not least the danger of understating the importance of the subjective experience of the supposed saboteur. Nevertheless, it is possible to classify acts of sabotage into two broad categories: a temporary expression of frustration or an attempt to assert control (classifications loosely based on Taylor and Walton, 1971). As with the case of humour, acts of sabotage may simultaneously have different meanings for different people involved, so in practice there is far more complexity than this simple typology might suggest. First, sabotage can represent a temporary expression of frustration with the work process, rules, managers, co-workers, or indeed any aspect of the organisation. In such circumstances sabotage is likely to be the wilful malicious act of a frustrated individual. The anger is placated and the tension dissipated through, for example, kicking the photocopier or being intentionally rude to a customer. Although undesirable in the eyes of management, the consequences of such sabotage are transient and generally offer no serious threat. Such incidents may even be seen as tolerable and necessary expressions of dissent which act as a kind of safety valve. Second, sabotage can be understood as an attempt to assert control over the work process, thus presenting a direct challenge to authority, and consequently far more serious for management. In some circumstances such sabotage may be expressed as individual action (for example, halting a machine by, quite literally, 'putting a spanner in the works'); in others, a meaningful challenge can only be orchestrated through collective action (for example, customs officers at an airport 'working to rule' by checking every passenger, thus causing enormous disruptions).

The difficulty is that in practice many acts of sabotage do not easily fit these categories, but are located in a grey area between the two. Consider the following example cited by Taylor and Walton (1971: 228).

When 600 shipyard workers employed on the new Cunarder Q.E.2 finished on schedule they were promptly sacked by John Brown's, the contractors involved. With what looked like a conciliatory gesture they were invited to a party in the ship's luxurious new bar, which was specially opened for the occasion. The men became drunk, damaged several cabins, and smashed the Royal Suite to pieces.

One interpretation might be that this was a rational act of reasserting control by a group of workers reflecting their alienation from the product of their labour. Another interpretation: the frustration of the sacking, linked to the indignity of being invited to 'celebrate' this, unleashed a temporary destructive urge. Then again, perhaps the men became so drunk that they lost any sense of rational intent and would have gone on the rampage irrespective of where they were drinking. All three interpretations might be correct. Indeed, each might be applicable to different workers: the behaviour may have been the same, but the reasons behind it may have differed, and if questioned, the workers might have attributed different meanings and significance to their behaviour.

Analysing sabotage becomes even more confusing because some actions may have destructive or damaging results without there being any malevolence in the minds of the perpetrators. Indeed, there are numerous instances when attempts to adjust the work process to achieve productivity targets, and thus 'make out', carry the risk of potential negative long-term consequences. For example, Taylor and Walton (1971: 232) cite the practice in aircraft assembly of using an instrument called a 'tap' which allows the wing bolts to be more easily inserted but potentially weakens the overall structure. Using the tap is strictly prohibited by factory rules, yet its use continues covertly because without it production cannot function effectively. So, should the workers who use 'taps' be described as saboteurs? Or are they merely irresponsible workers? Are they even irresponsible if their ingenuity in making out by using the tap results in increased production? Or do they become irresponsible saboteurs only if a plane crashes as a result of their short cuts?

In the following example there is little evidence of malicious intent behind the worker's actions; he is easing the work, making out as best he can within the rules set by management.

> The engines passed the [worker] rapidly on a conveyor. His instructions were to test all the nuts and if he found *one* or *two* loose to tighten them, but if three or more were loose he was not expected to have time to tighten that many. In such cases he marked the engine with chalk and it was later set aside from the conveyor and given special attention. The superintendent found that the number of engines so set aside reached an annoying total in the day's work. He made several unsuccessful attempts to locate the trouble. Finally, by carefully watching all the men on the conveyor line, he discovered that the [worker] was unscrewing a *third* nut whenever he found two already loose. It was easier to loosen *one* nut than to tighten two. (Mathewson, 1931: 238, emphasis in original, cited in Hodson, 1991: 281.)

Similarly, in the next example the employee's behaviour reflects a frustration with the conditions of work imposed by management. It is irresponsible behaviour, but is it sabotage?

> One of the young male workers [in the brewery] took a bottle in his hand and made a throwing motion with it. Later, on break, I asked him what he was throwing at. He replied that he was not throwing at anything in particular.... He said that he didn't want to do any damage, that he was just bored and that it would be fun to lob bottles out like grenades and watch them crash and blow up.... He added, 'It's so dull out there I'd just like to make something happen, to have something interesting to do or see' (Molstad, 1986: 231.)

Moreover, there may be occasions where the consequence of an act of sabotage is separated in time and space from the saboteur. For example, devising and intentionally spreading computer viruses is a malicious act of sabotage, yet the perpetrators may have no specific organisational target for their actions. Their motives seem to be the challenge of creating something that frequently destroys the work of others, but the consequences of their actions may never be known to the perpetrators as they remain unaware of how extensively and to whom the virus spreads.

In trying to generalise about sabotage, as in the case of joking, we are faced with the difficulty of interpreting the behaviour of individuals and understanding the meaning those individuals attribute to it. It is impossible to interpret all acts that have destructive consequences as being planned, rational behaviour with malicious intent. Indeed, stupidity, thoughtlessness and irrationality may better explain the behaviour in some circumstances. However, whilst making out, joking and, to some extent, fiddling are widely tolerated by management, sabotage is not. It is viewed as a negative activity, perhaps because it presents a direct challenge to authority, and carries a more easily quantifiable cost: the damage and loss of production, customers, and so on. Nevertheless, consistent with the other forms of informal behaviour, sabotage can also be interpreted as a way that employees (individually and collectively) respond to alienating tendencies at work.

ESCAPING

The term 'escape' can be applied in two ways that are relevant for our present discussion: physical escape through (temporarily or permanently) quitting the job, or mental escape through withdrawing into one's own thoughts. Physical escape is more easy to identify as it can be represented in job turnover figures and levels of absence. A high labour turnover indicates some dissatisfaction with the job – although sources of this dissatisfaction may be diverse and difficult to pinpoint: pay, conditions, job content, promotion opportunities, superordinates, co-workers, recognition, equity, or some combination of these. Similarly, as noted in Chapter 4, voluntary absence is used by a significant proportion of people as a temporary respite from the pressures and frustrations contained within many work settings.

Mental withdrawal is more complex in that it can take a variety of forms. One way of coping with boredom, for example, is to retreat from conscious activity into the realms of daydream. The work is performed in an automaton-like fashion, relying on internalised routines (as discussed in Chapter 5) which act to free the person to concentrate on thoughts outside of work. In this sense, the person can 'escape' into a world of their own; indeed, this can be the only way of coping for some service sector workers (such as flight attendants) who are obliged to maintain a cheerful façade for hours on end (discussed further in Chapter 7).

Physical and mental withdrawal are not mutually exclusive categories. For example, a person may drift into a daydream, planning how to escape from a particular job, and subsequently enact this plan, perhaps by gaining qualifications at night school, or securing a small business grant, or playing the lottery. So the daydream may be an outlandish fantasy or an attainable goal. Others might want escape not for themselves but for their family, so people find themselves engaging in stoic tolerance of their particular work circumstances in the hope that this will secure a better future for daughters and sons. As Westwood (1984: 235) observes from her study of hosiery workers, '[the] women wanted their daughters to have the opportunity to pursue education and training as a means to a life which would be more autonomous. There was a strong sense from the women that they did not want their daughters to be undervalued or wasted in the way they had been.' A similar attitude is evident amongst male workers, particularly for their sons. To take an example from Collinson's (1992) study of engineering workers.

[Alf, 30 years old] feels imprisoned on the shopfloor with little possibility of promotion.... Investing in the self-sacrificing role of parental breadwinner, Alf holds on to a belief in 'personal success' and dignity.... He insists, 'I've not done too bad, I keep me family. But it's too late for me. I've been telling the lad I want him to do better than I've done. He'll have every opportunity I didn't have. I'm probably more ambitious for the kids than I am for me. If I could give them my ambition, I'd consider myself a success then. Some, if they got a lad in here [the factory] would think it were a success, me, I'd consider it a failure.' (Collinson, 1992: 185.)

These views represent a type of deferred gratification or success by proxy, and bring together the two parts of escaping: the mental escape of oneself through dreaming of, and planning for, the physical escape of one's offspring from similar future conditions of boredom and oppression.

The instances of withdrawal contained in these examples reflect a way of coping with work that accommodates the existing circumstances facing employees – a coping strategy based on resigned acceptance of the status quo. Whilst it is likely that such employees would display neither a very high commitment to the organisation nor an enthusiasm for their work, it does not automatically follow that they would perform their tasks incompetently or carelessly. This being the case, the withdrawn, compliant employee does not necessarily present a problem for management: unlike making out, fiddling, joking, sabotage and even physical escape, the mental escape from work does not present management with an alternative discourse, and in this sense offers no challenge. It is the most passive of the informal behaviours explored, yet, more poignantly than any of the others, suggests accommodation with the various aspects of estrangement that constitute alienation.

CONCLUSION: SURVIVING BY CONSENT AND RESISTANCE

The discussion has highlighted five principal strategies that employees can adopt to deal with the alienating tendencies of work: making out, fiddling, joking, sabotage and escaping. It is clear that these represent 'unofficial' behaviours at work: they demonstrate the importance of looking below the surface into the depths of the workplace where other complex patterns of action and meaning can be found. To explore this domain, it is necessary to use research methods based on getting close to the subject, either through direct involvement (participative observation, sometimes covert) or detailed case-study analysis (semi-structured interviews and close observation). Such methods were employed by all the researchers cited in this chapter, and their subsequent analyses have helped to illuminate a side of work previously shaded by management rhetoric. In other words, alternative behaviours are being enacted on a daily basis by employees in a bid to survive the worse aspects of their working days.

Table 8.3 *Interpretation of the five survival strategies*

| | Survival strategy | | | | |
	'Making out'	*Fiddling*	*Joking*	*Sabotage*	*Escaping*
Consent	Game playing within rules (mutual benefit)	'Deserved' perk	Regulation: preserves the status quo	Expression of frustration	Passive acceptance of status quo (esp.mental)
Resistance	Undermining of rules (threat to management control	Theft	Subversion of management authority	Assertion of control	Withdrawal of goodwill (esp.physical)

But caution needs to be taken: to explain work as a struggle for survival may be melodramatic. Moreover, to characterise the five survival strategies as *always* problematic for management is, as has been noted already, an untenable proposition. What seems to be occurring is that each of the strategies can represent (and be interpreted as) consent *or* resistance to management. This warrants some explanation, so to assist in this, Table 8.3 summarises the different behaviours that could be interpreted as representing consent or resistance for each of the five survival strategies.

There are two important points to think about when looking at Table 8.3. First, there is the issue of who is doing the interpretation. One person might interpret a particular piece of behaviour performed as part of a survival strategy as representing consent, whilst another might see the same behaviour as representing resistance. For example, a builder who steals a few bags of cement might consider this a permissible 'perk', whilst the site manager may interpret it as theft from the company (a sackable offence); conversely the builder may be thieving the cement to spite the employer, whilst the site manager simply turns a blind eye, believing it to be a way of circumventing demands for better pay. So, the *same* fiddling behaviour might represent an expression of either consent or resistance (by the builder); equally, it may be interpreted (by the site manager) as either an expression of resistance (therefore a problem) or consent (no problem). Furthermore, the interpretations by the builder and site manager might coincide or differ, thus potentially adding greater complexity to the situation.

The second point to note is that some aspects of behaviour associated with a particular survival strategy may be more closely equated with consent or resistance than others. Indeed, there may develop some consensus as to what a particular piece of behaviour means. For example, as noted earlier, making out in Burawoy's (1979) study had its limits: there were boundaries across which the employees did not step in their bid to 'find the angles', because to do so would directly challenge management, and perhaps spoil the opportunity to make out for everyone else. Of course, such boundaries between consent and resistance are not fixed, and are always open to reinterpretation. In practice, even where a particular behaviour seems clearly to fall into one category or the other, there are frequently alternative interpretations. Take, for example, the escape strategy of absence from work. It has been noted how regularly taking days off is generally seen as unacceptable by management and is often viewed with disdain by fellow employees (especially those with a strong work ethic). However, suppose a secretary was absent from the office the first Monday in every month in order to take an elderly parent to the hospital for a regular check-up. Should these extra 12 days paid unofficial leave be construed as resistance; or might such regular absences enhance the secretary's consent to managerial authority when in work? Similarly, are all jokes innocuous ways of coping by letting off steam, or might the pointed humorous comments aimed at the supervisor slowly erode his or her status and authority? Even sabotage poses problems of interpretation: for instance, does the photocopier fail to work because it has been kicked by an employee, or does an employee kick the photocopier because it fails to work?

Once again, as in previous chapters, a complex picture emerges which requires the analysis of work to incorporate a plurality of interpretations, experiences and behaviours. It forces us to question unreflective, supposedly 'common sense' understandings that frequently litter management textbooks and the popular press. The foregoing analysis puts us in a position to challenge the dogmatic viewpoints of those who state that all rule-bending is problematic; all fiddling is costly; all sabotage is destructive; all joking is fun; or all absence is simply laziness.

9 Unfair Discrimination at Work

Imagine you are scanning the appointments section of a newspaper and come across the following advertisement. As you read it, ask yourself the question: what aspects of the advert are discriminatory?

> Sales executive required for a medium-sized electronics firm wanting to expand its customer base into Japan. Applicants must have at least five years previous experience of international sales and be aged between 28 and 35. Fluency in Japanese is essential. The job requires energy, dedication, and adaptability, as considerable periods of time will be spent outside the UK. Starting salary will be commensurate with age and experience, and a mixed benefits packet will be offered in line with personal requirements.

The answer is: all of it! The company's management is seeking to discriminate between people on the basis of whether or not they have the appropriate attributes to carry out the job. The important issue, however, is not whether discrimination is occurring (it certainly is) but whether the discrimination is based on *fair criteria*. For example, the requirement of fluency in Japanese is obviously a criterion which discriminates in favour of people who can speak the language; if you cannot speak Japanese you will not get the job and therefore will be discriminated against. Yet, the company managers who have made 'fluency in Japanese' a criterion for choosing between people are likely to argue that this is fair because it is an essential requirement to performing the job well. However, if you are of the opinion that 'fluency in Japanese' is *not* a necessary requirement to do the job well, then you could argue that this is an unfair criterion on which to discriminate between people. Similarly, the advert stipulates that the applicants must be aged between 28 and 35, therefore people are being discriminated against on the basis of age; as indeed they are on 'previous experience' and less tangible qualities, such as 'energy, dedication and adaptability'. Judgements about whether any of these are justifiable criteria upon which to discriminate between potential applicants will influence opinions about the overall fairness of the recruitment. At issue, therefore, is not the question of discrimination itself (selecting suitable from non-suitable applicants) but the *fairness* of the discrimination (whether the grounds for discriminating between the applicants are legitimate and justifiable). The problem is, of course, that when people talk of 'discrimination' they invariably mean *unfair* discrimination; as a consequense, the word is frequently used only in a pejorative sense. Typically, therefore, if someone described the advert as 'discriminatory', they are likely to mean that they consider it unfair in the ways in which it discriminates between people. In this respect, the word 'discrimination' has lost its literal sense, and, in its vernacular form, implies criticism.

To summarise: discrimination is about applying various criteria to choose between people, so the key issue becomes the fairness of the criteria upon which the discrimination is based. Fair criteria lead to discrimination that is justifiable (fair discrimination), whereas unfair criteria lead to unfair discrimination, which is unjustifiable and about which something needs to be done. But this presents us with three fundamental questions that this chapter will address. First, how is discrimination experienced in contemporary workplaces? Second, why might the concept of fairness differ from context to context and person to person, and why might any consensus about fairness differ between social groups? Third, how have policy initiatives so far addressed unfair discrimination and attempted to ensure equality of opportunity, and to what overall effect?

EXPERIENCING DISCRIMINATION

Commentators on discrimination have identified five categories which dominate the extent of unfair discrimination: sex/gender, race/ethnicity, disability, sexual orientation and (most recently) age. Clearly, these are not mutually exclusive categories, so some people find themselves experiencing unfair discrimination from several different directions. The extent to which different individuals experience one or several sources of disadvantage serves to underline a central theme running through the book: the plurality of human work experience. Nevertheless, the experience of discrimination also has some common manifestations which transcend these individual categories. To explore the key features of how discrimination is experienced, this section draws mainly on examples of race and ethnicity. This is not to imply that this category of discrimination is more important than the others – indeed, later in the chapter gender is brought into the analysis. Race and ethnicity, like gender, deserve increased status as analytical constructs central to understanding work in organisations (Nkomo, 1992), but this is necessarily limited (at the present) by the ethnocentric tendency of most academics in framing theoretical and research questions. Yet, there is a richness of empirical enquiry on which we can draw in this section, even if, as Nkomo argues, there remains a need for an alternative paradigm for future analysis of race in organisations (1992: 505–6).

Defining Race and Ethnicity

First, it is important to clarify what is meant by race and ethnicity. As noted in other chapters, many of the concepts encountered when studying work can be identified as being socially constructed, and in this way changeable and negotiable - the most vivid example of this being 'skill' (see Chapter 5). It can be argued that race and ethnicity are in many ways similarly socially constructed: they are concepts used by a particular group to define themselves and thereby identify their difference from 'the other'. In this case, the process of social construction involves a particular dominant group focusing on elements of a person's behaviour, appearance, attitude, belief or biography which identifies them as in some way different from the dominant group and belonging to a separate group (usually a minority). Of course, everyone differs from other people in some way, but only certain differences are perceived to be relevant – these 'relevant' differences have been arrived at through common agreement and understandings by members of the particular setting, and reinforced through the values, beliefs and norms of the group. Racial differences are related to physical features, the most obvious example being skin colour, whilst ethnic differences are related to cultural features such as language, customs and religion. A particular group of people (ranging from a nation state to a small team of workers in a factory) will therefore come to some common understanding as to what racial and/or ethnic differences are of relevance in distinguishing themselves from others. From context to context, and group to group, racial and ethnic boundaries are drawn differently and have varying relevance.

There is considerable debate about the concept of 'race' because it has been discredited by biological science: everyone is of mixed 'race'. Politically, however, it remains important because, as Mason (1994) points out, some people behave as though clearly identifiable groups do exist, hence racism (for a fuller review of this detailed debate see Anthias, 1992; Anthias and Yuval-Davis, 1992; Miles, 1993). The controversy over race has led to increasing focus by social scientists on the utility of 'ethnicity' as a way of defining difference. But the concept of ethnicity is not problem free (for a full discussion see Yinger, 1986). It has led to some anomalous legalistic distinctions in the UK: for example, gypsies constitute an ethnic group but Rastafarians do not (Forbes and Mead, 1992). The current situation is that the law recognises an ethnic group as one which has a long shared history and a cultural tradition of its own, and that this might be identified through characteristics such as: a common geographical origin; a common language; a common literature; a common religion; and the characteristic of being a minority in a larger community (Forbes and Mead, 1992: 23). However, much of the categorisation of 'ethnicity' tends to rely on a more limited definition based on race: primarily skin colour and, within the non-white group, a subdivision into geographical origin. Thus, Figure 9.1 shows the categories recommended by the Commission for Racial Equality (CRE) which were used in the 1991 Census of Great Britain. It underlines the way skin colour dominates, and ethnic differences within the white population tend to be ignored; the 'white' category would subsume, for example, anyone who is Irish, Polish or Jewish; similarly the categorisation does not acknowledge the fervent ethnic identity of many Welsh or Scottish people.

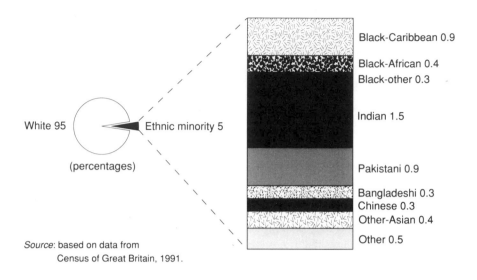

Black-Caribbean 0.9

Black-African 0.4
Black-other 0.3

Indian 1.5

White 95   Ethnic minority 5

(percentages)

Pakistani 0.9

Bangladeshi 0.3
Chinese 0.3
Other-Asian 0.4

Other 0.5

Source: based on data from
Census of Great Britain, 1991.

Figure 9.1   *Ethnic composition of Britain*

Disadvantage in Getting Work

A principal way that ethnic minorities experience discrimination at work is through a lack of equality of opportunity in getting jobs. According to estimates produced by the UK Government, the rate of unemployment for the ethnic minority population remains constantly higher (more than half as high again) than the white population (*Employment Gazette*, 1990 and 1993). This structural disadvantage means that in times of recession, when competition for jobs intensifies, the ethnic minority population tends to suffer more, whilst in periods of recovery, it gains proprotionately less than the white population (Brah, 1986; Dex, 1983; Rhodes and Braham, 1986; D.J. Smith, 1981).

Exclusion from employment is also a reflection of the relevance of the skills possessed by an individual, so access into jobs is likely to be related to the extent of training and retraining undertaken. Access to training schemes is particularly important for people from ethnic minorities backgrounds because it provides a vital means of improving employment prospects in a labour market already biased against them through unfair discrimination. However, research reveals that just as there are barriers to employment, there are also barriers for ethnic minorities within government training schemes designed to improve employment prospects. For example, an analysis of the provision of training schemes for unemployed adults (Ogbonna and Noon, 1995) revealed that ethnic minorities were joining the scheme in representative proportions, yet they did not enjoy the positive outcomes (jobs and qualifications) experienced by their white counterparts. Through detailed interviews with the providers of the training and the trainees themselves, two types of disadvantage were revealed. The first occurred among the training providers (private firms providing off-the-job instruction). Here, unfair discrimination was experienced in terms of the time spent with each trainee (ethnic minorities receiving less attention), the stereotyping of ability, and, in a few cases, verbal abuse. The second type of disadvantage occurred amongst the placement providers (local organisations who provided hands-on experience). Placements were generally difficult to secure for all trainees, and faced with direct competition from white trainees, ethnic minorities were less successful (the providers could pick and choose, and some were found to be using overtly racist criteria) (Ogbonna and Noon, 1995: 551–6). Furthermore, when placements were secured, ethnic minority trainees were less likely to be placed in major institutions like banks, insurance companies and department stores. Instead, there was a tendency for them to be sent to (or only be accepted by) small companies (many of whom saw this as useful 'free labour') and voluntary organisations. Whilst at least providing some work experience, both of these types of organisation had neither the resources to provide adequate on-the-job training to back up the skills learned in the classroom, nor the staffing vacancies to offer employment following the completion of the placement period. These findings echo earlier studies that have similarly revealed unfair discrimination in training (see, for example, Cross, 1987; Cross *et al.*, 1990; Lee and Wrench, 1987).

Another key area where disadvantage is experienced by ethnic minorities is in the process of recruitment and selection. Studies have revealed discriminatory practices both in the private and public sectors (Brown and Gay, 1985; Jenkins, 1986; Jewson *et al.*, 1990), in white-collar and professional occupations (Firth, 1981; Hubbuck and Carter, 1980), and amongst graduate recruiters (Brennan and McGeevor, 1987; Noon, 1993). The problem for researchers, however, is how to identify discrimination in recruitment and selection, particularly if, as Jenkins (1986: 240) argues, the majority of discrimination amongst employers 'is neither strikingly visible nor necessarily self-consciously prejudiced'. One way of tackling this problem is by undertaking research using covert methods. For example, research reported by one of the authors (Noon, 1993) used a quasi-experimental design which involved sending speculative letters of application to the UK's top 100 companies from two fictitious MBA students – one whose name identified him as Asian, and the other as most likely white. The factual content of the letters was identical and the 'candidates' were equally qualified (a matched sample); this allowed the responses to be compared using statistical analysis. This analysis revealed that the treatment of the two 'candidates' differed according to ethnic grouping, but the prejudice was not blatant. They were equally likely to receive a reply to their speculative letter, but an analysis of the content of the replies revealed that the companies were acting more positively to the white 'candidate' by sending a more encouraging reply. Theoretically, both 'candidates' should have been treated the same, as there was substantively no difference between them, other than their implied ethnic group. The analysis went on to compare the responses of the companies with their declared statements on equal opportunities. It was discovered that those companies with equal opportunity statements in their annual reports were more likely to treat both 'candidates' the same; however, where discrimination in this group of companies did occur, it tended to favour the 'white' candidate. This suggests that a gap exists between company policy and practice (Noon, 1993).

Case study research based on interviews has similarly found evidence of racial and ethnic discrimination. Frequently, this appears to be the result of negative stereotypes held by managers in charge of the selection process (see for example, Hubbuck and Carter, 1980; Jenkins, 1986; Jewson *et al.*, 1990). Indeed, Ram (1992) found that the necessity to access the white-dominated business society has even led some Asian employers to discriminate against ethnic minorities in favour of whites. However, unfair discrimination can also occur unintentionally as a result of bad or inappropriate selection methods. A particularly notable example (*Labour Research*, 1990) is the case of British Rail where, as part of the selection process for train drivers, personality questionnaires were used which were supposed to reveal strengths in terms of 'relationships with people', 'thinking style' and 'feelings and emotions'. The results were controversial, however, because they profiled all the white candidates positively and all the black candidates negatively. The reason for this is that personality tests are culturally bound because they rely on values, beliefs and norms that are reflected in the dominant culture; so people from a different cultural background are more likely to fall outside the acceptable profile. Although the managers at British Rail had no intention of discriminating against ethnic minority candidates, the use of the personality test produced that effect. This problem of unintentional indirect discrimination is returned to below, when the liberal perspective on equal opportunities is examined.

Disadvantage in Work

Having secured a job, people from ethnic minority backgrounds can experience further unfair discrimination in terms of full recognition of achievement and promotion. Jones's (1993) analysis of occupational structure, for example, revealed that ethnic minorities were disproportionately clustered in jobs deemed lower skilled, and were notably under-represented in senior management grades in large organisations – a situation similarly experienced by women. This structural disadvantage only serves to perpetuate the situation because those most likely to change policies within organisations regarding equal opportunities are denied access to decision-making processes. Likewise, many of those who control policy – predominantly white, able-bodied men – have little incentive to change a system (albeit unfair) from which they benefit.

Irrespective of the type of work being undertaken, it is evident that many ethnic minorities experience discrimination from their co-workers on a regular basis. Whilst some of the harassment becomes so severe that it is brought to public attention, much of it remains hidden and perniciously erodes the morale and self-worth of its victims, similar to the way persistent bullying can break the spirit of a child. A particularly vivid example is the case of the UK fire service where a confidential Home Office report in 1994 revealed an alarming amount of racial and sexual harassment, ranging from verbal abuse and being ostracised to physical attacks. For instance, it highlighted the experience of an Afro-Caribbean fire-fighter: 'The first day, the blokes tricked us.... They threw a bucket of water over us. We laughed our heads off and I thought "I've been accepted"' *(The Observer*, 10 April 1994). Clearly this could be construed as an initiation ritual (the sort of event explored when analysing humour in Chapter 8) but wheras the 'ragging' continued for this particular fire-fighter, it stopped for his white colleague. He goes on to explain how the attacks increased in severity.

> They dragged me out of my bed, put me under the shower. They tied me up, they put me under the water tower and filled it with water. I nearly drowned. They grabbed me and set me head-first in a fire bin. They set my shoes on fire, whacked me in the head. They'd tell me to do things to test my strength, and then while I was exercising try and trip me up, knock my hands away. *(The Observer*, 10 April 1994.)

Examples such as this illustrate the way certain groups are exposed through work to hostile social environments. Similar experiences can be found in the relatively small but growing body of research concerning disability, sexual orientation and age (see for example, Hearn and Parkin, 1987; Hearn *et al.*, 1989; D. Hill, 1985; Lonsdale, 1990; Oliver, 1990). For many people, the harsh reality is that work becomes a domain of unpleasant social interaction: unfair discrimination, in its various guises and manifestations, is entrenched as part of everyday life. But this raises some important issues about how to theorise the nature of discrimination, and how this can be linked with policy to eliminate unfairness and promote equality of opportunity.

THEORISING DISCRIMINATION

Fairness is, as discussed at the start of this chapter, a subjective concept. At its root are moral assumptions about how people ought to be treated so that equal opportunity prevails. Should people be treated the same, or should they be treated differently? On which criteria should they be treated the same or differently? This is not as straightforward an issue as it may first appear because a person can be the victim of unfair discrimination through receiving the same treatment or different treatment, depending on the circumstances. For example, take the criteria of age and sex: in the earlier advertisement, age is used to discriminate between people; in other words, people are treated *differently* according to age, so applicants older than 35 could be rejected, even if they satisfied the other criteria, such as previous work experience. On the other hand, the advert does not use gender as a criterion to discriminate, so (theoretically) applicants will be treated the *same* regardless of their sex. However, by ignoring differences between genders, potential women applicants who have taken time out of work to have children are likely to have accumulated less previous work experience than men of an equivalent age; indeed, it could transpire that many potential women applicants who meet the (legitimate) previous work experience criteria are older than 35, and therefore fall outside the age band required. Thus, by treating applicants differently with regard to age, and the same with regard to sex, the advert may well be unfairly discriminating against potential women applicants who satisfy all the other criteria.

To reiterate the problem: unfair discrimination can occur by ignoring differences and giving people equal treatment, *or* by identifying differences and giving (some) people special treatment. This can be illustrated with a further, more blatant, example: the case of South Africa. Under the old regime of apartheid, an employer recognised racial differences and the white population was given special treatment (especially through education) which meant privileged access to prestigious jobs: unfair discrimination prevailed. In contemporary South Africa, an employer may now ignore racial differences and treat everyone the same, but in so doing overlooks the existing disadvantaged position of the black population with regard to prestigious jobs. The existing structural disadvantage means that unfair discrimination continues.

This issue of recognising how unfair discrimination can emerge from the concepts of 'sameness' and 'difference' is addressed by Liff and Wajcman (1996) in an analysis of equal opportunity policy and gender. They reach the conclusion that attention must be paid to both because they reflect different forms of disadvantage.

> Sometimes women are disadvantaged by being treated differently when in fact they are the same (e.g. denied a job for which they are perfectly well qualified) and at other times by being treated the same when their difference needs to be taken into account (e.g. having their absence to look after a sick child treated the same way as a man who is absent with a hangover). (Liff and Wajcman, 1996: 86.)

Recognising the way that the dominant group (in this case, male employers) selectively use the concepts of sameness and difference to construct disadvantage against women, Liff and Wajcman (following Bacchi, 1990, and Cockburn, 1991) suggest that the arguments can be turned back on the dominant group using a similar logic of selectivity, but with the purpose of eliminating disadvantage for women.

> [Equal treatment] is entirely appropriate for tackling some types of

discrimination and can be expected to have brought benefits. Here the best way forward is for women to be treated the same as men, for example by ensuring that selection and appraisal methods are free from bias. In other cases, where women have been excluded from certain types of experience or qualification, or where they have specific demands placed on them from the home which impinge on their work, this difference should be acknowledged. Appropriate equality initiatives [special treatment] in this context would include targeted training courses, childcare or the opportunity for men and women to work different hours. (Liff and Wajcman, 1996: 86.)

As can be seen, the issue of discrimination becomes more complex when it is applied to work organisations. Indeed, we are faced with a veritable Gordian knot of logic: it is possible to argue that to ensure fairness people need to be treated both similarly and differently, and that paradoxically, similar and different treatment can also undermine fairness. Figure 9.2 represents an attempt to cut through the knot. It shows the relationships between the concepts in the context of an organisation, and the discussion that follows seeks to elaborate the various components of the diagram.

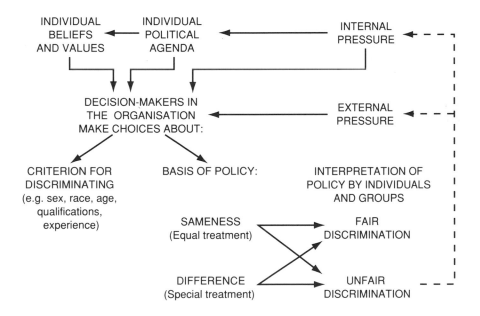

Figure 9.2   *The process of discrimination in an organisation*

The critical group are the decision-makers (typically managers at all levels) who have the power to exercise choices in line with their own beliefs and their own political agenda, although within constraints set by external pressures (for

example, legislation, public opinion and labour supply) and internal pressures
(for example, other managers, employees, trade unions, and key individuals such
as the manager's own boss). This is very similar to the strategic choice thesis
suggested by Child (1972) which emphasised the political and ideological
aspects of decision-making by managers. Figure 9.2 is just concerned with
the range of management decisions that directly affect other people (usually
subordinates): for example, deciding who to appoint; who to allocate to a
particular shopfloor task or team; who to promote; whether to give someone a
pay rise; who needs training; who to make redundant; and so on. In decisions
such as these, important choices are made in two respects: first, over the criteria
on which to discriminate between people (age, race, qualifications, experience,
performance, gender, personality, physical appearance, or whatever); second,
over how to apply each selected criterion, that is, whether to adopt a policy of
sameness (equal treatment) or difference (special treatment). As the earlier
discussion highlighted, managers tend to identify a particular criterion and decide
whether there should be equal treatment or special treatment; in other words,
whether their policy is to be based on the principle of sameness or difference for
that particular criterion. To illustrate: in promoting someone, senior managers
might decide that work experience with the firm is important whereas
educational qualifications are not; in this case employees who have given many
years of service to the firm will be looked on more favourably than newcomers
(a policy based on difference leading to special treatment with regard to work
experience); conversely, employees with a university degree will not be looked
upon more favourably than those without a degree (a policy based on sameness
leading to equal treatment with regard to educational qualification). It can be
seen, therefore, that a policy based on sameness or difference can be applied to
any criterion, and the decision-makers are the key actors in both identifying the
criteria and relating a policy of sameness or difference to it.

These choices made over criteria and policy are judged by other members of
the organisation: people will be assessing whether the discrimination is fair or
unfair. If a person feels there were justifiable criteria with an appropriate policy,
then the perception is likely to be of fairness. On the other hand, if it is felt that
there were unjustifiable criteria or that a justifiable criterion had been distorted
through an inappropriate policy, then the perception of unfairness is likely to
prevail. Such interpretations can be made by individuals or may be negotiated by
groups (for example, work teams, trade unions, professionals, informal social
cliques). Thus, for any policy or action associated with any criterion of discrimination there is likely to be a plurality of responses: some individuals and groups
will interpret it as fair and others as unfair. Thus competing interpretations can
occur. The extent to which people concern themselves with issues of fairness will
vary according to the circumstance and is likely to reflect the extent to which they
are directly involved with, or affected by, the outcome. Similarly, the
diagram cannot reflect the power or the will of individuals and groups to take
action. However, when unfairness is perceived, this might lead to greater internal

and/or external pressure in an attempt to influence future decisions (shown by the feedback loop in Figure 9.2).

The map of the process of discrimination suggests the relationships between various concepts that have been explored in this chapter so far. It is descriptive in that it attempts to encapsulate the importance of structural constraints, agency (through the choices of decision-makers) and subjectivity (especially through interpretation of discrimination). It is not normative, and cannot be used as a diagnostic tool because it does not show *how* choice or action can affect the direction of interpretation (that is, whether a policy is fair or unfair). Indeed, the subjectivity of the process militates against theorising in such a way. This is an important point because it suggests that policy initiatives aimed at eliminating interpretations of unfair discrimination will need to address the structural, moral and political issues embedded in the process of discrimination. So how have policy initiatives been addressing the problem?

THREE PERSPECTIVES ON EQUAL OPPORTUNITIES

Devising policy to ensure equal opportunities is rife with controversy, due to the inevitable way it is entwined with political and moral beliefs. The notion of what constitutes fairness, and how policy can be constructed to enhance this, will differ from person to person. It is possible, however, to identify three broad perspectives on equality. The first two perspectives, *liberal* and *radical*, are based on concepts developed by Jewson and Mason (1986); the third perspective, *reactionary*, is an attempt to complete the spectrum by briefly assessing the view that rejects interference by policy-makers. Each perspective is examined in turn.

The Liberal Perspective

From this perspective, 'equal opportunity exists when all individuals are enabled freely and equally to compete for social rewards' (Jewson and Mason, 1986: 313). The role of policy-makers is therefore to ensure that the rules are fair. 'It is not their job to determine who are the winners and losers, but to ensure only that the social mechanisms by which winners and losers select themselves are based on principles of fairness and justice' (ibid.). Policy is therefore concerned with devising *fair procedures*, so that justice is seen to be done.

In the UK, this liberal perspective has informed legislation which requires employers to act according to certain guidelines, a breach of which might make them liable to prosecution for unfair practice (see Figure 9.3 for a summary of the legislative provision). Whilst this legal framework sets some boundaries, it would be misleading to suggest that it clearly establishes fair rules. As with any legalistic solution, interpretation of the rules becomes a problem, and nowhere is this more vividly illustrated than in the concept of discrimination itself. The

Table 9.1   *Summary of main equal opportunities legislation in the UK*

Equal Pay Act 1970/Equal Value (Amendment) Regulations 1983
Equal pay and conditions for men and women engaged in:
    same or similar work
    work rated as equivalent (by job evaluation)
    work of equal value.

Sex Discrimination Acts 1976, 1986
Unlawful to discriminate against people on the basis of sex or married status.
• Covers recruitment, promotion, training, working conditions and dismissal
• Exemptions allowed for genuine occupational qualifications
• Special treatment permitted due to pregnancy and childbirth
• Positive action initiatives encouraged to reverse under-representation
• Equal Opportunities Commission established with responsibilities to:
    monitor the implementation of the Sex Discrimination Act and Equal Pay Act
    give advice to employers on reviewing their practice
    give advice to complainants
    investigate organisations breaching the legislation.
• Extends power of industrial tribunals to deal with sex discrimination.

Race Relations Act 1976 (Britain only)
Unlawful to discriminate on grounds of race, colour, nationality, ethnic or national origins.
• Covers recruitment, promotion, training, working conditions and dismissal.
• Exemptions allowed for genuine occupational qualifications.
• Positive action initiatives encouraged to reverse under-representation.
• Commission for Racial Equality established with responsibilities to:
    monitor the implementation of the Race Relations Act
    give advice to employers on reviewing their practice
    give advice to complainants
    investigate organisations breaching the legislation.
• Extends power of industrial tribunals to deal with race discrimination.

Fair Employment (Northern Ireland) Act 1989
Unlawful to discriminate against people on the basis of religious or political belief or affiliation.
• Obliges employers to:
    monitor the 'community affiliations' of employees and job applicants
    review periodically employment practices (recruitment, training and promotion)
    take affirmative action where the review suggests that one community is under-
        represented
    adopt 'goals and timetables' where a relevant notice has been served by the Fair
        Employment Commission.

- Fair Employment Commission established with responsibilities to:
  promote affirmative action and work towards eliminating discrimination
  maintain a code of practice
  collect annual monitoring data from firms of over 250 employees
  give advice to employers on reviewing their practice
  give advice to complainants
  investigate organisations and issue legally enforceable orders.
- Separate tribunal established to deal with Fair Employment cases.

Disability Discrimination Act 1995
Unlawful to discriminate against people with a disability: physical or mental impairment which has a substantial and long-term effect on a person's ability to carry out normal day-to-day activities.
- Applies to all employers with 20 or more employees.
- Covers recruitment, promotion, training, working conditions and dismissal.
- Obliges employers to make 'reasonable adjustment' to their premises and working arrangements.
- Complaints are heard by industrial tribunals.
- National Disability Council acts as an advisory body, but does not have powers of investigation.

---

legislation identifies two types of discrimination. The first, *direct discrimination*, occurs when the treatment of, or attitude towards, a person is less favourable because of their sex, race or disability. For example, if the advertisement at the beginning of this chapter had asked for a salesman or implied that only male applicants would be considered, then the company would have been in breach of the Sex Discrimination Act 1975 because it directly discriminates against women. Direct discrimination is therefore relatively easy to detect, and so relatively easy for employers to avoid, providing they are well informed about their legal requirements.

In contrast, the second type of discrimination, *indirect discrimination*, is a legalistic minefield. It stipulates that indirect discrimination occurs when a requirement or condition is applied equally but has the consequence of disadvantaging a particular group (sex or race, but not disability). This means that there does not necessarily have to be an *intention* to discriminate – it is not the action itself, but the *effect* of the action that matters. The example of British Rail's personality tests cited earlier illustrates the problem. However, in practice the law tends to favour the employer because, as Jenkins (1986: 250) argues, 'for particular policies or conditions to be indirectly discriminatory, it is necessary that they cannot be shown to be justifiable'. Consequently, selection criteria such as labour market history or relevant experience, or practices such as word-of-mouth recruitment, may fall outside the definition, in spite of the fact that they are likely to disadvantage ethnic minorities. Furthermore, Jenkins suggests that white managers, in a white-dominated business, may make ethnocentric judgements about who will 'fit in', which may be legally justifiable in terms of the 'business necessity' to employ manageable workers (Jenkins, 1986: 78). To take another example: it will be recalled from the earlier discussion that the advertisement at the beginning may be discriminating against women because it stipulates an age range for applications. It is immaterial whether the managers intended to discriminate against women in this way when they placed the advert: the effect is still indirect discrimination. However, as a defence, the managers might argue that this age range is justifiable on the basis of the demands of the job, proven to them by their past experience of employees. It would be very difficult to argue against this.

As well as setting the legalistic framework, the liberal perspective on equal opportunities has made it permissible in the UK for organisations to embark upon *positive action* programmes. These are initiatives designed to counteract the effects of past discrimination and seek to redress the gender and ethnic profile of the workforce. This is frequently confused with positive discrimination (preferential treatment for disadvantaged groups, discussed below), but it is vital to recognise the difference: in the UK, positive action is lawful whereas positive discrimination is not. The most typical examples of positive action initiatives are the provision of company crèches, advertising campaigns aimed at specific groups, career-break schemes, and awareness training for managers.

An important feature, critical to the success of positive action initiatives, is *equal opportunity monitoring*. Essentially, monitoring is a process of data collection and analysis (particularly with regard to the composition of the workforce, recruitment and promotion) which can be used as part of the policy formation process (for an assessment of current practice, see Industrial Relations Review and Report, 1990; Jewson *et al.*, 1992). Although monitoring is voluntary at present, groups like the Commission for Racial Equality are increasingly convinced that the way forward is to make monitoring compulsory. In fact, the Government has accepted the principle of compulsory monitoring by passing the Fair Employment (Northern Ireland) Act 1989, which requires organisations in the province to keep records of the composition of their workforce in terms of religious affiliation. There is mixed opinion about monitoring; a debate which is summarised in Table 9.2. Those commentators who remain sceptical about monitoring, tend to argue that it is costly, highly bureaucratic and unworkable. Webb and Liff (1988: 550) suggest that 'merely processing the numbers of applications generated by the use of such procedures in the current climate is likely to be beyond the resources of many employers. The result is that the policy is circumvented and derided.' More cynically, it can be argued that monitoring can become 'a smoke-screen behind which discrimination continues to flourish' (Jenkins, 1987: 118).

In a critique of the liberal approach to equal opportunities, Webb and Liff (1988) argue that it is not enough to view unfair discrimination as an essentially technical problem that can be rectified through fair procedures – not least because

Table 9.2 *The pros and cons of equal opportunities monitoring*

The case for monitoring	*The case against monitoring*
It allows an organisation to demonstrate what they are doing and identify particular problem areas.	It stirs up trouble and discontent, and can create problems that would otherwise not arise.
It encourages managers to think creatively about positive action initiatives. It removes the need for stronger legislation such as quotas (positive discrimination).	It puts undue pressure on managers, and might encourage them to lower standards or appoint for the wrong reasons. It is positive discrimination by the back door.
The data can be kept confidential, just like any other information.	It is an invasion of privacy and open to abuse.
It provides useful information to help management decision-making.	It creates unnecessary information.
Organisations conducting their activities in line with the legal requirements have nothing to fear.	Organisations with no problems regarding equal opportunities do not need this burdensome bureaucratic mechanism.
The costs are modest.	It is an unnecessary expenditure.
It is good business practice.	The business needs to focus on its commercial activities.

of the paradox of sameness and difference, explored in the previous section. They suggest that because inequality is deeply embedded, it is insufficient to see the solution lying with simply rectifying unfair discrimination in recruitment, selection, training and promotion.

> Women fail not because they are less able to carry out the tasks; they are excluded because of the way that necessary qualifications are defined. The competition is structured against women because the job is perceived as requiring skills, experiences and working patterns far more likely to be found amongst men, or indeed seen as inherently male. (Webb and Liff, 1988: 549.)

This resonates with the discussion in Chapter 5 concerning how notions of skill are often constructed to the disadvantage of women. Managers in organisations need to reassess job requirements which may have been historically developed and bear little relation to current needs. This, argue Webb and Liff, would include the structuring and grading of jobs and the terms on which they are offered. 'What should be asked of employers is not that they accept less qualified, less able women in preference to men but that they rethink what the job requires in ways that do not rule out competent women' (Webb and Liff, 1988: 549). Therefore, this 'job audit' approach goes much further than the typical positive action programmes of the liberal perspective described above, yet, as we shall see, rejects the solution proposed by the radical approach, to which the discussion now turns.

The Radical Perspective

The dilemma for more radically minded policy-makers in addressing equal opportunities was eloquently summed up by US President Lyndon Johnson in 1965, with the following analogy.

> Imagine a hundred yard dash in which one of the two runners has his legs shackled together. He has progressed 10 yards, while the unshackled runner has gone 50 yards. At that point the judges decide that the race is unfair. How do they rectify the situation? Do they merely remove the shackles and allow the race to proceed? Then they could say that 'equal opportunity' now prevailed. But one of the runners would still be forty yards ahead of the other. Would it not be the better part of justice to allow the previously shackled runner to make up the forty yard gap; or to start the race all over again? (Quoted in Bell, 1973: 429.)

As has been noted, the liberal perspective would suggest that it is enough to remove the shackles, and ensure that henceforth there is no unfair advantage. However, as President Johnson pointed out, this does not rectify the existing situation of inequality. In other words, policy should address any extant structural disadvantage as well as ensure greater equality of opportunity in the future. This represents a more radical approach because it suggests that policy makers should be concerned with the *outcome*, rather than the *process*, and should therefore be seeking to ensure a *fair distribution of rewards*. Consequently, there is a requirement to intervene directly through policies of *positive discrimination* (known as affirmative action in the US). The most typical example of this is setting quotas for disadvantaged groups, which organisations must achieve or face legal penalties. For example, there could be a requirement for an organisation to have 30 per cent of its workforce from a particular ethnic minority group in line with the ethnic profile of the local community from which it recruits its employees. This means that the recruiters can discriminate in favour of someone *because* they are from an ethnic minority.

Obviously the policy of positive discrimination is not without its critics. First, there are those who argue that it merely shifts the unfairness from one group to another. In particular, it means that white, able-bodied, heterosexual men may find themselves victims of discrimination; this has led to a backlash in the US, with right-wing politicians seeking to revoke the affirmative action legislation. The backlash is very much a phenomenon of the 1990s which demonstrates how, in the US, equal opportunity policy is inextricably tied to politics. As *The Guardian* (20 June 1995) reported:

> No one can pin-point the exact moment, but the beginning of the end came in the autumn of 1990. No one knew it at the time, but in a single TV image the death of affirmative action was foretold. The moment came at the end of a campaign commercial for veteran rightwing Senator Jesse Helms. Trailing behind his Democratic opponent, Helms played the race card by zeroing in on affirmative action.... 'You know you deserved that job,' intoned the voice-over ominously, showing a pair of white hands clutching a rejection letter. 'But they had to give it to a minority,' the ad said, showing a pair of black hands grasping a letter of appointment. It was blatant, it was condemned as racist, but the TV spot – with its implication that white men were losing out to blacks because of reverse discrimination – struck a nerve. Helms came from behind and won. The advert has entered US political history, as the debut of the backlash against affirmative action – a movement which has now reached the Congress, the White House and... the Supreme Court.

A second group of critics of affirmative action are members of disadvantaged groups themselves who condemn the policy because it devalues their achievements by raising the suspicion that they did not really deserve the job, promotion or whatever. For example, even if positive discrimination played no part in the selection process, and the female candidate genuinely was the best qualified for the job, she will always be faced with those who begrudgingly mutter, 'She only got the job because she's a woman and it helps achieve the quota'.

In the UK, positive discrimination is unlawful, and policy suggestions towards it have been condemned by the Institute of Personnel and Development, who label it 'reverse discrimination'. Ironically, legislation introduced by a Conservative Government committed to deregulating employment comes the closest to positive discrimination. The Fair Employment Act (Northern Ireland) 1989 (summarised earlier in Table 9.1) obliges employers to monitor their employees and job applicants in terms of their 'community affiliations' (religious and political beliefs). In particular, if a notice has been served by the Fair Employment Commission, the employer is obliged to set goals and timetables to redress the imbalance in the composition of the workforce – in effect, it is a legally enforceable quota, although it is never labelled as such. In this respect the legal precedent has been set for putting positive discrimination on the statute books. But such a development is highly unlikely, given that neither the

Commission for Racial Equality nor the Equal Opportunties Commission believe
it an appropriate way forward, and a ruling by the European Court of Justice
(1995) that the use of quotas for women, operated by some public sector
organisations in Germany, contravened the EU equal treatment Directive.

The Reactionary Perspective

This third perspective is concerned less with equality than inequality. It emanates
from notions of biological essentialism, and postulates the natural inequality of
people due to genetic differences. Proponents of this view tend to argue that
'natural selection' will prevail, and such notions as 'the law of the jungle' and 'the
survival of the fittest' are evoked as explanations as to why policy-makers should
not intervene. This perspective, in practice, covers a broad range of
opinion, from the backlash 'victims' noted above, to the most abhorrent racists,
and is therefore a melting pot of stereotypical views, prejudice and arbitrary
judgements. A contemporary expression of this perspective is embraced by the
'new right', the generic term for an ideology that reflects a 'curious and unstable
combination of the market mechanism, moral authoritarianism and the racially
based theory of national identity' (Parekh, 1986, quoted in Allen and Macey,
1990: 385). In the United States, this has found expression most vividly amongst
the fundamentalist cable TV preachers, but, as Allen and Macey (1990: 385–7)
note, the ideology has achieved a ready outlet in the press and amongst some
academics within Europe, especially in Britain, France and Germany.

This perspective need not detain us further, but it is perhaps the one that
most vividly highlights the moral and political dimension of equal opportunities.
The question of whether and how to rectify unfair discrimination is one that
impassions people. Understanding a person's perspective on equality is, therefore, an important stage in predicting their opinions on the fairness of policies,
and perhaps reducing the unpredictability implied by the diagram in Table 9.2.
Almost everyone has an opinion; most are willing to state it; few are in a
position to enact it. It is to the latter group the discussion now turns in drawing
some conclusions about the future of equal opportunities.

CONCLUSION: PROSPECTS FOR EQUAL OPPORTUNITIES

The importance of the political context is a theme that has emerged throughout
the book, yet the issue of equal opportunities brings it into sharper focus. If
policy-makers in government have a political commitment to freeing up the
labour market through deregulation of employment (as has been the case with
Conservative Governments in the UK since 1979) then any intervention through
equal opportunities legislation would be anathema to them. Indeed, policy-
makers might even want to enervate existing laws to provide more freedom for

employers. As noted in Chapter 2, this commitment to removing constraints on employers and allowing market forces to dictate terms of employment has led the UK Government to withdraw from the EU social chapter. It is highly unlikely that any strengthening of the existing legislation will occur in the foreseeable future. Moreover, across Europe, the UK stands out as having the most robust legislative protection for ethnic minorities (European Commission, 1992; Forbes and Mead, 1992) although this is not the case for gender, disability, age and sexual orientation.

There is a further way that the commitment to a less regulated free market affects equal opportunities. The policy of 'rolling back the state' has led to a programme of privatisation and compulsory competitive tendering (CCT) that has dramatically reduced the government's role as a direct employer. It was in the public sector that many equal opportunity positive action initiatives were enacted; the demise of the public sector also means a reduction of such initiatives. In some local authorities (particularly Labour Party dominated ones) private companies were often obliged to demonstrate their own commitment to equal opportunities when tendering for contracts, but CCT regulations now limit the extent to which non-economic factors can be taken into account when awarding contracts.

The declining role of the state as employer, coupled with the political commitment to market forces, has meant that equal opportunities policy has increasingly been left to the discretion of individual employers. Although this voluntarist approach in the UK has to take account of the legislative framework outlined above, it can lead to a wide spectrum of responses from employers. At one extreme there will be those who do nothing other than the minimum required under the law, whilst at the other extreme will be organisations championing the cause of equal opportunities by implementing very progressive positive action programmes. The bulk of organisations are likely to lie between these two points and restrict themselves to developing aspects of equal opportunities that are good for business. For example, a company might pay lip service to equal opportunities because it presents a good image for the organisation, although there is little substance and commitment lying behind the words. Alternatively, an organisation's human resource department might be keen to develop fair and thorough recruitment procedures and target unrepresented groups, thereby tapping a rich source of otherwise neglected talent.

A further possible development is that managers in organisations increasingly recognise the diversity of the workforce, and move towards a greater recognition of individual differences. This shifts the debate away from the recognition of disadvantages shared by different groups (a collective focus) to an emphasis on the unique attributes and requirements of each employee (individual focus). In the words of the earlier discussion: the notion of 'sameness' and equal treatment disappears because 'difference' is celebrated, and policy is based on special treatment for all. Such an approach has already begun in the United States under the banner of 'managing diversity' and may well gain purchase in the increasingly individualised employment context in the UK. If this were to occur, then unfair discrimination at work might be recognised more widely, but at a price: it would no longer be acknowledged as the common experience of disadvantaged groups of people, but the private experience of isolated individuals.

10 Hidden Work

INTRODUCTION

Up to now, our examination of the realities of work has concentrated on those activities taking place within what might be termed the 'formal' or 'visible' work sector, that is where the goods and services produced are included in official statistics, such as the calculation of a country's Gross National Product (GNP), and where workers involved in the production of those goods and services receive a wage, which in turn is subject to tax. Yet, to focus all our attention here would be to misrepresent the totality of work and work experience. For as well as productive activity that takes place within the formal economy, there are other contexts in which productive activity also occurs but which do not figure in national accounts of production or earnings. Thus, for example, whilst a joiner working for a firm producing windows creates output and earns a wage, both of which are 'visible' in terms of production and earnings accounts, if that same individual repairs a window in their own home or voluntarily assists in making a new door for a local youth club, none of this work will be visible in terms of being included in any national accounts. Similarly, if someone minds a friend's child for a day, who pays cash in return, which is not declared to the tax authorities, this income and the work for which the payment was received will not figure in national accounts. Each of these aspects of work – in the domestic and voluntary spheres, and receiving payment for work which is not declared for tax – are hidden, but they are unquestionably work, nonetheless.

Work that occurs outside the formal work sector can be 'hidden' from public gaze in one of two ways. First, it might be explicitly concealed from the state authorities because it involves illegal activity (either the activity itself is a crime, such as drug dealing, or the income deriving from a legal activity is not declared for tax, thereby representing the illegal act of tax evasion). In this general category too is work activity, such as prostitution, which involves some activities which are illegal (e.g. soliciting) but which is also hidden because of its widespread social status as stigmatised work. Secondly, work undertaken may be 'hidden' in a more implicit way, by it not being generally recognised as 'real' work at all, primarily because those performing the tasks do not receive payment: the archetypal case here is housework. Each of these two general categories – work which is either explicitly or implicitly hidden – in turn are comprised of a range of individual activities. Yet, at the same time, these various activities hold certain key elements in common: for example, as well as each being 'hidden' for one reason or another, they all exhibit significant (albeit varied) links with the

formal or visible work sector. To explore the different aspects and implications of
hidden work, the chapter is divided into three further sections. The first
examines the main dimensions of hidden work and considers some of the
attempts to measure the size of, and trends within the hidden work sector.
Sections two and three consider the two main areas of hidden work in more
detail, identifying some of the broader issues concerning the significance of
hidden work for the totality of work experience.

DEFINING AND MEASURING HIDDEN WORK

Consider a household where Jeremy, an employee at a firm of estate agents, has
decided to build an extension to his house. The additional space will provide an
extra bedroom to house his elderly mother, Doris, who has suffered a stroke and
is no longer able to look after herself in her own home. Faced with this situation,
Jeremy and his wife Joanne have decided that the best thing would be for Doris
to live with them so they can be on hand to give her the care she needs.

Given the urgency of the situation and the inevitable delays of 'red tape',
Jeremy decided to get the plans for the extension through the local authority
Planning Committee more quickly than was usual. Fortunately, his membership
of the local golf club had helped him to develop a number of 'useful' contacts,
one of which was the local government officer in the Planning Department whose
job it was to draw up the lists of property development for consideration by the
Planning Committee. After an informal chat and a gift of a couple of bottles of
whisky, the plans were put forward for consideration (and passed) very speedily.

Lacking the finances to pay a firm of builders to do the extension, Jeremy
started on the work himself at weekends. However, he soon fell behind his
schedule, not least because every other weekend he had custody of the two
children by his first marriage, which occupied most of his time. To free up some
of these weekends, Joanne (a nursery nurse by training) would spend a good part
of her time amusing the children. She also kept Jeremy supplied with numerous
cups of tea and a cooked lunch, as well as completing various other domestic
chores (such as the ironing and cleaning) that were usually left until the
weekend.

Even though Jeremy was freed from the childcare and domestic chores, he still
found himself making little headway with the work at weekends and soon began
to put in an hour or two on the building work during the week, by pretending to
his boss that he was leaving the office early to do a house evaluation, or have a
meeting with a prospective vendor. However, after a few weeks it was clear that
not even this extra time was progressing the work fast enough, so one evening
Jeremy called up various contacts in the building trade to try to find someone to
help. He was put in touch with a building labourer called Ron who agreed to give
him a hand, working at weekends. Ron made it clear that he would want to be
paid in cash, with no receipts, but that in return he would 'borrow' the equipment

they would need from his employer – an excavator to dig the trench for the foundations and a concrete mixer – provided that any equipment was back on his firm's building site before Monday morning.

With the added help of Ron, the extension was soon finished and Doris duly moved in. Yet, while the arrangement of having Doris under the same roof meant that there was now less travelling involved in visiting her, Joanne soon found that the combination of tasks of keeping her own household going, looking after her mother-in-law and doing her job at a local nursery school, were getting too much for her. As a result, she gave up her job at the nursery, although to keep some interest outside the home she carried on doing some voluntary work in the evenings which involved organising fund-raising activities for a local hospital.

The most remarkable aspect of this account is that although there is a large amount of 'work' being done, only two of the activities figure as part of the formal economy: Jeremy's job at the estate agents, and Joanne's job at the nursery school. The remaining work all takes place within the domains of hidden work. For example, as well as Jeremy's DIY building activities, there is the care dispensed by Joanne to her mother-in-law and to her husband's children, together with the work involved in her keeping the men supplied with food and drink as well as undertaking the other domestic tasks of cleaning and ironing, not to mention the voluntary work done in the evening for the hospital charity. In addition, the work done by Ron is also hidden in that his requirement for cash-in-hand payments with no receipts suggests an intention not to declare some or all of this income to the tax authorities. The account also contains examples of some of the fiddles which are often associated with the hidden work sphere: for example, the planning officer taking a 'backhander' to push Jeremy's application up the queue, Jeremy's use of office hours to work on the extension, and Ron's unauthorised 'borrowing' of his employer's equipment (see Chapter 8 for a more detailed discussion of workplace fiddling). This account also underlines the need for some means of categorising the diverse activities which fall under the general heading of hidden work.

Categorising Hidden Work

There are various ways of categorising the hidden work sphere. The preference here is for one based on the distinction indicated earlier. First, there are those activities which are explicitly 'concealed' because they are illegal, because they contain illegal aspects and attract social stigma, or because the income deriving from legal activities is not declared to the tax authorities. Second, there is a variety of 'unrecognised' work which is more implicitly hidden as a result of not generally being performed for payment, thus placing those work activities not only outside market relations but also outside the range of activity widely considered to constitute 'real' work.

As Figure 10.1 indicates, under each of the two main categories, different

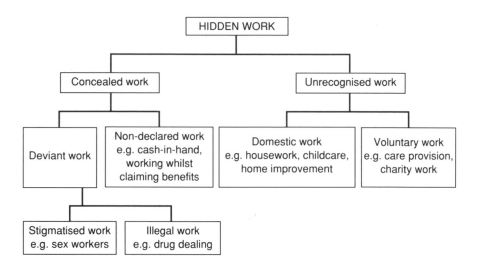

Figure 10.1 *Dimensions of hidden work*

individual work activities may be located; the examples given do not represent an
exhaustive list but are indicative of the sorts of activity to be found within each
of the general areas of hidden work. Further, the distinction between
different activities and categories will, in practice, often be blurred by
individuals simultaneously pursuing more than one aspect of hidden work: for
example, by performing work activities which benefit both the household and a
wider group (e.g. by gardening and growing flowers which are used to decorate
both the home and the local church). However, whilst recognising the existence
of overlaps, this does not invalidate the main distinction between concealed and
unrecognised work, as this distinction is based on the fundamentally different
causes of their hiddenness.

Other commentators have drawn broadly similar distinctions between the
main categories of hidden work, though there is some variation in the labels
used and the degree to which some of the categories (notably the domestic and
voluntary spheres) are treated separately or as elements of a single category.
For example, while Gershuny (1983) distinguishes between the 'household',
'communal' and 'underground' economies, and Handy (1984) refers to the
'household', 'voluntary' and 'black' economies, Smith and Wied-Nebbeling
(1986) in their work on Britain and Germany, make a distinction only between
the 'black' and the 'self-service' economies in the two countries, while R. Rose
(1985) distinguishes between the 'unofficial' and 'domestic' economies.
Following writers such as Felt and Sinclair (1992: 45) the terminology preferred
here is concealed and unrecognised *sectors* rather than 'economies' to emphasise
that these areas do not represent activities completely separate from a formal,
visible economy. Indeed, in various ways (discussed below) the hidden work

sector is inextricably tied to the formal work sector, and many people are, to a greater or lesser extent, active in both visible and hidden sectors.

Problems of Measurement

As most researchers in this area have acknowledged, a number of inherent measurement problems exist in relation to hidden work, so much so that anything approaching an accurate quantification of the scale of hidden work as a whole, is virtually impossible. Three distinct measurement problems become immediately apparent. First, what is to be included? Most measurement attempts, for example, have been undertaken with a view to estimating how much revenue is lost to the Exchequer as a result of concealed market activities. By definition, those seeking to calculate such estimates are not interested in non-market activities which make up the unrecognised work sector. As a result, the latter has been the subject of far fewer attempts to quantify and measure. Secondly, in those few attempts which have been made to measure both the concealed and the unrecognised work sectors, a key problem has been how to quantify non-market activities: that is, how to put a monetary value on activities which are not paid for. Thirdly, is the problem of how to measure work activities accurately which are concealed because they are illegal.

It is not the intention here to examine these measurement issues in great detail (for a lengthier discussion, see for example, Fiege, 1989; Smith and Wied-Nebbeling, 1986: 27–42; and Thomas, 1992). As regards estimating the value of the concealed sector, attempts have included: undertaking small-scale, ethno-graphic studies of concealed work activities and scaling up the results; aggregating up from the results of investigations of single cases by the Inland Revenue where discrepancies are revealed between declared and actual income; and seeking to establish differences between levels of income and expenditure in the economy as a whole, or among samples of households (using surveys such as the Family Expenditure Survey) on the assumption that if total expenditure is greater than declared income, the additional income required for this expenditure will have been acquired through concealed activities. Attempts have even been made to measure the concealed sector by the amount of cash in circulation (based on an assumption that transactions in the concealed sector are conducted in cash); indeed, particular attention has been given to the amount of large denomination bank notes in circulation, on an assumption that these figure disproportionately in concealed transactions. Despite the variety in these attempts to measure the concealed-work sector, however, it remains the case that 'a considerable margin of error surrounds all estimates of the scale of concealed transactions' (Smith and Wied-Nebbeling, 1986: 40). This is probably putting it mildly: all the measurement instruments applied to the concealed sector are extremely blunt, making the practice of estimation highly unreliable, if not altogether impossible. As a result, it is difficult to challenge (or improve upon) estimates such as the much-quoted one by the Inland Revenue (1981) which estimated in the late 1970s that the value of non-declared work in the UK was around 7.5 per cent of GNP. Over the intervening period, others have concluded fairly similar estimates; R. Rose (1985: 125), for example, estimates that between 4 and 7.2 per cent of total labour time may be spent in concealed work. Similarly, calculating the average of nine studies identified by R. Rose (1985: 126) gives a mean estimate of the value of undeclared work of just under 6.5 per cent of Gross Domestic Product (GDP).

As noted above, while the core problem of measuring concealed work is the reluctance of those taking part to have their activities made visible, the main difficulty in measuring the unrecognised work sector is one of establishing an accurate valuation. Since those performing household and voluntary work do not normally receive payment, these activities do not have a readily calculable monetary value. There are, of course, methods of conferring a money value on these tasks. In relation to household-based work activities, for example, these methods fall into two general categories. The first involves calculating the cost of purchasing the various tasks from the formal or visible work sector – what Chadeau (1985: 242) refers to as measuring the 'foregone expense'. In terms of domestic work activities, for example, this may be calculated either on the basis of the cost of employing a general housekeeper, or the cost of hiring the specialist services of a cook, cleaner, gardener, and so on. Secondly, estimates can be made on the basis of the lost income incurred by the person who is under-taking the domestic work, who could otherwise devote an equivalent amount of time to paid work (what Chadeau terms, measuring the 'foregone wage'). Yet, while both these methods of calculation produce a monetary value for household domestic work, both contain measurement problems. The most prominent of these is that the alternative methods of calculation are likely to yield quite different values. Nevertheless, while such problems indicate a need to treat any calculations with caution, it remains equally clear that *irrespective of the method of calculation, the monetary value of work activities in the unrecognised work sector is very high.* Chadeau (1985: 245–6), for example, reports over thirty studies undertaken in various countries mainly between 1960 and 1980 which used a variety of bases on which to estimate the value of domestic work. The combined average estimate for all these studies is that domestic work is equivalent to over one third (34.7 per cent) of GNP. Other estimates have put the figure even higher. Handy (1984: 19) for example, comments that over half the country's total labour time is devoted to productive activity in or around the household and that if this work were charged it could amount to 40 per cent of the formal economy (see also R. Rose, 1985: 133). As Handy (1984) points out, when combined with the extent of voluntary work which is undertaken this would make the size of the unrecognised work sector as much as *half* the total economy. For the present discussion, it is sufficient to note that whatever the measurement problems, the value of unrecognised work is vast. Further, given the number of people involved and the time spent on domestic and other non-market activities, the monetary value of the unrecognised work sector almost certainly dwarfs the value of activities in the concealed sector by a large margin.

Just as it is almost impossible to establish an accurate valuation of hidden work, it is also difficult to draw definitive conclusions about likely overall trends: is the size of the hidden work sphere changing over time and are some aspects changing more or less rapidly, and in the same or different direction, as others? The problem here is more than one of establishing reliable benchmarks from which to estimate change. Other problems include the diversity of the hidden work sector, the range of possible influencing variables, and the possibility that single variables will have contrasting effects on different aspects of hidden work.

Take the example of the relationship between the amount of hidden work and the state of the economy. It has been argued, for example, that during periods of strong economic growth, the scope for concealed work activity will tend to rise as people have more money to purchase goods and services, and the formal economy is less able to keep up with the total level of demand. Correspondingly, it is argued that economic recession will tend to dampen concealed work activities, as the amount of money to spend on goods and services diminishes (O'Higgins, 1989: 175). Yet, an opposite argument would seem to be equally plausible. In periods of economic recession when levels of disposable income are depressed, people could conceivably increase their efforts to obtain the goods and services they require more cheaply by entering into more 'cash-in-hand' transactions. Also, if unemployment rises as a result of recession, this could increase the amount of time spent on domestic and voluntary activities (MacDonald, 1996). It may also be the case that some aspects of concealed work – such as 'earning whilst claiming' (claiming welfare payments while concealing additional income being earned from cash-in-hand activity) – increase during recessions when unemployment is greater (though the overall importance of earning whilst claiming has been exaggerated in the past, particularly in comparison to other undeclared income fraud). Further, if one of the outcomes of recession and a lack of employment opportunities is to stimulate a growth in self-employment (as was particularly the case in Britain in the 1980s, for example), as different writers have pointed out (for example, Thomas, 1992) it is the self-employed sector which accounts for a high proportion of concealed work through failing to declare all the income earned. Similarly, whilst it is arguable that a growth in participation rates in the formal work sector could act to limit the amount of time available for activity in the unrecognised work sphere (e.g. voluntary work) at the same time it is evident that some aspects of concealed work thrive on the income, contacts, opportunities and skills deriving from paid employment (Pahl, 1984 and 1988).

Another example of the difficulties of projecting possible trends in hidden work is that while some long-term factors may have stimulated a growth in hidden work during the twentieth century, others may have acted in favour of a decline in aspects of hidden work. For example, an overall rise in levels of taxation over a long period potentially acts to increase the incentive for undertaking non-declared work. Further, the long-term decline in the basic working week in the visible work sector has potentially increased opportunities for workers to devote more time to additional activities in the hidden sector. And, following Gershuny's (1983) argument, the decline in the total number of domestic servants in the early decades of the twentieth century was accompanied by a growth in the proportion of households performing their own domestic tasks. In contrast, other long-term developments such as a rise in women's labour market participation and the growth in the welfare state (the latter providing care in the formal sector to augment existing family and communal care of the elderly, sick and disabled) potentially acted, over a long period, in favour of reducing the total time devoted to domestic and voluntary activities.

These countervailing influences on hidden work, however, are yet further complicated if shorter time horizons are taken into account. For example, while the development of the welfare state in the UK over the last fifty years may have altered the balance between care being provided in the formal or the domestic and voluntary work spheres, recent legislation in the UK (notably the National Health Service and Community Care Act 1990) has resulted, in latter years, in a shift of emphasis back towards more care being dispensed in the domestic and voluntary spheres, rather than in the formal work sector. As a result of this policy, local authorities are now required both to take account of caring provision already being given in their assessments of individuals' care needs, and to promote the development of domiciliary care rather than residential care.

Overall, the different measurement problems and the variety of possible influences on the scale and development of hidden work as a whole, suggest that any general conclusion cannot safely go beyond saying that though overall trends cannot clearly be defined, it is evident that the amount of hidden work performed remains very substantial and is unlikely to be declining significantly (or will do so in the foreseeable future) and could grow further beyond its current size.

EXPLORING HIDDEN WORK (1) CONCEALED WORK

'Concealed' work is one of many labels which have been applied to the area of hidden work which directly or indirectly involves illegal activities; other terms include the 'black', 'shadow', 'submerged', 'irregular', 'underground', 'unobserved', 'unofficial', 'illicit', 'subterranean' and 'informal' sector (see, for example, Feige, 1989; Gershuny, 1983; M. Rose, 1985; Smith and Wied-Nebbeling, 1986; and Thomas, 1992). Our choice of the 'concealed' sector reflects the fact that this aspect of hidden work involves market transactions which are purposely concealed from view, either because they are illegal in themselves, because they contain illegal aspects and are subject to a social stigma, or because they are associated with fraudulent behaviour, such as the evasion of taxes or working whilst claiming state unemployment benefit (Smith and Wied-Nebbeling, 1986: 2). Though relatively simple, this categorisation is not problem-free, however, partly because it covers such a wide scale of activities (e.g. from small-scale cash-in-hand transactions to multi-million-pound drug-dealing) and also, by ring-fencing behaviours and applying particular labels to denote them, this conveys an impression that it is possible to draw a clear and definite distinction between the 'concealed' and the 'visible' sectors. In practice, however, this distinction tends to be much more blurred.

Deviant Work

One of the main reasons why some people conceal the work they are engaged in is because it is illegal. Some of the categories more commonly used in visible work also apply, however. For some, for example, criminal activity is a part-time pursuit, a supplement to income acquired through legal channels. For others, however, crime is their full-time 'occupation'. Indeed, references are commonly made to some individuals being 'professional' criminals, and pursuing a criminal 'career' (for a discussion of crime as alternative work behaviour, see Ferman, 1983: 217).

Not all deviant work is wholly illegal, however. The sex industry, for example, comprises various forms of work (for example, prostitution and the production of pornography) some aspects of which are legal, others not. As regards prostitution, for example, in the UK it is illegal 'to loiter or solicit in a street or public place for the purpose of prostitution' (Street Offences Act 1959, quoted in Lacey *et al.*, 1990: 362). However, the label of deviant work reflects not only these aspects which are illegal, but also the degree to which sex workers are stigmatised by the rest of society (Goffman, 1963; Woollacott, 1980). These social stigma and legal pressures combine to cast prostitutes (and other sex workers) as 'outsiders' in the world of work (H. Becker, 1963). At the same time, this shared experience as outsiders helps to generate a supportive work culture among many of the workers themselves (Woollacott, 1980: 198), a workgroup culture further strengthened by the constant danger of abuse and injury which sex workers face from their clients (see also Adkins, 1995).

Non-Declared Work

For many people, their main experience of concealed work will be work undertaken for payment but which is hidden from the tax authorities. It is widely believed that the biggest source of untaxed income is that accruing to the self-employed, whose income is not subject to tax collection through Pay-As-You-Earn (PAYE) arrangements. On the basis of the findings of individual investigations by the Inland Revenue, it is evident that a significant proportion of the self-employed fail to declare all their income to the tax authorities. This not only includes those owning businesses but also those self-employed individuals who contract themselves to larger organisations (see Chapter 2 for discussion of the growth of self-employment). Away from the self-employed, however, in recent periods of high unemployment, undeclared income deriving from 'working and claiming' has regularly become a *cause célèbre* of (particularly Conservative) Governments, with clamp-downs on the 'benefit-fraud' stemming from those claiming unemployment and/or other welfare payments whilst also acquiring income from work which is not declared to the authorities. This governmental selective attention – pursuing the small-scale frauds of the unemployed with a vigour hardly shown towards their richer counterparts engaging in large-scale tax evasion – probably reflects not only a class bias and the political appeal of lowering social security costs by removing those caught 'fiddling benefit', but also a *realpolitik* of the benefit fiddlers being much easier to catch than their larger-scale and more sophisticated tax-dodging counterparts. In this endeavour, governments have also been assisted by the periodic involvement of sections of the press (such as the *Sun* newspaper's 'Split on a Scrounger' campaign, with a telephone hotline for anonymous callers) and by a willingness among some to 'shop' neighbours who they suspect of benefit offences, to the local social security office (see also Pahl, 1984: 95). What these government and press campaigns reflect too, is a perception that the unemployed are particularly the ones involved in cash-in-hand activities: that they are available for such work by virtue of not having a formal job, and are successful in obtaining cash-in-hand work because they can afford to take jobs at a lower payment than would be offered in the visible work sector, because any wage is supplemented by the welfare benefits also being claimed.

Clearly, a proportion of the total cash-in-hand work *is* undertaken by the unemployed, though often for very small payment (MacDonald, 1994). The growth of small subcontracting firms in both manufacturing and services has probably extended the availability of cash-in-hand work into a wider range of sectors over the past two decades. What Pahl (1984) and others have shown, however, is that it is a far from accurate picture to portray most cash-in-hand work activities as being undertaken by the unemployed. On the contrary, much of this work is carried out by people who are already in employment and are undertaking additional work in their spare time (like Ron in our earlier example). For Pahl (1984) and others, it is the extra resources available to those in employment which increases their access to additional work: employment provides contacts as well as sufficient financial resources to acquire the equipment and materials necessary for undertaking other work (garden machinery, power tools, transport, or whatever) together with the skills necessary for conducting other activity. Unemployment, on the other hand, is for many not only an intensely isolating experience (whatever contacts that might have been made while in employment are soon lost) but also that the (low) level of unemployment income restricts the unemployed in extending their own concealed activity, other than in those areas requiring little or no capital expenditure, such as labouring for others or cleaning windows (Pahl, 1984: 97). What this also indicates is that just as the distinction between employed and unemployed confers income and status on the former rather than the latter, in the same way, employment – and the benefits stemming from employment – provide access to more highly rewarded areas of concealed work, than those available to the unemployed, who are largely restricted to lower-paying activities.

EXPLORING HIDDEN WORK (2) UNRECOGNISED WORK

Domestic Work

The hidden work sphere is dominated, in terms of the volume of activity, number of people involved, total time spent and overall value of activities, by domestic labour within the household. It is domestic work too, which has particularly significant implications for the pattern and experience of work in the visible work sector. Here, there is space to explore only certain aspects of domestic work, but even a brief examination provides ample indication of the various points at which work in the domestic sphere touches upon and shapes the broader realities and experiences of work, and more generally underlines the continued prominence of domestic work in overall work experience. A number of these points of contact between domestic work and paid employment have already been noted in earlier chapters. In the discussion of attitudes towards time-discipline in Chapter 4, for example, it was noted how the household, together with schools and other institutions, has played an important part in the development and internalisation of values towards regularity, punctuality and time thrift. More broadly, the domestic sphere represents a key location for childhood socialisation, including socialisation relating to work values (see Chapter 3). The domestic sphere is more than a context for the development of values towards work, however: it also represents an important source of material support for those working in paid employment. The household acts to deliver labour to the workplace in a condition fit for work: clothed, fed, rested. Over and above these physical contributions, the domestic sphere also provides an important source of psychological support for those in paid work: a context in which they can relax, 'wind down', and 'switch off' from the pressures of their job.

As well as the different aspects of this support role *vis-à-vis* the formal work sector, the domestic sphere also exerts a major influence on the overall pattern of labour market participation. At its simplest, the large amount of time expended on housework and childcare limits the time available for other activities, including paid employment. But of course, the main point here is that domestic work has not simply limited the labour market participation of people in general: it has especially limited the participation of women in paid work. For it is women who disproportionately continue to shoulder the responsibilities for domestic work. As industrialism developed, the increased prominence of the male 'breadwinner' left women with the larger part of the domestic responsibilities. And, even though the participation rates of women in the labour market have risen considerably since the post-1945 period, and especially since the 1960s (see Chapter 2) this has not been matched by a corresponding sharing of the tasks of household work between men and women, or an equalising of the overall responsibility for the domestic sphere (Horrell, 1994). As Morris (1990: 102), reviewing the evidence on domestic work comments, 'none of the data seems to warrant any suggestion that the traditional female responsibility for household work has been substantially eroded'. Moreover, as writers such as Duncombe and Marsden (1995) points out, this continuing inequality spans not only the distribution of physical work tasks, but also the emotional work that takes place in the household, with women continuing to shoulder a disproportionate amount of the emotional caring work, with their male partners giving priority to their paid work roles (see also the discussion of emotional labour in Chapter 7). For many women, therefore, taking on paid employment has added to their sum of total work, rather than brought about any equalising of work responsibilities with their male partners. 'Married women in employment bear a disproportionate "dual burden" of paid and unpaid work' (Gershuny *et al.*, 1994: 152). Time-budget surveys conducted in the UK in 1974/5 and 1987 discussed by Gershuny and his colleagues (1994: 176–7) do in fact suggest that husbands' proportion of household work had risen by 1987 compared with 1975, particularly where their wives were in full-time employment. However, overall a significant gap still remains, particularly where women have not been in paid employment for a long period. Gershuny and colleagues (1994: 179) argue that this may reflect a process of 'lagged adaptation' with husbands (and wives) moving only slowly away from their former assumptions about domestic responsibilities (see also Horrell, 1994).

Their disproportionate share of responsibilities for housework and childcare has various implications for women's position in the labour market: for example, a degree of discontinuity in labour market activity (with periods of employment interspersed with periods of childcare) which in turn contributes both towards a lower rate of progression within internal career hierarchies and a resulting disproportionate occupancy by women of lower-level and more poorly paid jobs (see also Chapter 9). With women more likely to be occupying less well-paid jobs than their male partners, this tends to lead to any mobility among many couples being male-driven: couples relocate on the basis of the labour market for the male's job. Such mobility patterns in turn potentially further exacerbate women's position in the labour market, since they are forced to seek employment in labour markets that have been chosen more to suit the job requirements of their male partners rather than themselves.

The ways in which women's domestic work responsibilities influence their pattern of labour market participation is particularly represented by the nature and growth of part-time working. Over four-fifths of part-time workers are women and more than two-fifths of female employees work part-time (see Chapter 2). One of the factors accounting for why employers, seeking to expand part-time working, have met with an adequate supply of available labour, has been the requirement for many women to combine a desire or need for paid employment with their continuing domestic responsibilities: a combination which for many can best or only be achieved by engaging in part-time rather than full-time employment.

Various factors make women's disproportionate involvement in household work problematic. For example, much of the activity which comprises household work is both highly repetitive (cooking, cleaning, washing and ironing, for example) and immensely time-consuming. Indeed, as Oakley (1974: 45) points out, the virtually continuous nature of domestic work for many women is summed up in such traditional phrases as 'a woman's work is never done'. The housewives in Oakley's own study worked, on average, 77 hours per week – double the working week of many workers in full-time paid employment (Oakley, 1974: 93). Further, for much of the time, housework activities are performed in isolation, and at times under considerable time pressures. The combined effect of these factors is that many find housework a source of frustration, dissatisfaction and low self-esteem. The strength of these negative feelings are, for many, seemingly stronger than the positive aspects of domestic work deriving from, for example, a degree of autonomy, or involvement with child development.

What exacerbates and encapsulates the problematic nature and status of domestic work is that it is work which is unpaid. As noted earlier, it is this absence of payment which is a key factor in making this aspect of work 'hidden'. In addition, the fact that, for the most part, domestic work remains practically as well as metaphorically hidden (since much of it takes place 'behind closed doors') adds to the 'invisible' nature of this aspect of work. Thus, overall, domestic work is hidden in terms of status and social recognition, in terms of national accounts of total work output, and by the private nature of much of household life.

Voluntary Work

Like unpaid domestic labour, voluntary work – which has also been referred to by such terms as 'communal' work (Gershuny, 1983) and 'gift work' (Handy, 1984) – is generally (though not exclusively) characterised by an absence of money payment for work undertaken. For Gershuny (1983) one of the long-term factors stimulating the growth of voluntary work has been the rising cost of buying in services from the formal economy, leading to an increased self-provisioning from within the community. However, it is important not to overlook the fact that the exchange of unpaid work has always been a basis on which communities, particularly rural communities, have functioned (see, for example, Felt and Sinclair, 1992). And, like other aspects of hidden work, voluntary work is characterised by its scale and diversity. A survey of volunteering conducted in the UK in the early 1990s, for example, indicates that up to 23 million adults are involved in voluntary work of one sort or another each year, and that around 100 million hours may be spent on organised and unorganised voluntary activity every week (Joseph Rowntree Foundation, 1991).

The range of activity which constitutes voluntary work is vast and incorporates informal activities (such as doing an elderly neighbour's shopping) and various social exchange or mutual self-help activities (such as participating in a baby-sitting circle) as well as work in the more 'organised' voluntary work sector which itself is composed of an almost endless range of activities: from the St John Ambulance Association to prison visiting, from voluntary fire services to charity shops, and from canvassing during elections to serving on the local Neighbourhood Watch committee. As Harding and Jenkins (1989: 119) point out, the nature of voluntary work is also diverse in terms of the levels at which activities take place: while some voluntary activities are local in character, others are part of national or even multinational voluntary organisations. The study of voluntary activity in the UK quoted above found that the most common activities within the organised voluntary work sector include raising money, running an event, serving on a committee and providing transport, while the most common foci for voluntary activity relate to sports and exercise, children's education and health and welfare (Joseph Rowntree Foundation, 1991).

Rather than attempt to consider all the many facets of voluntary work, it is more useful here to take one example to illustrate a broader argument concerning the relevance of this aspect of hidden work for the visible work sphere. Given its growing prominence in public debate in recent years, a useful example is that of the voluntary provision of care for someone who is elderly, sick or disabled. Historically, tending the sick and elderly represented a major aspect of voluntary activity: prior to the introduction of a welfare state, much of the tending of the old and infirm took place within the household and the community. The rise of state-funded care reduced (but by no means totally eliminated) this reliance on care from within the community. In recent years, however, various factors have once again increased the significance being placed on care provided within the community rather than by the state. One of these factors is the general increase in life expectancy which has taken place, resulting in a larger proportion of the population living into very old age: estimates relating to Britain, for example, suggest that the proportion of the population over the age of 85 years may be 50 per cent higher by the year 2031 than it was in the early 1990s (Corti and Dex, 1995: 101). Second, as noted above, at the same time as the proportion of elderly people in the population is rising, the state (through legislation such as the National Health Service Care and Community Act) has increased the emphasis placed on the self-provisioning of care needs by the families and others close to those requiring care, rather than care being dispensed directly by state-funded professional care facilities.

Clearly, caring for someone who is old, disabled or ill could, depending on the circumstances, be categorised as either domestic work or voluntary work. Attending to an infirm spouse in one's own home, for example, is part of many individuals' everyday domestic routine. On the other hand, many people provide care for someone in the latter's home, for example by paying regular visits to an elderly neighbour. This overlap of categories should not delay us unduly, however; as noted earlier, in practice many activities straddle boundaries within the overall hidden work sector. What is more important here is the relevance of caring for a broader understanding of work as a whole.

There are several issues arising from the relationship between the voluntary dispensing of care and the formal work sector. These include, for example, whether or not voluntary care activity undermines the role and status of those performing a care function as part of their paid employment, or whether a willingness among the public to perform some tasks voluntarily has restricted the growth of occupations which otherwise would have expanded to meet a greater demand for care provision. Probably the most important aspect of the interaction between caring and employment, however, is the potential impact which providing care has on the carer's own labour market situation and employment experience. It is clear that, in many cases, looking after a sick or elderly person is very time-consuming and significantly influences a carer's activity and career in the formal work sector. According to data from the British Household Panel Study (a regular survey of over 5000 households in Britain) in the early 1990s, almost one in seven adults was providing informal care for someone sick, disabled or elderly (Corti *et al.*, 1994; Corti and Dex, 1995: 101). Just under one-third of the carers were looking after someone in their own home, whilst two-thirds provided care for someone living elsewhere. Whilst a higher proportion of carers were women (17 per cent of the female adult population), the proportion of men (12 per cent of the male adult population) providing care is still significant. Over a third (35 per cent) of all co-resident carers (those looking after someone in their own home) spent at least 50 hours per week on caring; women spent more time on care than men, both inside and outside the household.

Given the amount of time devoted to providing care, it is only to be expected that this will significantly affect carers' patterns of paid employment. This is indeed what Corti and her colleagues found (Corti *et al.*, 1994). For example, overall participation rates of women and men carers in the formal work sector were significantly lower than their counterparts not involved in caring; further, among those carers in employment, the likelihood of working part-time rather than full-time was significantly higher. Carers were also more likely to occupy lower level jobs than their counterparts not involved in caring. Many involved in co-resident care, in particular, indicated that family responsibilities had prevented them from either looking for a job, accepting a full-time job, or changing jobs; caring responsibilities had also required many to leave paid employment altogether, or work fewer hours (Corti *et al.*, 1994: 28, 38). Such effects are not surprising, given the time spent on caring. In the study by Corti *et al.* (1994: 37), for example, two-fifths of the male and female co-resident carers who held full-time jobs also spent 20 hours or more a week on caring. Overall, it is clear from this study (as well as from others: see, for example, Arber and Ginn, 1995; Parker 1988) the extent to which carers are forced to forgo employment opportunities, or change their working patterns to fit in with their caring responsibilities.

Conclusion

Overall, probably as much work activity takes place outside the formal work sector as inside. This albeit brief examination of the dimensions of hidden work indicates how, for many, the realities of work are shaped by experiences away from 'visible' employment. What is more, these hidden work realities are clearly very diverse: the woman at home caring for a young family; the unemployed person working voluntarily to maintain some routine and a sense of purpose; the older individual discouraged from seeking paid employment, using time available for house repairs and DIY; the daughter or son working part-time whilst at the same time caring for an elderly parent; the individual who secures an income through illegal activity of one sort or another. The range of activities is as great, if not greater, than the diversity of work experiences in the visible work sector. Each of these areas of hidden work deserves greater recognition and more careful analysis to reflect their significance in many people's lives. In this chapter, it has been possible only to touch upon the diverse realities of hidden work. What is clear even from this brief examination, however, is not only the scale and importance of hidden work, but also the degree to which the hidden and visible work spheres interrelate. Indeed, so extensive is this degree of interrelatedness that any analysis of one cannot be satisfactorily undertaken without due recognition being given to the significance of the other. Further, the diversity of hidden work adds significantly to the overall diversity in work experiences and work realities. This theme of diversity is one that has been evident throughout the book and is a theme we comment further upon in the concluding chapter.

11 Conclusion: The Realities of Work

The exploration of the realities of work in western capitalist society has taken us through a century of industrial history and fifty years of empirical research, a variety of sectors in differing economic and political contexts, a range of work settings and processes, and a plethora of experiences and understandings of working. The constant theme has been one of plurality: in theories, research methods and analyses as well as findings, observations and understandings. This is a valuable conclusion in its own right because it alerts us to the importance of acknowledging that different explanations are possible for the same phenomenon, because it is experienced and interpreted differently. In turn, this allows us to draw conclusions about four themes that have emerged from foregoing chapters: change and continuity; informality and subcultures; (managerial) rationalities and (employee) counter-rationalities; and analytical complexity.

CHANGE AND CONTINUITY

An abiding theme within the study of work is the extent to which there has been a change from, or continuity with, the past. It has already been observed that some commentators have argued how specific periods can delineate one stage of society from the next: for example, the theories of industrial and post-industrial society (Chapter 3) or Fordist, neo-Fordist and post-Fordist production (Chapter 6). Others argue that the changes are in fact so great as to constitute a new paradigm that represents not only a marked economic, political, institutional, cultural and social shift, but a quantum leap in the way we understand the world: a leap from modernist to postmodernist conceptions of the world (for a full discussion see Harvey, 1989; Lyon, 1994; also, for an analysis linked to human resource management, see Legge, 1995: 286–328).

In the preceding chapters, there is evidence of both continuity *and* change. It has been shown that in the workplace there have been new theories, ideas, technologies and practices to replace the old ones; but so too there have continued to be important resonances with the past. Table 11.1 illustrates some of the principal areas of change and continuity that have been explored in the preceding chapters. It suggests how change in one aspect of work can produce continuity in another. Indeed, the extent to which work overall in contemporary society can be characterised as being radically different, or ostensibly the same, depends largely upon which themes are being focused upon. A focus on the

203

features illustrated by the left-hand side of Table 11.1 would lead to the conclusion that work has undergone notable change, whilst a focus on the right-hand side would suggest a pattern of continuity.

Table 11.1   *Change and continuity in work*

Notable CHANGE yet...	also CONTINUITY
New patterns of production and consumption	Persistence of work ethic
Rise of service sector	Continued existence of routine, boring jobs
Technological change with some growth of high skilled jobs	New types of low-skill, low-discretion jobs
Increase of emotional labour	Undervaluing of social abilities as skill
More women in the labour market (feminisation)	Gendered division of labour Unfair discrimination
New forms of work (flexibility) and working-time patterns	Traditional working methods and forms of control
New management initiatives for work intensification	Traditional methods of control and reliance on employee consent
Emergence of Post-Fordist organisations	Taylorist/Fordist organisations remain

It seems to us that there is an important reality of work that *has* changed dramatically because it is being experienced by increasing numbers of people: a declining sense of employment security. This is particularly the case in the UK where a number of factors have converged to reduce the employment security of large sections of the working population. First, there has been the political/ideo-logical commitment to the supremacy of market forces and the concomitant deregulation of employment, coupled with the Conservative Government's refusal to accept the European social chapter. Second, there has been a weakening of the influence of trade unions, with fewer workers now represented by unions and thereby enjoying a protection against the worst excesses of exploitation that unions offer. Third, there has been the expansion of multinational organisations, so local economies (and particularly employment opportunities and working conditions) are increasingly dependent on organisations with a global perspective, and with a single-minded pursuit of the most favourable return on investment. Fourth, new working-life patterns are emerging, which means that the 9 to 5, five-day week from leaving school until retirement at 65 is not the common pattern of employment. Increasingly, people fail to get jobs when leaving school, must undertake part-time work, are placed on fixed-term contracts, are faced with periods of unemployment through redundancy, and are pressed into early retirement. For the employer, this means flexibility, but for the employee it means vulnerability.

Just as increasing employment insecurity constitutes a significant change, there is equally an important reality of work that represents continuity: unfair discrimination within labour markets and employing organisations. This discrimination manifests itself in a number of ways, but most notably means some groups have greater access to higher-level, more prestigious, better-paid jobs than others. It is evident that for many in the workforce, the reality of their work experience is one of inequitable treatment, compared with groups which have been more favoured in the labour market. The question of discrimination was addressed directly in Chapter 9, but at other points in the book, too, the way that social arrangements have favoured some groups rather than others has been clear. Three of these points were the discussion of how the notion of skill is, in important part, socially constructed (Chapter 5), the comparative lack of skill attributed to jobs involving emotional labour, particularly in comparison with jobs perceived as more 'rational' in character (Chapter 7); and the ways that the work performed in households importantly influences access to, and success within, the paid employment sector (Chapter 10). In each of these, the different realities for women, compared to their male counterparts, have been emphasised. Women are the ones holding skills which have disproportionately failed to be recognised as deserving skilled status; women are disproportionately involved in emotional labour jobs, where the content of those jobs tends to receive only limited recognition; and it remains women who carry a disproportionate share of responsibility for household tasks, to the detriment of their involvement in paid employment. This continuing difference in the realities of work of men and women is made more salient by the increasing feminisation of the workforce.

INFORMALITY AND SUBCULTURES

A common theme that emerges from various chapters is how employees cope with the realities of work by developing informal rules and a shared identity. Although work can require individual as well as collective behaviours, there exist underpinning values, which are shared and negotiated collectively, and from which norms of informal behaviour develop. In other words, the broad patterns of behaviour are framed within negotiated orders which constitute workplace subcultures. A subculture is characterised by sets of meanings that are shared by a particular group, and reinforced through beliefs, values and norms. Newcomers must learn the norms of behaviour and in so doing begin to understand the meanings and become imbued with the values and beliefs, eventually internalising them. This concept of subculture is important because it highlights the need to treat organisations as pluralist rather than unitary entities: a collection of subcultures rather than a single culture. In this sense, there may be a formal organisational culture proclaiming common values and beliefs, but behind this façade there are likely to be different informal subcultures reflecting distinct values and beliefs.

Over a period of time, strong subcultures may become embedded into the work organisation. It was noted in Chapter 5 the impact this has on conceptions of skill, particularly perpetuating assumptions about what constitutes men's and women's work. Similarly, subcultures may have a powerful impact (either positive or negative) on the process of discrimination at work (explored in Chapter 9) by promoting a collective understanding of fairness and unfairness in the treatment of various individuals and groups by managers. More generally, it was noted how the economic necessity of both visible work (Chapter 3) and hidden work (Chapter 10) was guided by a moral dimension, which itself often reflects dominant cultural values and beliefs.

Subcultures represent collective interests that are *different* from the formal management ideology and structures within an organisation. This arises from the pluralistic nature of all organisations. However, the types of informal, unofficial behaviours associated with coping with alienation (Chapter 8), time-discipline (Chapter 4) and stress from emotional labour (Chapter 7) are themselves often regulated by the subculture; in turn, this assists in the production of consent, thus helping to obscure the exploitative nature of the capitalist labour process. The subculture provides the mechanism for this informal regulation, so cannot really be construed as acting against profitable production; in this sense such subcultures are not usually counter-capitalism. They may perhaps be seen as counter-managerial in that they challenge aspects of control, but even then management prerogative is not opposed.

RATIONALITIES AND COUNTER-RATIONALITIES

Modern texts on managing tend to paint too uniform a view of work and workers, and by extension, too uniform a view on what constitutes 'effective' management. This view, we believe, in turn reflects an over-developed sense of the omnipotence of managerial rationality pervading the workplace: that is, that the rules as defined by management are the ones strictly adhered to by the workforce. What has been demonstrated at different points in the book, however, is the simultaneous existence of a strong workers' counter-rationality, reflecting the different interests which management and workforce bring to the workplace. Put simply, for management it is the *output* from work which is the central issue, while for the workforce the *process* of working is an end in itself, as well as the main means of gaining income. As discussed in Chapter 3, notwithstanding any increased emphasis on consumerism and the construction of identity around consumption rather than production ('I am what I buy', rather than ' I am what I do') workers continue to go to work for more than just money. The sheer amount of time spent working, and thus the centrality of work in the majority of adults' waking hours, means that the experience of work, and the process of working, remain important. What this reinforces is how the strategies which workers adopt function in various ways towards a counter-rationality, and towards making work as 'humane' as possible: by easing workloads, breaking up a monotonous day, creating fun, generating interaction, building up group identities, maintaining self-esteem.

As we have also seen, in the main these counter-rationalities function not only for workers but also indirectly for management, and for the maintenance of capitalist wage relations. For, in ways much discussed in industrial sociology, by challenging and subverting the margins of managerial rationality, workers establish a broader consent to the core of that rationality. Rarely is there evidence of counter-rationalities going beyond fairly confined boundaries: the occasional unauthorised absence, the limited time taken up by practical jokes, the minor deviations from management's requirements over emotional labour. These do not add up to a fundamental challenge to, or rejection of, a system, more a way of making that system more acceptable and creating a feeling that workers can exercise a measure of control over managerial definitions of work reality. Therefore, workers' counter-rationality does not typically represent a fundamental challenge to managerial authority. Workers may 'misbehave', but they do so, for the most part, within tacitly agreed and narrow limits.

This is not to say that such behaviour remains unproblematic for management. We can see how, for example, in various ways management are seeking to tighten up the utilisation of working time (see Chapter 4). But, we can also see the *limited* nature of these managerial attempts to tighten up organisational regimes. Such a limitation is borne partly out of a recognition that the costs (for example, in terms of worker morale) of suppressing all 'indulgencies' are probably greater than the sum of any ensuing benefits. The limited assault on employees' counter-strategies are probably also borne out of an awareness that a complete suppression is simply not possible.

The foregoing comments differ from a view of the workplace as a site where surveillance and compliance have reached near total levels. For the most part, such workplaces would seem to remain a small minority; most workplaces appear to operate not on a basis of management seeking total and continuous conformity with detailed sets of prescribed rules governing all aspects of behaviour at work, but rather more of a system of negotiated order, whereby tacit agreements are established as to what levels of deviation from formal rules are allowed. These levels are not fixed or constant – customs and practices are subject to modification over time – and periodically give rise to tension, as each side attempts to shift the boundary or respond to the other's attempts to shift it. But the complex requirement of capital from wage labour – the need for consent as well as control, for active cooperation rather than merely passive compliance in translating labour power into productive labour – gives rise to a management –workforce relationship based on negotiation and a tension between the two different interest groups and the twin rationalities, rather than the uniform imposition of a dominant rationality.

ANALYTICAL COMPLEXITY

It is a truism that life is complex, so why should it be presumed that working life is simple? Why do managers believe in the quick-fix or the latest buzz-word? Why do students seek neatly packaged answers? Why do management texts produce six-step solutions to ubiquitous problems? Why do lecturers resort to key-word acronyms to explain a multitude of varied human behaviour? It is because they are all in search of 'the simple answer', when the real answer is: there is no simple answer. Engaging with complexity is time-consuming, costly, confusing and frequently disillusioning, yet it is the only satisfactory way of exploring work.

If there are no simple solutions to complex problems, then either the complexity must be engaged with, or the problem redefined to simplify the challenge. Frequently, academics employ the latter method, but with varying degrees of success. To analyse helps to understand the problem, but not necessarily to find a solution. For example, Chapter 5 revealed how different ways of 'measuring' skill were used by different researchers. None of the methods was without its limitations, and each led to different conclusions about how the concept of skill should be understood. The solution (if it can be described as such) was to examine the complexity of the concept, and an attempt to integrate all the approaches in an effort to arrive at a multi-faceted 'measure' of skill: and ultimately, an explanation so complex that it would be of virtually no 'practical' use in the workplace. It is this last point that alerts us to a particular problem with accepting complexity: it does not provide what the market wants. Because people (managers especially) want simple solutions and explanations there is a pressure to produce them. Complexity is simplified, the nostrum emerges and the quick-fix solution is invented. So, it is of little wonder that the realities of work invariably fail to match up with the descriptions included or implied in many management texts.

Engaging with complexity also requires a more open-minded approach to the nature of problems. If a person is looking for 'the logical solution', in the same way as, for example, Taylor (Chapter 6) believed that scientific management was the answer to all productivity problems, then the mind is closed to the equally logical possibility that there is no single solution. Indeed, the emergent picture is that the realities of work are characterised by contradiction, dilemma and paradox. For example, it was discussed in Chapter 8 how the contradictions embedded in the capitalist labour process produce the dilemma of control for managers, and how, through the process of 'making out', employees paradoxically consent to their own subordination and exploitation. Throughout the analysis, the importance of contradictory theories and interpretation has surfaced: for example, the question of the demise or survival of the work ethic (Chapter 3); the theses of deskilling, upskilling or reskilling work (Chapter 6); the significance of emotional labour (Chapter 7); the forms of survival strategy to cope with alienation (Chapter 8); and the liberal, radical and reactionary perspectives on equal opportunities (Chapter 9).

By acknowledging and confronting complexity throughout the chapters, it has been possible to show the richness and variety of the experience of work. Moreover, the pluralist approach we have taken has meant that these complex realities can be explored without the discussion flitting through a postmodern carnival or being constrained by a structuralist prison.

WORK - A MYTH OF THE FUTURE

The myth of work that we began this book with has been dispelled. The different chapters have revealed the diversity of work experience. It is a diversity borne partly out of the multitude of different contexts within which work takes place, together with the very many occupations and tasks that people perform at work, and the different work schedules and contractual arrangements that employees are engaged on. However, at the same time, the diversity also derives from the different ways that people construct meaning and identity in their roles as workers: the different values they attach to work, the ways they behave and interact at work and the different strategies they employ to adjust to and ameliorate the pressures of work in contemporary industrial society.

If one myth of work can be castigated as being too simplistic and too generalist, we should be cautious of those who would seek to replace it with a new myth about how work will be transformed in the twenty-first century. So, by way of warning, here is a possible myth about work in the future. Work will become increasingly information-intense, requiring high-level, conceptual skills and a highly educated workforce. The physical workplace will be replaced with the virtual workplace, characterised by the way it links employees, based at home, via the Internet. These will not be employees in the traditional sense of the word, but rather subcontracted, self-employed workers on flexible hours. The working lifetime will be reconfigured to provide working opportunities for all; work centrality will diminish, and leisure hours will be extended in which to consume a wide variety of individually specified, enriching and entertaining pursuits on offer in the information society. But whilst this is just speculation, there is one factor we can be sure of: complexity and diversity will continue to characterise the future realities of work.

Bibliography

Adam, B. (1990) *Time and Social Theory*, Cambridge: Polity.

Adkins, L. (1995) *Gendered Work: Sexuality, Family and the Labour Market*, Milton Keynes: Open University Press.

Aglietta, M. (1979) *A Theory of Capitalist Regulation*, London: New Left.

Allen, J. and Henry, N. (1996) 'Fragments of industry and employment', in R. Crompton, D. Gallie and K. Purcell (eds) *Changing Forms of Employment*, London: Routledge, pp. 65–82.

Allen, S. and Macey, M. (1990) 'Race and ethnicity in the European context', *British Journal of Sociology*, 41 (3): 375–93.

Anthias, F. (1992) 'Connecting "race" and ethnic phenomena', *Sociology*, 26 (3): 421–38.

Anthias, F. and Yuval-Davis, N. (1992) *Racialized Boundaries*, London: Routledge.

Anthony, P. D. (1977) *The Ideology of Work*, London: Tavistock.

Applebaum, H. A. (1981) *Royal Blue: The Culture of Construction Workers*, New York: Holt, Rinehart and Winston.

Arber, S. and Ginn, J. (1995) 'Gender differences in the relationship between paid employment and informal care', *Work, Employment and Society*, 9 (3): 445–71.

Armstrong, P. (1988) 'Labour and monopoly capital', in R. Hyman and W. Streeck (eds) *New Technology and Industrial Relations*, Oxford: Blackwell, pp. 143–59.

Armstrong, P. (1989) 'Management, labour process and agency', *Work, Employment and Society*, 3 (3): 307–22.

Armstrong, P. (1995) 'Accountancy and HRM', in J. Storey (ed.) *HRM: A Critical Text*, London: Routledge, pp. 142–63.

Ashforth, B. and Humphrey, R. (1993) 'Emotional labour in service roles: the influence of identity', *Academy of Management Review*, 18 (1): 88–115.

Ashforth, B. and Humphrey, R. (1995) 'Emotion in the work place: a reappraisal', *Human Relations*, 48 (2): 97–125.

Atkinson, J. (1984) 'Manpower strategies for flexible organisation', *Personnel Management*, August: 28–31.

Attewell, P. (1990) 'What is skill?', *Work and Occupations*, 17 (4): 422–48.

Bacchi, C. (1990) *Same Difference: Feminism and Sexual Difference*, Sydney: Allen and Unwin.

Batstone, E. and Gourlay, I. (1986) *Unions, Unemployment and Innovation*, Oxford: Blackwell.

Batstone, E., Gourlay, S., Levie, H. and Moore, R. (1987) *New Technology and the Process of Labour Regulation*, Oxford: Clarendon.

Becker, G. (1964) *Human Capital*, New York: National Bureau of Economic Research.

Becker, H. (1963) *Outsiders: Studies in the Sociology of Deviance*, New York: Free Press.

Beechey, V. (1982) 'The sexual division of labour and the labour process: a critical assessment of Braverman', in S. Wood (ed.) The *Degradation of Work?*, London: Hutchinson, pp. 54–73.

Bell, D. (1973) *The Coming of Post-Industrial Society*, New York: Basic.

Bell, D. (1974) *The Cultural Contradictions of Capitalism*, London: Heinemann.

Best, S. and Kellner, D. (1991) *Postmodern Theory: Critical Interrogations*, London: Macmillan.

Beynon, H. (1973) *Working for Ford*, Harmondsworth: Penguin.

Blauner, R. (1964) *Alienation and Freedom*, Chicago: University of Chicago Press.

Blyton, P. (1985) *Changes in Working Time: An International Review*, London: Croom Helm.

Blyton, P. (1992) 'The search for workforce flexibility', in B. Towers (ed.) *Handbook of Human Resource Management*, Oxford: Blackwell, pp. 295–318.

Blyton, P. (1994) 'Working hours', in K. Sisson (ed.) *Personnel Management*, 2nd edn, Oxford: Blackwell, pp. 495–526.

Blyton, P. (1995) *The Development of Annual Working Hours in the United Kingdom*, Geneva: International Labour Organization.

Blyton, P. and Trinczek, R. (1995) 'Working time flexibility and annual hours', *European Industrial Relations Review*, no. 260, September: 13-14.

Blyton, P. and Turnbull, P. (eds) (1992) *Reassessing Human Resource Management*, London: Sage.

Blyton, P. and Turnbull, P. (1994) *The Dynamics of Employee Relations*, Basingstoke: Macmillan.

Blyton, P. and Turnbull, P. (1996) 'Confusing convergence: industrial relations in the European airline industry', *European Journal of Industrial Relations*, 2 (1): 7–20.

Blyton, P., Bacon, N. and Morris, J. (1996) 'Working in steel: steelworkers' attitudes to change 40 years on', *Industrial Relations Journal*, 27(2): 155–65.

Boland, R. J. and Hoffman, R. (1983) 'Humor in a machine shop', in L. Pondy, P. Frost, G. Morgan and T. Dandridge (eds) *Organizational Symbolism*, Greenwich, CT: JAI, pp. 187–98.

Bosworth, D. (1994) 'Shiftwork in the UK: evidence from the LFS', *Applied Economics*, 26 (6): 617–26.

Boyer, R. (ed.) (1988) *The Search For Labour Market Flexibility*, Oxford: Clarendon.

Bradley, H. (1989) *Men's Work, Women's Work*, Oxford: Blackwell.

Bradney, P. (1957) 'The joking relationship in industry', *Human Relations*, 10 (2): 179–87.

Brah, A. (1986) 'Unemployment and racism: Asian youth on the dole,' in S. Allen, A Watson, K. Purcell and S. Woods (eds) *The Experience of Unemployment*, London: Macmillan, pp. 61–78.

Bratton, J. (1992) *Japanization at Work*, London: Macmillan.

Braverman, H. (1974) *Labor and Monopoly Capital*, New York: Monthly Review.

Brennan, J. and McGeevor, P. (1987) *Employment of Graduates from Ethnic Minorities*, London: Commission for Racial Equality.

Brown, C. and Gay, P. (1985) *Racial Discrimination: 17 Years after the Act*, London: Policy Studies Institute.

Browning, H. L. and Singelmann, J. (1978) 'The transformation of the US labour force', *Politics and Society*, 8 (3): 481–509.

Brunhes, B. (1989) 'Labour flexibility in enterprises: a comparison of firms in four European countries' in Organisation for Economic Cooperation and Development (ed.) *Labour Market Flexibility: Trends in Enterprises*, Paris: OECD, pp. 11–36.

Buchanan, D. A. (1986) 'Management objectives in technical change', in D. Knights and H. Willmott (eds) *Managing the Labour Process*, Aldershot: Gower, pp. 67–84.

Buchanan, D. A. and Boddy. D. (1983) *Organisations in the Computer Age: Technological Imperatives and Strategic Choice*, Aldershot: Gower.

Burawoy, M. (1979) *Manufacturing Consent*, Chicago: University of Chicago Press.

Burawoy, M. (1985) *The Politics of Production*, London: Verso.

Burchell, B., Elliott, J., Rubery, J. and Wilkinson, F. (1994) 'Management and employee perceptions of skill', in R. Penn, M. Rose and J Rubery (eds) *Skill and Occupational Change*, Oxford: Oxford University Press, pp. 159–89.

Butcher, S. and Hart, D. (1995) 'An analysis of working time 1979–1994', *Employment Gazette*, May: 211–22.

Campbell, N. and Burton, F. (eds) (1994) *Japanese Multinationals: Strategies and Management in the Global Kaisha*, London: Routledge.

Capelli, P. (1995) 'Rethinking employment', *British Journal of Industrial Relations*, 33 (4): 563–602.

Carlzon, J. (1987) *Moments of Truth*, New York: Harper and Row.

Cavendish, R. (1982) *Women on the Line*, London: Routledge.

Chadeau, A. (1985) 'Measuring household activities: some international comparisons', *Review of Income and Wealth*, 31 (3): 237–53.

Charles, N. (1986) 'Women and trade unions', in Feminist Review (ed.) *Waged Work*, London: Virago, pp. 160-85.

Child, J. (1972) 'Organisation structure, environment and performance: the role of strategic choice', *Sociology*, 6 (1): 1–22.

Child, J. (1984) *Organisation: A Guide to Problems and Practice*, 2nd edn, London: Harper and Row.

Child, J. (1985) 'Managerial strategies, new technology and the labour process', in D. Knights, H. Willmott and D. Collinson (eds) *Job Redesign*, Aldershot: Gower, pp. 107–41.

Clarke, T. (1989) 'Imaginative flexibility in production engineering: the Volvo Uddevalla plant', paper presented to Employment Research Unit Conference, Cardiff Business School.

Clawson, D. and Fantasia, R. (1983) 'Beyond Burawoy: the dialectics of conflict and consent on the shop floor', *Theory and Society*, 12: 671–80.

Cockburn, C. (1983) *Brothers: Male Dominance and Technological Change*, London: Pluto.

Cockburn, C. (1985) *Machinery of Dominance*, London: Pluto.

Cockburn, C. (1986) 'The material of male power', in Feminist Review (ed.) *Waged Work*, London: Virago, pp. 93–113.

Cockburn, C. (1991) *In the Way of Women*, Basingstoke: Macmillan.

Cohen, S. and Taylor, L. (1976) *Escape Attempts*, Harmondsworth: Penguin.

Collinson, D. (1988) '"Engineering humour": masculinity, joking and conflict in shop-floor relations', *Organization Studies*, 9 (2): 181–99.

Collinson, D. (1992) *Managing the Shopfloor*, Berlin: de Gruyter.

Collinson, D. and Knights, D. (1986) '"Men only": theories and practices of job segregation in insurance', in D. Knights and H. Willmott (eds) *Gender and the Labour Process*, London: Sage, pp. 140–78.

Corti, L. and Dex, S. (1995) 'Informal carers and employement', *Employment Gazette*, March: 101–7.

Corti, L., Laurie, H. and Dex, S. (1994) *Caring and Employment*, Employment Department Research Series no. 39, London: HMSO.

Cressey, P. and MacInnes, J. (1980) 'Voting for Ford: industrial democracy and the control of labour', *Capital and Class*, 11: 5–33.

Crompton, R. (1987) 'Gender, status and professionalism', *Sociology*, 21 (3): 413-28.

Crompton, R. (1990) 'Professions in the current context', *Work, Employment and Society*, special issue, May: 147–66.

Cross, M. (1987) 'Equality of opportunity and inequality of outcome: the MSC, ethnic minorities and training policy', in R. Jenkins and J. Solomos (eds) *Racism and Equal Opportunity Policies in the 1980s*, Cambridge: Cambridge University Press, pp. 73–92.

Cross, M. (1988) 'Changes in working practices in UK manufacturing 1981–88', *Industrial Relations Review and Report*, no. 415: 2–10.

Cross, M., Wrench, J. and Barnett, S. (1990) *Ethnic Minorities and the Careers Service*, Research Paper no. 73, London: Department of Employment.

Crowther, S. and Garrahan, P. (1988) 'Corporate power and the local economy', *Industrial Relations Journal*, 19 (1): 51–9.

Crozier, M. (1964) *The Bureaucratic Phenomenon*, London: Tavistock.

Crusco, A. H. and Wetzel, C. G. (1984) 'The Midas touch: the effects of interpersonal touch on restaurant tipping', *Personality and Social Psychology Bulletin*, 10 (4): 512–17.

Cunnison, S. and Stageman, J. (1995) *Feminizing the Unions*, Aldershot: Avebury.

Dale, I. and Kerr, J. (1995) 'Small and medium sized enterprises: their numbers and importance to employment', *Labour Market Trends*, December: 461–5.

Davies, S. (1990) 'Inserting gender into Burawoy's theory of the labour process', *Work, Employment and Society*, 4 (3): 391–406.

Deery, S. J. and Mahony, A. (1994) 'Temporal flexibility: management strategies and employee preferences in the retail industry', *Journal of Industrial Relations*, 36 (3): 332–52.

Delbridge, R., Turnbull, P. and Wilkinson, B. (1992) 'Pushing back the frontiers: management control and work intensification under JIT/TQM factory regimes',

New Technology, Work and Employment, 7 (2): 97–106.

Deming, W. E. (1982) *Quality, Productivity and Competitive Position*, Cambridge, MA: MIT Press.

Denman, J. and McDonald, P. (1996) 'Unemployment statistics from 1881 to the present day', *Labour Market Trends*, January: 5–18.

Department for Education and Employment (1995a) 'Changes to the coverage of the monthly count of claimant unemployment', *Labour Market Trends*, November: 398–400.

Department for Education and Employment (1995b) 'New developments in the pattern of claimant unemployment in the United Kingdom', *Employment Gazette*, September: 351–8.

Department of Employment (1990) 'Ethnic origins and the labour market', *Employment Gazette*, March: 125–37.

Department of Employment (1993) 'Ethnic origins and the labour market', *Employment Gazette*, February: 25–33.

Department of Employment (1994) 'Historical supplement 4, employment statistics', *Employment Gazette*, October.

Dex, S. (1983) 'Recurrent unemployment in young black and white males', *Industrial Relations Journal*, 14 (1): 41–9.

Dickens, L. (1995) 'UK part-time employees and the law – recent and potential developments', *Gender, Work and Organization*, 2 (4): 207–15.

Dickens, R, Gregg., P., Machin, S., Manning, A. and Wadsworth, J. (1993) 'Wages councils: was there a case for abolition?', *British Journal of Industrial Relations*, 31 (4): 515–29.

Ditton, J. (1977) *Part-Time Crime: An Ethnography of Fiddling and Pilferage*, London: Macmillan.

Ditton, J. (1979) 'Baking time', *Sociological Review*, 27 (1): 157–67.

Doganis, R. (1994) 'The impact of liberalization on European airline strategies and operations', *Journal of Air Transport Management*, 1 (1): 15–25.

Douglas, M. (1975) *Implicit Meanings: Essays in Anthropology*, London: Routledge and Kegan Paul.

Dubois, P. (1979) *Sabotage in Industry*, Harmondsworth: Pelican.

Duncombe, J. and Marsden, D. (1995) '"Workaholics" and "whingeing women": theorising intimacy and emotion work – the last frontier of gender inequality?', *Sociological Review*, 43 (1): 150–69.

Edwards, P. K. and Scullion, H. (1982) *The Social Organisation of Industrial Conflict*, Oxford: Blackwell.

Edwards, P. K. and Whitston, C. (1991) 'Workers are working harder: effort and shop-floor relations in the 1980s', *British Journal of Industrial Relations*, 29 (4): 593–601.

Edwards, P. K. and Whitston, C. (1993) *Attending to Work: The Management of Attendance and Shopfloor Order*, Oxford: Blackwell.

Edwards, R. (1979) *Contested Terrain: the Transformation of the Workplace in the Twentieth Century*, London: Heinemann.

EIRR (European Industrial Relations Review) (1995) 'Annual working time in the European Union', *European Industrial Relations Reveiw*, no. 259: 17–19.

Ekman, P. (1973) 'Cross culture studies of facial expression', in P. Ekman (ed.) *Darwin and Facial Expression*, New York: Academic, pp. 169–222.

Eldridge, J. E. T. (1971) *Sociology and Industrial Life*, Middlesex: Nelson.

Eldridge, J. E. T. (1983) Book review, *British Journal of Industrial Relations*, 25 (1): 418–20.

Elger, T. (1990) 'Technical innovation and work reorganization in British manufacturing in the 1980s: continuity, intensification or transformation?', *Work, Employment and Society*, special issue, May: 67–102.

Elger, T. (1991) 'Task flexibility and the intensification of labour in UK manufacturing in the 1980s', in A. Pollert (ed.) *Farewell to Flexibility?*, Oxford: Blackwell, pp. 46–66.

European Commission (1992) *Legal Instruments to Combat Racism and Xenophobia*, Brussels: European Commission.

Evans, S. (1990) 'Free labour and economic performance: evidence from the construction industry', *Work, Employment and Society*, 4 (2): 239–52.

Featherstone, M. (1990) *Consumer Culture and Postmodernism*, London: Sage.

Feige, E. L. (1989) ' The meaning and measurement of the underground economy', in E. L. Feige (ed.) *The Underground Economies*, Cambridge: Cambridge University Press, pp. 175–96.

Felstead, A. and Jewson, N. (1995) 'Working at home: estimates from the 1991 census', *Employment Gazette*, March: 95–9.

Felt, L. F. and Sinclair, P. R. (1992) 'Everyone does it: unpaid work in a rural peripheral region', *Work, Employment and Society*, 6 (1): 43–64.

Ferguson, K. (1984) *The Feminist Case Against Bureaucracy*, Philadelphia: Temple University Press.

Ferman, L. A. (1983) 'The work ethic in the world of informal work', in J. Barbash, R. J. Lampman, S. A. Levitan and G. Tyler (eds) *The Work Ethic - A Critical Analysis*, Wisconsin: Industrial Relations Research Association.

Filby, M. P. (1992) '"The figures, the personality and the bums": service work and sexuaity', *Work, Employment and Society*, 6 (1): 23–42.

Fineman, S. (ed.) (1993) *Emotion in Organizations*, London: Sage.

Firth, M. (1981) 'Racial discrimination in the British labor market', *Industrial and Labor Relations Review*, 34 (2): 265–72.

Forbes, I. and Mead, G (1992) *Measure for Measure: A Comparative Analysis of Measures to Combat Racial Discrimination in the Member Countries of the European Community*, Research Series no. 1, Sheffield: Employment Department.

Fox, A. (1966) *Industrial Sociology and Industrial Relations*, Research Paper no. 3, Royal Commission on Trade Unions and Employers' Associations, London: HMSO.

Fox, A. (1974) *Beyond Contract*, London: Faber and Faber.

Francis, B. and Penn, R. (1994) 'Towards a phenomenology of skill', in R. Penn, M. Rose and J. Rubery (eds) *Skill and Occupational Change*, Oxford: Oxford University Press, pp. 223–43.

Friedman, A. (1977a) *Industry and Labour: Class Struggle at Work and Monopoly Capitalism*, London: Macmillan.

Friedman, A. (1977b) 'Responsible autonomy versus direct control over the labour process', *Capital and Class*, 1 (Spring): 43–57.

Friedman, A. (1990) 'Managerial activities, techniques and technology: towards a complex theory of the labour process', in D. Knights and H. Willmott (eds) *Labour Process Theory*, London: Macmillan, pp. 177–208.

Friedmann, G. (1961) *The Anatomy of Work*, London: Heinemann.

Fuchs, V. (1968) T*he Service Economy*, New York: Basic.

Gallie, D. (1991) 'Patterns of skill change: upskilling, deskilling or the polarization of skills?', *Work, Employment and Society*, 5 (3): 319–51.

Gallie, D. and White, M. (1993) *Employee Commitment and the Skills Revolution*, London: Policy Studies Institute.

Gershuny, J. (1978) *After Industrial Society? The Emerging Self-Service Economy*, London: Macmillan.

Gershuny, J. (1983) *Social Innovation and the Division of Labour*, Oxford: Oxford University Press.

Gershuny, J. and Miles, I. (1983) *The New Service Economy: The Transformation of Employment in Industrial Societies*, London: Pinter.

Gershuny, J. and Pahl, R. (1980) 'Britain in the decade of the three economies', *New Society*, 51: 7-9.

Gershuny, J., Godwin, M. and Jones, S. (1994) 'The domestic labour revolution: a process of lagged adaptation', in M. Anderson, F. Bechhofer and J. Gershuny (eds) *The Social and Political Economy of the Household*, Oxford: Oxford University Press, pp.151–97.

Goffman, E. (1963) *Stigma*, Harmondsworth: Penguin.

Goffman, E. (1969) *The Presentation of Self in Everyday Life*, London: Allen Lane.

Goffman, E. (1971) *Relations in Public*, New York: Basic.

Goodwin, M. and Duncan, S. (1986) 'The local state and local economic policy: political mobilisation or economic regeneration', *Capital and Class*, 27: 14–36.

Gorz, A. (1982) *Farewell to the Working Class*, London: Pluto.

Gorz, A. (1985) *Paths to Paradise: On the Liberation from Work*, London: Pluto.

Guest, D. (1990) 'Have British workers been working harder in Thatcher's Britain? - A re-consideration of the concept of effort', *British Journal of Industrial Relations*, 28 (3): 293–312.

Hakim, C. (1991) 'Grateful slaves and self-made women: fact and fantasy in women's work orientations', *European Sociological Review*, 7 (2): 101–21.

Hales, C. P. (1986) 'What do managers do? A critical review of the evidence', *Journal of Management Studies*, 23 (1): 88–115.

Hall, E. (1993) 'Smiling, deferring and flirting: doing gender by giving good service', *Work and Occupations*, 20 (4): 452–71.

Handy, C. (1984) *The Future of Work*, Oxford: Blackwell.

Harding, P. and Jenkins, R. (1989) *The Myth of the Hidden Economy*, Milton Keynes: Open University Press.

Hartmann, H. (1979) 'Capitalism, patriarchy and job segregation', in Z. Eisenstein (ed.)

Capitalist Patriarchy and the Case for Socialist Feminism, New York: Monthly Review, pp. 206–47.

Harvey, D. (1989) *The Condition of Postmodernity*, Oxford: Blackwell.

Hassard, J. (1989) 'Time and industrial sociology', in P. Blyton, J. Hassard, S. Hill and K. Starkey (eds) *Time, Work and Organization*, London: Routledge, pp. 13–34.

Hearn, J. and Parkin, W. (1987) *'Sex' at 'Work': The Power and Paradox of Organization Sexuality*, Brighton: Wheatsheaf.

Hearn, J., Sheppard, D. L., Tancred-Sheriff, P. and Burrell, G. (eds) (1989) *The Sexuality of Organization*, London: Sage.

Hewitt, P. (1993) *About Time: The Revolution in Work and Family Life*, London: Rivers Oram.

Hill, D. (1985) 'Employment of the disabled', *Industrial Relations Journal*, 16 (1): 78–83.

Hill, S. (1991) 'Why quality circles failed but Total Quality Management might succeed', *British Journal of Industrial Relations*, 29 (4): 541–68.

Hochschild, A. R. (1979) 'Emotion work, feeling rules and social structure', *American Journal of Sociology*, 85 (3): 551–75.

Hochschild, A. R. (1983) *The Managed Heart: Commercialization of Human Feeling*, Berkeley: University of California Press.

Hochschild, A. R. (1989) *The Second Shift*, New York: Viking.

Hodson, R. (1991) 'Workplace behaviors', *Work and Occupations*, 18 (3): 271–90.

Hoggert, P. (1996) 'New modes of control in the public services', *Public Administration*, 74 (1): 9–36.

Horrell, S. (1994) 'Household time allocation and women's labour force participation', in M. Anderson, F. Bechhofer and J. Gershuny (eds) *The Social and Political Economy of the Household*, Oxford: Oxford University Press, pp. 198–224.

Horrell, S. and Rubery, J. (1991) *Employers' Working Time Policies and Women's Employment*, London: HMSO.

Horrell, S., Rubery, J. and Burchell, B. (1994) 'Gender and skills', in R. Penn, M. Rose and J. Rubery (eds) *Skill and Occupational Change*, Oxford: Oxford University Press, pp. 189–222.

Hubbuck, J. and Carter, S. (1980) *Half a Chance? A Report on Job Discrimination Agains Young Blacks in Nottingham*, London: Commission for Racial Equality.

Hutton, W. (1995) *The State We're In*, London: Cape.

Hyman, R. (1987) 'Strategy or structure? Capital, labour and control', *Work, Employment and Society*, 1 (1): 25–55.

Hyman, R. (1991) 'Plus Ça change? The theory of production and the production of theory', in A. Pollert (ed.) *Farewell to Flexibility?*, Oxford: Blackwell, pp. 259-83.

Incomes Data Services (1996) 'UK to toe the line on working time limits', *Employment Europe*, no. 413: 26–28.

Industrial Relations Review and Report (1990) 'Ethnic monitoring - policy and practice', *IRS Employment Trends*, 478: 4–11.

Ingram, A. and Sloane, P. (1984) 'The growth of shiftwork in the British food, drink and tobacco industries', *Managerial and Decision Economics*, 5 (3): 168–76.

Inland Revenue (1981) *Annual Report*, no. 123, London: HMSO.

Jackall, R. (1988) *Moral Mazes: The World of Corporate Managers*, New York: Oxford University Press.

Jahoda, M. (1979) 'The impact of unemployment in the 1930s and the 1970s', *Bulletin of the British Psychological Society*, 32: 309–14.

Jahoda, M. (1982) *Employment and Unemployment*, Cambridge: Cambridge University Press.

James, N. (1989) 'Emotional labour: skill and work in the social regulation of feelings', *Sociological Review*, 37 (1): 15–42.

Jaques, E. (1956) *Measurement of Responsibility*, London: Tavistock.

Jaques, E. (1967) *Equitable Payment*, rev. edn, Harmondsworth: Penguin.

Jenkins, R. (1986) *Racism and Recruitment*, Cambridge: Cambridge University Press.

Jenkins, R. (1987) 'Equal Opportunities in the private sector: the limits of voluntarism', in R. Jenkins and J. Solomos (eds) *Racism and Equal Opportunity Policies in the 1980s*, Cambridge: Cambridge University Press, pp. 110–24.

Jenson, J. (1989) 'The talents of women, the skills of men', in S. Wood (ed.) *The Transformation of Work?*, London: Unwin Hyman, pp. 141–55.

Jewson, N. and Mason, D. (1986) 'The theory and practice of equal opportunity policies: liberal and radical approaches', *Sociological Review*, 34 (2): 307–34.

Jewson, N., Waters, S. and Harvey, J. (1990) *Ethnic Minorities and Employment Practice: A Study of Six Employers*, Research Paper no. 76, Sheffield: Employment Department.

Jewson, N., Mason, D., Lambkin, C. and Taylor, F. (1992) *Ethnic Monitoring Policy and Practice: A Study of Employers' Experiences*, Research Paper no. 89, London: Department of Employment.

Jones, T. (1993) *Britain's Ethnic Minorities*, London: Policy Studies Institute.

Joseph Rowntree Foundation (1991) *National Survey of Volunteering*, Social Survey Research Findings no. 22, York: Joseph Rowntree Foundation.

Juran, J. M. (1979) *Quality Control Handbook*, New York: McGraw-Hill.

Keen, S. (1995) 'British working week is longest of EU countries', *People Management*, 1 (3): 13–15.

Keep, E. (1989) 'Corporate training strategies: the vital component?', in J. Storey (ed.) *New Perspectives on Human Resource Management*, London: Routledge, pp. 109–25.

Keep, E. (1994) 'Vocational education and training for the young', in K. Sisson (ed.) *Personnel Management*, 2nd edn, Oxford: Blackwell, pp. 299–333.

Kelly, J. (1982) *Scientific Management, Job Redesign and Work Performance*, London: Academic.

Kelly, J. (1985) 'Management's redesign of work: labour process, labour markets and product markets', in D. Knights, H. Willmott and D. Collinson (eds) *Job Redesign*, Aldershot: Gower, pp. 30–51.

Kerr, C., Dunlop, J. T., Harbison, F. H. and Myers, C. A. (1960) *Industrialism and Industrial Man*, London: Heinemann.

Knights, D. and Willmott, H. (eds) (1986) *Managing the Labour Process*, Aldershot: Gower.

Knights, D. and Willmott, H. (eds) (1990) *Labour Process Theory*, London: Macmillan.

Knights, D., Willmott, H. and Collinson, D. (eds) (1985) *Job Redesign: Critical*

Perspectives on the Labour Process, Aldershot: Gower.

Koestler, A. (1976) *The Ghost in the Machine*, London: Picador.

Kreckel, R. (1980) 'Unequal opportunity structure and labour market segmentation', *Sociology*, 14 (4): 525–50.

Kusterer, K. (1978) *Know How on the Job*, Boulder, CO: Westview.

Labour Research (1990) 'The right personality for the job?', *Labour Research*, September: 15–16.

Lacey, N., Wells, C. and Meure, D. (1990) *Reconstructing Criminal Law*, London: Weidenfeld and Nicolson.

Lazonick, W. (1978) 'The subjection of labour to capital: the rise of the capitalist system', *Review of Radical Political Economics*, 10 (1): 1–31.

Lee, D. (1982) 'Beyond deskilling: skill, craft and class', in S. Wood (ed.) *The Degradation of Work?*, London: Hutchinson, pp. 146–62.

Lee, G. and Wrench, J. (1987) 'Race and gender dimensions of the youth labour market: from apprenticeship to YTS', in G. Lee and R. Loveridge (eds) *The Manufacture of Disadvantage*, Milton Keynes: Open University Press, pp. 83–99.

Legge, K. (1995) *Human Resource Management: Rhetorics and Realities*, Basingstoke: Macmillan.

Lessor, R. (1984) 'Social movements, the occupational arena and changes in career consciousness: the case of women flight attendants', *Journal of Occupational Behaviour*, 5: 37–51.

Lewis, A. (1995) 'The deskilling thesis revisited: on Peter Armstrong's defence of Braverman', *Sociological Review*, 43 (3): 478–500.

Litt, S. and Wajcman, J. (1996) '"Sameness" and "difference" revisited: which way forward for equal opportunity initiatives?', *Journal of Management Studies*, 33 (1): 79–94.

Linhart, R. (1981) *The Assembly Line*, London: Calder.

Linstead, S. (1985a) 'Jokers wild: the importance of humour in the maintenance of organizational culture', *Sociological Review*, 33 (4): 741–67.

Linstead, S. (1985b) 'Breaking the "purity rule": industrial sabotage and the symbolic process', *Personnel Review*, 14 (3): 12–19.

Linstead, S. (1995) 'Averting the gaze: gender and power on the perfumed picket line', *Gender, Work and Organization*, 2 (4): 190–206.

Littler, C. R. (1982) *The Development of the Labour Process in Capitalist Societies*, Aldershot: Gower.

Littler, C. R. (1985) 'Taylorism, Fordism and job design', in D. Knights, H. Willmott and D. Collinson (eds) *Job Redesign*, Aldershot: Gower, pp. 10-29.

Littler, C. R. and Salaman, G. (1982) 'Bravermania and beyond: recent theories of the labour process', *Sociology*, 16 (2): 251–69.

Lonsdale, S. (1990) *Women and Disability*, London: Macmillan.

Lynch, J. J. (1992) *The Psychology of Customer Care*, London: Macmillan.

Lyon, D. (1994) *Postmodernity*, Buckingham: Open University Press.

MacDonald, R. (1994) 'Fiddly jobs, undeclared working and the "something for nothing" society', *Work, Employment and Society*, 8 (4): 507–30.

MacDonald, R. (1996) 'Labours of love: voluntary working in a depressed local economy', *Journal of Social Policy*, 25 (1): 1–21.

Mangham, I. L. and Overington, M. A. (1987) *Organizations as Theatre*, Chichester: Wiley.

Manwaring, T. and Wood, S. (1985) 'The ghost in the labour process', in D. Knights, H. Willmott and D. Collinson (eds) *Job Redesign*, Aldershot: Gower, pp. 171–96.

Mars, G. (1982) *Cheats at Work: An Anthropology of Workplace Crime*, London: Allen and Unwin.

Mars, G. and Nicod, M. (1984) *The World of Waiters*, Boston, MA: George Allen and Unwin.

Marsh, C. (1991) *Hours of Work of Women and Men in Britain*, London: HMSO.

Marx, K. (1930) *Capital*, London: Dent

Marx, K. (1969) 'Alienated labour', in T. Burns (ed.) *Industrial Man: Selected Readings*, Harmondsworth: Penguin, pp. 95–109.

Marx, K. (1976) Capital, vol. 1, Harmondsworth: Penguin.

Mason, D. (1994) 'On the dangers of disconnecting race and racism', *Sociology*, 28 (4): 845–58.

Massey, D. (1988) 'What's happening to UK manufacturing?', in J. Allen and D. Massey (eds) *The Economy in Question*, London: Sage, pp. 45–90.

Mathewson, S. B. (1931) *Restriction of Output among Unorganized Workers*, New York: McGraw-Hill.

Matthaei, J. (1982) *An Economic History of Women in America*, Brighton: Harvester.

Mayo, E. (1933) *The Human Problems of an Industrial Civilisation*, New York: Macmillan

McClelland, K. (1987) 'Time to work, time to live: some aspects of work and the re-formation of class in Britain 1850–1880', in P. Joyce (ed.) *The Historical Meanings of Work*, Cambridge: Cambridge University Press, pp. 180–209.

McCormick, B. J. (1979) *Industrial Relations in the Coal Industry*, London: Macmillan.

McKee, L. and Bell, C. (1986) 'His unemployment, her problem: the domestic and marital consequences of male unemployment', in S. Allen, A. Waton, K. Purcell and S. Wood (eds) *The Experience of Unemployment*, Basingstoke: Macmillan, pp. 134-49.

McLennan, G. (1995) *Pluralism*, Buckingham: Open University Press.

McLoughlin, I. and Clark, J. (1994) *Technological Change at Work*, 2nd ed, Milton Keynes: Open University Press.

Metcalf, D. (1989) 'Water notes dry up: the impact of the Donovan reform proposals and Thatcherism at work on labour productivity in British manufacturing industry', *British Journal of Industrial Relations*, 27 (1): 1–31.

Meyer, S. (1981) *The Five-Dollar Day: Labor Management and Social Control in the Ford Motor Co., 1908–21*, Albany: SUNY.

Miles, R. (1993) *Racism after 'Race Relations'*, London: Routledge.

Miller, D. and Form, W. (1963) *Industrial Sociology*, New York: Harper and Row.

Millward, N., Stevens, M., Smart, D. and Hawes, W. R. (1992) *Workplace Industrial Relations in Transition*, Aldershot: Dartmouth.

Molstad, C. (1986) 'Choosing and coping with boring work', *Urban Life*, 15 (2): 215–36.

Moorhouse, H. F. (1984) 'American automobiles and workers' dreams', in K. Thompson (ed.) *Work, Employment and Unemployment*, Milton Keynes: Open University Press, pp. 246–60.

Moorhouse, H. F. (1987) 'The "work" ethic and "leisure" activity: the hot rod in post-war America', in P. Joyce (ed.) *The Historical Meanings of Work*, Cambridge: Cambridge University Press. pp. 237–57.

More, C. (1980) *Skill and the English Working Class 1840-1914*, London: Croom Helm.

More, C. (1982) 'Skill and the survival of apprenticeship' in S. Wood (ed.) *The Degradation of Work?*, London: Hutchinson, pp. 109-22.

Morgan, G. (1986) *Images of Organization*, London: Sage.

Morris, L. (1990) *The Workings of the Household*, Cambridge: Polity.

MOW International Research Team (1987) *The Meaning of Working*, London: Academic.

Mumby, D. and Putnam, L. (1992) 'The politics of emotion: a feminist reading of bounded rationality', *Academy of Management Review*, 17 (3): 465–86.

Mumford, L. (1934) *Technics and Civilisation*, New York: Harcourt, Brace and World.

Naylor, K. (1994) 'Part-time working in Great Britain - an historical analysis', *Employment Gazette*, December: 473–84.

Neathey, F. (1992) 'Job assessment, job evaluation and equal value', in P. Kahn and E. Meehan (eds) *Equal Value/Comparable Worth in the UK and the USA* Basingstoke: Macmillan, pp. 65–81.

New Earnings Survey (1995) *Part A: Streamlined and Summary Analysis*, London: HMSO.

Nicholson, N. (1977) 'Absence behaviour and attendance motivation: a conceptual synthesis', *Journal of Management Studies*, 14 (3): 231–52.

Nicholson, N. and Johns, G. (1985) 'The absence culture and the psychological contract - who's in control of absence', *Academy of Management Review*, 10 (3): 397–407.

Nkomo, S. (1992) 'The emperor has no clothes: rewriting "race in organizations"', *Academy of Management Review*, 17 (3): 487–513.

Nolan, P. (1989) 'Walking on water? performance and industrial relations under Thatcher', *Industrial Relations Journal*, 20 (2): 81–92.

Noon, M. (1992) 'HRM: a map, model or theory', in P. Blyton and P. Turnbull (eds) *Reassessing Human Resource Management*, London: Sage, pp. 16–32.

Noon, M. (1993) 'Racial discrimination in speculative application: evidence from the UK's top 100 firms', *Human Resource Management Journal*, 3 (4): 35–47.

Noon, M. (1994) 'From apathy to alacrity: managers and new technology in provincial newspapers', *Journal of Management Studies*, 31 (1): 19–32.

Noon, M. and Delbridge, R. (1993) 'News from behind my hand: Gossip in organizations', *Organization Studies* 14 (1): 23-36.

O'Higgins, M. (1989) 'Assessing the underground economy in the United Kingdom', in E. L. Feige (ed.) *The Underground Economies*, Cambridge: Cambridge University Press, pp. 175–96.

Oakland, J. S. (1989) *Total Quality Management*, Oxford: Butterworth-Heinemann.

Oakley, A. (1974) *The Sociology of Housework*, London: Martin Robertson.

Oakley, A. (1982) *Subject Woman*, London: Fontana.

OECD (Organization for Economic Cooperation and Development) (1995), *Employment Outlook 1995*, Paris: OECD.

Offe, C. (1985) *Disorganised Capitalism*, Cambridge: Polity.

Ogbonna, E. and Noon, M. (1995) 'Experiencing inequality: ethnic minorities and the Employment Training scheme', *Work, Employment and Society*, 9 (3): 537–58.

Ogbonna, E. and Wilkinson, B. (1990) 'Corporate strategy and corporate culture: the view from the checkout', *Personnel Review*, 19 (4): 9–15.

Oliver, M. (1990) *The Politics of Disablement*, London: Macmillan.

Pahl, R. (1984) *Divisions of Labour*, Oxford: Blackwell.

Pahl, R. (1988) 'Some remarks on informal work, social polarization and the social structure', *International Journal of Urban and Regional Research*, 12: 247–67.

Palmer, B. (1975) 'Class, conception and conflict', *Review of Radical Political Economics*, 7 (2): 31–49.

Parekh, B. (1986) 'The New Right and the politics of nationhood', in G. Cohen (ed.) *The New Right, Image and Reality*, London: Runnymead Trust.

Parker, G. (1988) 'Who cares? A review of empirical evidence from Britain', in R. Pahl (ed.) *On Work*, Oxford: Blackwell, pp. 496–512.

Parkin, F. (1979) *Marxism and Class Theory: A Bourgeois Critique*, London: Tavistock.

Penn, R. (1982) 'Skilled manual workers in the labour process, 1856–1964', in S. Wood (ed.) *The Degradation of Work?*, London: Hutchinson, pp. 90–108.

Penn, R. (1983) 'Theories of skill and class structure', *Sociological Review*, 31 (1): 22–38.

Penn, R. (1990) *Class, Power and Technology*, Cambridge: Polity.

Penn, R. and Scattergood, H. (1985) 'Deskilling or enskilling? An empirical investigation of recent theories of the labour process', *British Journal of Sociology*, 36 (4): 611–30.

Penn, R., Gasteen, A., Scattergood, H. and Sewel, J. (1994a) 'Technical change and the division of labour in Rochdale and Aberdeen', in R. Penn, M. Rose and J. Rubery (eds) *Skill and Occupational Change*, Oxford: Oxford University Press, pp. 130–56.

Penn, R., Rose, M. and Rubery, J. (eds) (1994b) *Skill and Occupational Change*, Oxford: Oxford University Press.

Peters, T. and Austin, N. (1985) *A Passion for Excellence*, New York: Random House.

Peters, T. and Waterman, R. H. (1982) *In Search of Excellence*, New York: Harper and Row.

Phillips, A. and Taylor, B. (1986) 'Sex and skill', in Feminist Review (ed.) *Waged Work – A Reader*, London: Virago, pp. 54–66.

Pickard, J. (1991) 'Annual hours: a year of living dangerously', *Personnel Management*, August: 38–43.

Piore, M. J. and Sabel, C. F. (1984) *The Second Industrial Divide*, New York: Basic.

Pollard, S. (1963) 'Factory discipline and the industrial revolution', *The Economic History Review*, 16: 254–71.

Pollard, S. (1965) *The Genesis of Modern Management: A Study of the Industrial Revolution in Great Britain*, Harmondsworth: Penguin.

Pollert, A. (1981) *Girls, Wives, Factory Lives*, London: Macmillan.

Pollert, A. (1988) 'The "flexible firm": fixation or fact?', *Work, Employment and Society*, 2 (3): 281–316.

Pollert, A. (ed.) (1991) *Farewell to Flexibility?*, Oxford: Blackwell.

Pollitt, H. (1940) *Serving My Time: An Apprenticeship to Politics*, London: Lawrence and Wishart.

Polyani, M. and Prosch, H. (1975) *Meaning*, Chicago: University of Chicago Press.

Poor, R. (ed.) (1972) *4 Days, 40 Hours*, London: Pan.

Pringle, R. (1989) 'Bureaucracy, rationality and sexuality: the case of secretaries', in J. Hearn, D. L. Sheppard, P. Tancred-Sheriff and G. Burrell (eds) *The Sexuality of Organization*, London: Sage, pp. 158–77.

Prins, R. and de Graaf, A. (1986) 'Comparison of sickness absence in Belgian, German and Dutch firms', *British Journal of Industrial Medicine*, 43: 529–36.

Purcell, J. (1989) 'The impact of corporate strategy on human resource management', in J. Storey (ed.) *New Perspectives on Human Resource Management*, London: Routledge. pp. 67–91.

Purcell, J. (1995) 'Corporate strategy and its link with human resource management strategy', in J. Storey (ed.) *Human Resource Management: A Critical Text* London: Routledge. pp. 63–86.

Radcliffe-Brown, A. R. (1952) *Structure and Function in Primitive Society*, London: Cohen and West.

Rafaeli, A. and Sutton, R. I. (1987) 'Expression of emotion as part of the work role', *Academy of Management Review*, 12 (1): 23–37.

Rafaeli, A. and Sutton, R. I. (1989) 'The expression of emotion in organizational life', in L. L. Cummings and B. M. Staw (eds) *Research in Organizational Behaviour*, Greenwich, CT: JAI, pp. 1–42.

Ram, M. (1992) 'Coping with racism: Asian employers in the inner city', *Work, Employment and Society*, 6 (4): 601–18.

Reed, M. (1989) *The Sociology of Management*, Brighton: Harvester Wheatsheaf.

Reid, D. A. (1976) 'The decline of Saint Monday', *Past and Present*, no. 71: 76–101.

Rhodes, E. and Braham, P. (1986) 'Equal opportunity in the context of high levels of unemployment', in R. Jenkins and J. Solomos (eds) *Racism and Equal Opportunity Policies in the 1980s*, Cambridge: Cambridge University Press, pp. 189–209.

Riemer, J. W. (1977) *Hard Hats: The Working World of Construction Workers*, Beverly Hills, CA: Sage.

Ritzer, G. (1993) *The McDonaldization of Society*, Thousand Oaks, CA: Pine Forge.

Rodgers, D. (1978) *The Work Ethic in Industrial America 1850-1920*, Chicago: University of Chicago Press.

Roethlisberger, F. J. and Dickson, W. J. (1966) *Management and the Worker*, Harvard: Harvard University Press.

Rogoff, B. and Lave, J. (eds) (1984) *Everyday Cognition: Its Development in Social Context*, Cambridge MA: Harvard University Press.

Rolfe, H. (1986) 'Skill, deskilling and new technology in the non-manual labour process', *New Technology, Work and Employment*, 1 (1): 37–49.

Rolfe, H. (1990) 'In the name of progress? Skill and attitudes towards technological change', *New Technology, Work and Employment*, 5 (2): 107–21.

Rose, M. (1985) *Re-Working the Work Ethic*, London: Batsford.

Rose, M. (1988) *Industrial Behaviour*, 2nd edn, Harmondsworth: Penguin.

Rose, M. (1994) 'Skill and Samuel Smiles: changing the British work ethic', in R. Penn, M. Rose and J. Rubery (eds) *Skill and Occupational Change*, Oxford: Oxford University Press, pp. 281–335.

Rose, R. (1985) 'Getting by in three economies: the resources of the official, unofficial and domestic economies', in J-E. Lane (ed.) *State and Market*, London: Sage, pp. 103–41.

Roy, D. (1952) 'Efficiency and "the fix": informal inter-group relations in a piecework machine shop', *American Journal of Sociology*, 57: 255–66.

Roy, D. (1953) 'Work satisfaction and social reward in quota achievement: an analysis of piecework incentive', *American Sociological Review*, 18: 507–14.

Roy, D. (1955) 'Quota restriction and goldbricking in a machine shop', *American Journal of Sociology*, 60: 427–42.

Roy, D. (1960) 'Banana time: job satisfaction and informal interaction', *Human Organization*, 18: 156–68.

Rubery, J. and Wilkinson, F. (1979) 'Notes on the nature of the labour process in the secondary sector', *Low Pay and Labour Market Segmentation Conference Papers*, Cambridge.

Rubinstein, M. (1984) *Equal Pay for Work of Equal Value*, London: Macmillan.

Sabel, C. F. (1982) *Work and Politics: the Division of Labour in Industry*, Cambridge: Cambridge University Press.

Sadler, P. (1970) 'Sociological aspects of skill', *British Journal of Industrial Relations*, 8 (1): 22–31.

Sayer, A. and Walker, R. (1992) *The New Social Economy: Reworking the Division of Labour*, Oxford: Blackwell.

Scase, R. and Goffee, R. (1989) *Reluctant Managers: Their Work and Lifestyles*, London: Unwin Hyman.

Schein, E. H. (1965) *Organizational Psychology*, Englewood Cliffs, NJ: Prentice-Hall.

Scott, A. (1994) *Willing Slaves: British Workers Under Human Resource Management*, Cambridge: Cambridge University Press.

Sewell, G and Wilkinson, B. (1992) 'Empowerment or emasculation? Shopfloor surveillance in a total quality organisation', in P. Blyton and P. Turnbull (eds) *Reassessing Human Resource Management*, London: Sage, pp. 97–115.

Seymour, W. D. (1966) *Industrial Skills*, London: Pitman.

Shutt, J. and Whittington, R. (1987) 'Fragmentation strategies and the rise of small units: cases from the north west', *Regional Studies*, 21: 13–23.

Smith, C. (1989) 'Flexible specialisation, automation and mass production', *Work, Employment and Society*, 3 (2): 203–22.

Smith, D. J. (1981) *Unemployment and Racial Minorities*, London: Policy Studies Institute.

Smith, S. and Wied-Nebbeling, S. (1986) *The Shadow Economy in Britain and Germany*,

London: Anglo-German Foundation.

Snyder, M. (1987) *Public Appearances, Private Realities*, New York: Freeman.

Sorge, A., Hartman, G., Warner, M. and Nicholas, I. (1983) *Microelectronics and Manpower in Manufacturing Applications of Computer Numerical Control in Great Britain and West Germany*, Aldershot: Gower.

Spradley, J. P. and Mann, B. J. (1975) *The Cocktail Waitress: Women's Work in a Man's World*, New York: Wiley.

Steiger, T. L. (1993) 'Construction skill and skill construction', *Work, Employment and Society*, 7 (4): 535–60.

Steinberg, R. J. (1990) 'Social construction of skill', *Work and Occupations*, 17 (4): 449–82.

Stopford, J. and Turner, L. (1985) *Britain and the Multinationals*, Chichester: Wiley.

Sweeney, K. and Davies, J. (1996) 'Labour disputes in 1995', *Labour Market Trends*, 104 (6): 271–85.

Tancred, P. (1995) 'Women's work: a challenge to the sociology of work', *Gender, Work and Organization*, 2 (1): 11–20.

Taylor, F. W. (1911) *The Principles of Scientific Management*, New York: Harper.

Taylor, L. and Walton, P. (1971) 'Industrial sabotage: motives and meanings', in S. Cohen (ed.) *Images of Deviance*, Harmondsworth: Penguin, pp. 219–45.

Thomas, J. J. (1992) *Informal Economic Activities*, Hemel Hempstead: Harvester Wheatsheaf.

Thomas, P. and Smith, K. (1995) 'Results of the 1993 Census of Employment', *Employment Gazette*, October: 369–77.

Thomason, G. F. (1980) *Job Evaluation: Objectives and Methods*, London: Institute of Personnel Management.

Thompson, E. P. (1967) 'Time, work-discipline and industrial capitalism', *Past and Present*, no. 38: 56–97.

Thompson, P. (1989) *The Nature of Work*, 2nd edn, London: Macmillan.

Thompson, P. (1993) 'Postmodernism: fatal distraction', in J. Hassard and M. Parker (eds), *Postmodernism and Organization*, London: Sage, pp. 183–203.

Tidd, K. L. and Lockard, J. S. (1978) 'Monetary significance of the affiliative smile', *Bulletin of the Psychonomic Society*, 11: 344–6.

Towers, B. (1992) 'Two speed ahead: social Europe and the UK', *Industrial Relations Journal*, 23 (2): 83–9.

Turnbull, P. (1988) 'The limits to "Japanisation" – just-in-time, labour relations and the UK automotive industry', *New Technology, Work and Employment*, 3 (1): 7–20.

Turner, B. A. (1971) *Exploring the Industrial Subculture*, London: Macmillan.

Turner, H. A. (1962) *Trade Union Growth, Structure and Policy*, London: Allen and Unwin.

Turner, R., Bostyn, A.-M. and Wight, D. (1985) 'The work ethic in a Scottish town with declining employment', in B. Roberts, R. Finnegan and D. Gallie (eds) *New Approaches to Economic Life*, Manchester: Manchester University Press, pp. 476–89.

Ursell, G. and Blyton, P. (1988) *State, Capital and Labour: Changing Patterns of Power and Dependence*, London: Macmillan.

Van Maanen, J. and Kunda, G. (1989) '"Real feelings": emotional expression and organizational culture', in L. L. Cummings and B. M. Staw (eds) *Research in Organizational Behaviour*, Greenwich, CT: JAI, pp. 43–103.

Veal, A. J. (1989) 'Leisure and the future: considering the options', in F. Coalter (ed.) *Freedom and Constraint: The Paradoxes of Leisure*, London: Routledge. pp. 264–74.

Waddington, J. and Whitson, C. (1996) 'Empowerment versus intensification: union perspectives of change at the workplace', in P. Ackers, C. Smith and P. Smith (eds), *The New Workplace and Trade Unionism*, London: Routledge, pp 149–77.

Wajcman, J. (1991) 'Patriarchy, technology and skill', *Work and Occupations*, 18 (1): 29–45.

Walby, S. (1986) *Patriarchy at Work*, Cambridge: Polity.

Walby, S. (1990) *Theorizing Patriarchy*, Oxford: Blackwell.

Wallace, C. and Pahl, R. (1986) 'Polarisation, unemployment and all forms of work', in S. Allen, A. Waton, K. Purcell and S. Wood (eds) *The Experience of Unemployment*, Basingstoke: Macmillan, pp. 116–33.

Wareing, A. (1992) 'Working arrangements and patterns of working hours in Britain' *Employment Gazette*, November: 88–100.

Warr, P. (1987) *Work, Unemployment and Mental Health*, Oxford: Clarendon.

Watson, G. (1994) 'The flexible workforce and patterns of working hours in the UK', *Employment Gazette*, July: 239–48.

Watson, T. J. (1986) *Management, Organisation and Employment*, London: Routledge.

Watson, T. J. (1987) *Sociology, Work and Industry* 2nd edn, London: Routledge & Kegan Paul.

Watson, T. J. (1994) *In Search of Management: Culture, Chaos and Control in Managerial Work*, London: Routledge.

Webb, J. and Liff, S. (1988) 'Play the white man: the social construction of fairness and competition in equal opportunity policies', *Sociological Review*, 36 (3): 532–51.

Weber, M. (1930) *The Protestant Ethic and the Spirit of Capitalism*, translated by Talcott Parsons, London: Allen and Unwin.

Weber, M. (1947) *The Theory of Social and Economic Organization*, ed. Talcott Parsons, London: Hodge.

Webster, F. (1995) *Theories of the Information Society*, London: Routledge.

Westwood, S. (1984) *All Day Every Day*, London: Pluto.

Wharton, A. (1993) 'The affective consequences of service work: managing emotions on the job', *Work and Occupations*, 20 (2): 205–32.

Wharton, A. and Erickson, R. (1993) 'Managing emotions on the job and at home: under standing the consequences of multiple emotional roles', *Academy of Management Review*, 18 (3): 457–86.

Whipp, R. (1987) 'A time to every purpose: an essay on time and work', in P. Joyce (ed.) *The Historical Meanings of Work*, Cambridge: Cambridge University Press, pp. 210–36.

White, M. (1987) *Working Hours: Assessing the Potential for Reduction*, Geneva: International Labour Organization.

Williams, C. (1988) *Blue, White and Pink Collar Workers in Australia*, Sydney: Allen and Unwin.

Williams, K., Cutler, T., Williams, J. and Haslam, C. (1987) 'The end of mass production?', *Economy and Society*, 16 (3): 405–39.

Williams, K., Haslam, C. and Williams, J. (1992) 'Ford versus "Fordism": the beginning of mass production?', *Work, Employment and Society*, 6 (4): 517–55.

Willis, P. (1977) *Learning to Labour*, Farnborough: Saxon House.

Wilson C. P. (1979) *Jokes: Form, Content, Use and Function*, London: Academic.

Wilson, D. F. (1972) *Dockers: The Impact of Industrial Change*, London: Fontana Collins.

Witz, A. (1992) *Professions and Patriarchy*, London: Routledge.

Wood, S. (1989) (ed.) *The Transformation of Work?*, London: Unwin Hyman.

Wood, S. (ed.) (1982) *The Degradation of Work? Skill, Deskilling and the Labour Process*, London: Hutchinson.

Woollacott, J. (1980) 'Dirty and deviant work', in G. Esland and G. Salaman (eds) *The Politics of Work and Occupations*, Milton Keynes: Open University Press, pp.192–212.

Worrell, D. L., Davidson, W. N. and Sharma, V. M (1991) 'Layoff announcements and stockholder wealth', *Academy of Management Journal*, 34 (3): 662–78.

Wouters, C. (1989) 'The sociology of emotions and flight attendants: Hochschild's Managed Heart', *Theory, Culture and Society*, 6: 95–123.

Yankelovich, D. (1973) 'The meaning of work', in R. Rosnow (ed.) *The Worker and the Job*, New York: Columbia University Press/Prentice Hall, pp. 19–47.

Yinger, M. (1986) 'Intersecting strands in the theorisation of race and ethnic relations', in J. Rex and D. Mason (eds) *Theories of Race and Ethnic Relations*, Cambridge: Cambridge University Press, pp. 20–41.

Zimbalist, A. (ed.) (1979) *Case Studies on the Labour Process*, New York: Monthly Review.

Zuboff, S. (1988) *In the Age of the Smart Machine*, Oxford: Heinemann.

Author Index

228

Subject Index